Daydreams and Diaries

www.**randomhousechildrens**.co.uk

Jacqueline Wilson

Daydreams and Diaries

Illustrated by Nick Sharratt

CORGI YEARLING

DAYDREAMS AND DIARIES
A CORGI YEARLING BOOK 978 0 440 87069 2

JACKY DAYDREAM
First published in Great Britain by Doubleday
Text copyright © Jacqueline Wilson, 2007
Illustrations copyright © Nick Sharratt, 2007

MY SECRET DIARY
First published in Great Britain by Doubleday
Text copyright © Jacqueline Wilson, 2009
Illustrations copyright © Nick Sharratt, 2009

First published as DAYDREAMS AND DIARIES by Corgi Yearling,
an imprint of Random House Children's Publishers UK,
A Random House Group Company

This edition published 2014

1 3 5 7 9 10 8 6 4 2

Text in this edition copyright © Jacqueline Wilson, 2014
Illustrations in this edition copyright © Nick Sharratt, 2014

Photographs from Daydreams and Diaries exhibition reproduced by permission
of Seven Stories – National Centre for Children's Books and the author.

The Random House Group Limited supports the Forest Stewardship
Council® (FSC®), the leading international forest-certification organisation.
Our books carrying the FSC label are printed on FSC®-certified paper. FSC is
the only forest-certification scheme supported by the leading environmental
organisations, including Greenpeace. Our paper procurement policy
can be found at www.randomhouse.co.uk/environment.

MIX
Paper from
responsible sources
FSC® C016897

Set in New Century Schoolbook LT

Corgi Yearling Books are published by Random House Children's Publishers UK,
61–63 Uxbridge Road, London W5 5SA

www.randomhousechildrens.co.uk
www.randomhouse.co.uk
www.totallyrandombooks.co.uk

Addresses for companies within The Random House Group Limited
can be found at: www.randomhouse.co.uk/offices.htm

THE RANDOM HOUSE GROUP Limited Reg. No. 954009

A CIP catalogue record for this book is available from the British Library.

Printed and bound in Great Britain by CPI Group (UK) Ltd, Croydon CR0 4YY

Jacqueline Wilson

Jacky Daydream

Illustrated by Nick Sharratt

For Emma, with all my love

17th December 1945

1
Birth!

I was more than a fortnight late for my own birth. I was due at the beginning of December and I didn't arrive until the seventeenth. I don't know why. It isn't at all like me. I'm always very speedy and I can't stand being late for anything.

My mum did her level best to get me going. She drank castor oil and skipped vigorously every morning. She's a small woman – five foot at most in her high heels. She was nearly as wide as she was long by this time. She must have looked like a beach ball. It's a wonder they didn't try to bounce the baby out.

When I eventually got started, I still took forty-eight hours to arrive. In fact they had to pull me out with forceps. They look like a medieval instrument of torture. It can't have been much fun for my mother – or me. The edge of the forceps caught my mouth. When I was finally yanked out into the harsh white light of the delivery room in the hospital, my mouth was lopsided and partially paralysed.

They didn't bother about mothers and babies bonding in those days. They didn't give us time to have a cuddle or even take a good look at each other. I was bundled up tightly in a blanket and taken off to the nursery.

I stayed there for four days without a glimpse of my mother. The nurses came and changed my nappy and gave me a bath and tried to feed me with a bottle, though it hurt my sore mouth.

I wonder what I thought during those long lonely first days. I'm sure babies *do* think, even though they can't actually say the words. What would I do now if I was lying all by myself, hungry and frightened? That's easy. I'd make up a story to distract myself. So maybe I started pretending right from the day I was born.

I imagined my mother bending over my cot, lifting me up and cradling her cheek against my wispy curls. Each time a nurse held me against her starched white apron I'd shut my eyes tight and pretend *she* was my mother, soft and warm and protective. I'd hope she'd keep me in her arms for ever. But she'd pop me back in my cot and after three or four hours another nurse would come and I'd have to start the whole game all over again.

So perhaps I tried a different tack. Maybe I decided I didn't need a mother. If I could only find the right spell, drink the necessary magic potion, my bendy baby legs would support me. I could haul myself out of the little metal cot, pack a bag with a spare nappy and a bottle, wrap myself up warm in my new hand-knitted matinée jacket and patter over the polished floor. I'd go out of the nursery, down the corridor, bump myself down the stairs on my padded bottom and out of the main entrance into the big wide world.

What was my mother thinking all this time? She was lying back in her bed, weepy and exhausted, wondering why they wouldn't bring her baby.

'She can't feed yet, dear. She's got a poorly mouth,' said the nurses.

My mum imagined an enormous scary wound, a great gap in my face.

'I thought I'd given birth to a monster,' my mum told me later. 'I wasn't sure I *wanted* to see you.'

But then, on the fourth day after my birth, one of the doctors discovered her weeping. He told her the monster fears were nonsense.

'I'll go and get your baby myself,' he said.

He went to the nursery, scooped me out of my cot and took me to my mother. She peered at me anxiously. My mouth was back in place, just a little sore at the edge. My eyes were still baby blue and wide open because I wanted to take a good look at my mother now I had the chance. I wasn't tomato red and damp like a newborn baby. I was now pink-and-white and powdered and my hair was fluffy.

'She's pretty!' said my mum. 'She's just like a little doll.'

My mum had always loved dolls as a little girl. She'd played with them right up until secondary school. She loved dressing them and undressing them and getting them to sit up straight. But I was soft flesh, not hard china. My mother cradled me close.

My dad came and visited us in hospital. Fathers didn't get involved much with babies in those days but he held me gently in his big broad hands and gave me a kiss.

My grandma caught the train from Kingston up to London, and then she got on a tube, and then she took the Paddington train to Bath, where we lived, and then a bus to the hospital, just to catch a glimpse of her new granddaughter. It must have taken her practically all day to get there because transport was slow and erratic just after the war.

She was a trained milliner, very nifty with a needle, quick at knitting, clever at crochet. She came with an enormous bag of handmade baby clothes, all white, with little embroidered rosebuds, a very special Christmas present when there was strict clothes rationing and you couldn't find baby clothes for love nor money.

I had my first Christmas in hospital, with pastel-coloured paperchains drooping round the ward and a little troop of nurses with lanterns singing carols and a slice of chicken and a mince pie for all the patients. This was considered a feast as food was still rationed too. Luckily my milk was free and I could feed at last.

Can you think of a Jacqueline Wilson book where the main character has a little chat even though she's a newborn baby?

It's Gemma, in my book *Best Friends*. Gemma chats a great deal, especially to Alice. They've been best friends ever since the day they were born. Gemma is born first, at six o'clock in the morning, and then Alice is born that afternoon. They're tucked up next to each other that night in little cots.

I expect Alice was a bit frightened. She'd have cried. She's actually still a bit of a crybaby now but I try not to tease her about it. I always do my best to comfort her.

I bet that first day I called to her in baby-coo language. I'd say, 'Hi, I'm Gemma. Being born is a bit weird, isn't it? Are you OK?'

I often write about sad and worrying things in my books, like divorce and death – though I try hard to be as reassuring as possible, and I always like to have funny parts. I want you to laugh as well as cry. One of the saddest things that can happen to you when you're a child is losing your best friend, and yet even the kindest of adults don't always take this seriously.

'Never mind, you'll quickly make a *new* best friend,' they say.

They don't have a clue how lonely it can be at school without a best friend and how you can ache with sadness for many months. In *Best Friends* I tried hard to show what it's really like – but because Gemma is pretty outrageous it's also one of my funniest books too. I like Gemma and Alice a lot, but I'm particularly fond of Biscuits.

He's my all-time favourite boy character. He's so kind and gentle and full of fun, and he manages not to take life too seriously. Of course he eats too much, but I don't think this is such an enormous sin. Biscuits will get tuned in to healthy eating when he's a teenager, but meanwhile I'm glad he enjoys his food. His cakes look delicious!

2

My Mum and Dad

I was fine. My mum was fine. We could go home now.

We didn't really have a *proper* home, a whole house we owned ourselves. My mum and dad had been sent to Bath during the war to work in the Admiralty. He was a draughtsman working on submarine design, she was a clerical officer. They met at a dance in the Pump Room, which sounds like part of a ship but is just a select set of rooms in the middle of the city where they had a weekly dance in wartime.

My mum and dad danced. My mum, Biddy, was twenty-one. My dad, Harry, was twenty-three. They went to the cinema and saw *Now, Voyager* on their first proper date. Biddy thought the hero very dashing and romantic when he lit two cigarettes in his mouth and then handed one to his girl. Harry didn't smoke and he wasn't one for romantic gestures either.

However, they started going out together. They went to the Admiralty club. They must have spun out a lemonade or two all evening because neither of them drank alcohol. I only ever saw them down a small glass of Harvey's Bristol Cream sherry at Christmas. They went for walks along the canal together. Then Harry proposed and Biddy said yes.

I don't think it was ever a really grand passionate true love.

'It wasn't as if you had much choice,' Biddy told me much later. 'There weren't many men around, they were all away fighting. I'd got to twenty-one, and in those days you were starting to feel as if you were on the shelf if you weren't married by then. So I decided your father would do.'

'But what did you like about Harry?'

My mum had to think hard. 'He had a good sense of humour,' she said eventually.

I suppose they did have a laugh together. Once or twice.

Harry bought Biddy an emerald and diamond ring. They were very small stones, one emerald and two diamonds, but lovely all the same.

They didn't hang about once they were engaged. They got married in December. Biddy wore a long white lace dress and a veil, a miracle during wartime, when many brides had to make do with short dresses made out of parachute silk. She had a school friend who now lived in Belfast, where you didn't need coupons for clothes. She got the length of lace and my grandma made it up for her.

She had little white satin shoes – size three – and a bouquet of white roses. Could they have been real roses in December during the war? No wonder my mother is holding her bouquet so proudly. Harry looks touchingly proud too, with this small pretty dark-haired girl holding his arm. They'd only known each other three months and yet here they were, standing on the steps of St John's Church in Kingston, promising to love and honour each other for a lifetime.

They had a few days' honeymoon in Oxford and then they went back to Bath. They'd lived in separate digs before, so now they had to find a new home to start their married life together. They didn't have any money and there weren't any houses up for sale anyway. It was wartime.

They went to live with a friend called Vera, who had two children, but when my Mum quickly became pregnant with me, Vera said they'd have to go.

'No offence, but there's not room for two prams in my hall. You'll have to find some other digs.'

They tramped the streets of Bath but my mother had started to show by this time. All the landladies looked at her swollen stomach and shook their heads.

'No kiddies,' each said, over and over.

They must have been getting desperate, and now

they only had one wage between them, because Biddy had to resign from work when people realized she was pregnant. There was no such thing as maternity leave in those days.

Eventually they found two rooms above a hairdresser's. The landlady folded her arms and sucked her teeth when she saw Biddy's stomach, but said they could stay as long as she didn't ever hear the baby crying. She didn't want her other lodgers disturbed.

Biddy promised I'd be a very quiet baby. I was, reasonably so. Harry came to collect Biddy and me from the hospital. We went back to our two furnished rooms on the bus. We didn't have a car. We'd have to wait sixteen years for one. But Harry did branch out and buy a motorized tandom bike and sidecar, a weird lopsided contraption. Biddy sensibly considered this too risky for a newborn baby.

I was her top priority now.

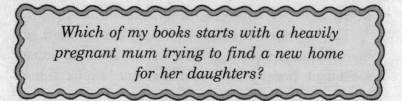

Which of my books starts with a heavily pregnant mum trying to find a new home for her daughters?

It's *The Diamond Girls*. That mum has four daughters already: Martine, Jude, Rochelle and Dixie. She's about to give birth to the fifth little Diamond and she's certain this new baby will be a boy.

'I've got a surprise for you girls,' said Mum. 'We're moving.'

We all stared at her. She was flopping back in her chair, slippered feet propped right up on the kitchen table amongst the cornflake bowls, tummy jutting over her skirt like a giant balloon. She didn't look capable of moving herself as far as the front door. Her scuffed fluffy mules could barely support her weight. Maybe she needed hot air underneath her and then she'd rise gently upwards and float out of the open window.

I'm very fond of that mum, Sue Diamond, but *my* mum would probably call her Common as Muck. Sue believes in destiny and tarot cards and fortune-telling. My mum would think it a Load of Old Rubbish.

I wonder which Diamond daughter you feel I'm most like? I think it's definitely dreamy little Dixie.

3

Babyhood

Biddy settled down happily to being a mother. I was an easy baby. I woke up at night, but at the first wail my mum sat up sleepily, reached for me and started feeding me. She had a lamp on and read to keep herself awake: *Gone with the Wind*; *Forever Amber*; *Rebecca*. Maybe I craned my neck round mid-guzzle and tried to read them too. I read all three properly when I was thirteen or so but I wasn't really a girl for grand passion. Poor Biddy, reading about dashing heroes like Rhett Butler and Max de Winter with Harry snoring on his back beside her in his winceyette pyjamas.

I didn't cry much during the day. I lay in my pram, peering up at the ceiling. At the first sign of weak sunshine in late February I was parked in the strip of garden outside. All the baby books reckoned fresh air was just as vital as mother's milk. Babies were left outside in their big Silver Cross prams, sometimes for hours on end. If they cried, they were simply 'exercising their lungs'. You'd never leave a pram outside in a front garden now. You'd be terrified of strangers creeping in and wheeling the baby away. But it was the custom then, and you 'aired' your babies just like you did your washing.

There was a *lot* of washing. There were no disposable nappies in those days so all my cloth nappies had to be washed by hand. There were no washing machines either, not for ordinary families like us, anyway. There wasn't even constant hot water from the tap.

Biddy had to boil the nappies in a large copper pan, stirring them like a horrible soup, and then fishing them out with wooden tongs. Then she'd wash them again and rinse them three times, with a dab of 'bluebag' in the last rinse to make them look whiter than white. Then she'd hang them on the washing line to get them blown dry and properly aired. Then she'd pin one on me and I'd wet it and she'd have to start all over again. She had all her own clothes to wash by hand, and Harry's too – all his white office shirts, and his tennis and cricket gear come the summer – and I had a clean outfit from head to toe every single day, sometimes two or three.

I wore such a lot of clothes too. In winter there was the nappy and rubber pants, and then weird knitted knickers called a pilch, plus a vest and a liberty bodice to protect my chest, and also a binder when I was a very young baby (I think it was meant

16

to keep my belly button in place). Then there was a petticoat, and then a long dress down past my feet, and then a hand-knitted fancy matinée jacket. Outside in winter there'd be woolly booties and matching mittens and a bonnet and several blankets and a big crocheted shawl. Perhaps it was no wonder I was a docile baby and didn't cry much. I could scarcely expand my lungs to draw breath wearing that little lot.

They were all snowy white and every single garment was immaculately ironed even though all I did was lie on them and crease them. My mother took great pride in keeping me clean. She loved it when people admired my pristine appearance when she wheeled me out shopping. She vaguely knew Patricia Dimbleby, Richard Dimbleby's sister, David and Jonathan Dimbleby's aunt (all three men are famous broadcasters), and plucked up the courage to ask her for tea.

I wonder what she gave her. Milk was rationed. Biscuits were rationed. Did she manage to make rock cakes using up her whole week's butter and sugar and egg allowance? Still, the visit was a success, whatever the sacrifice. Sixty years later my mum's face still glows when she talks about that visit.

'She positively *gushed* over you. She said she'd never seen such a clean baby, so perfectly kept, everything just so. She said I was obviously a dab hand at washing and ironing.'

It's interesting that the one children's classic picture book my mother bought for me was Beatrix Potter's *Mrs Tiggywinkle*. My mother didn't like animals: 'Too dirty, too noisy, too smelly.' She usually turned her nose up at children's books about animals, but though Mrs Tiggywinkle was undoubtedly a hedgehog, she was also a washerwoman, and a very good one too.

Which baby in one of my books is discovered without any clothes at all on the day she is born?

It's April, in *Dustbin Baby*. She's abandoned by her mother, thrust into a dustbin the moment she's born.

I cry and cry and cry until I'm as red as a raspberry, the veins standing out on my forehead, my wisps of hair damp with effort. I am damp all over because I have no nappy. I have no clothes at all and if I stop crying I will become dangerously cold.

I've always wondered what it must be like not to know your own family. Imagine being told to crayon your family tree at school and not having a single name to prop on a branch. April doesn't know who her mother is, who her father is. She doesn't know who *she* is. So she sets out on her fourteenth birthday to find out.

4

Housewife's Choice

Biddy didn't just keep me sparkling clean. She fussed around our rented flat every day after breakfast, dusting and polishing and carpet-sweeping. She didn't wear a turban and pinny like most women doing dusty work. She thought they looked common.

She listened to the Light Programme on the big wooden radio, tuning in to *Housewife's Choice*, singing along to its signature tune, *doobi-do do doobi-do*, though she couldn't sing any song in tune, not even 'Happy Birthday'.

When she was done dusting, we went off to the shops together. You couldn't do a weekly shop in those days. We didn't have a fridge and there was so little food in the shops, you couldn't stock up. You had to queue everywhere, and smile and simper at the butcher, hoping he might sell you an extra kidney or a rabbit for a stew. Biddy was pert and pretty so she often got a few treats. One day, when he had no lamb chops, no neck or shoulder, he offered my mum a sheep's head.

She went home with it wrapped in newspaper,

21

precariously balanced on the pale green covers of my pram. She cleaned the head as best she could, holding it at arm's length, then shoved it in the biggest saucepan she could find. She boiled it and boiled it and boiled it, then fished it out, hacked at it and served it up to Harry with a flourish when he came back from work.

He looked at the chunks of strange stuff on his plate and asked what it was. She was silly enough to tell him. He wouldn't eat a mouthful. I was very glad I still had milk for my meals.

She couldn't go back to the butcher's for a few days as she'd had more than her fair share of meat, so she tried cutting the head up small and swooshing it around with potatoes and carrots, turning it into sheep soup.

Harry wasn't fooled. There was a big row. He shouted that he wasn't ever going to eat that sort of muck. She screamed that she was doing her best – what did he expect her to do, conjure up a joint of beef out of thin air? He sulked. She wept. I curled up in my cot and sucked my thumb.

There were a lot of days like that. But in the first photos in the big black album we are smiling smiling smiling, playing Happy Families. There are snapshots of days out on the tandem, blurred pictures of me squinting in the sunlight but still smiling. I'm in my summer woollies now, still wearing several layers, but at least my legs are bare so I can kick on my rug.

There are professional photos of me lying on my tummy, stripped down to my knitted knickers, smiling obediently while Biddy and the photographer clapped and cavorted. There are pictures of me sitting up on the grass but I always have a little rug under me to keep me clean. There's even a photo of me in my tiny tin bath. What a palaver it must have been to fill it up every day and then lug it to the lavatory to empty it.

My grandma must have been stitching away as I'm always wearing natty new outfits. By the autumn I'm wearing a tailored coat with a silky lining, a neat little hood and matching buttoned leggings, with small strappy shoes even though I can't walk properly yet.

I had my first birthday. Biddy and Harry gave me a book – not a baby's board book, a proper child's history book, though it had lots of pictures. Biddy wrote in her elaborately neat handwriting: *To our darling little Jacqueline on her first birthday, Love from Mummy and Daddy.*

I don't think I ever *read* my first book, but when I was older, I liked to look at the pictures, especially the ones of Joan of Arc and the little Princes in the Tower. I think my grandma might have made me felt toy animals because there's a photo of me sitting on the rug between Biddy and Harry, playing with a horse with a felt mane and a bug-eyed fawn.

The local paper did a feature on young married couples living in Bath and Biddy and Harry were picked for it. She's wearing a pretty wool dress embroidered with daisies and thick lisle stockings. Harry is wearing a smart suit with a waistcoat, probably his year-old wedding suit, but he's got incongruous old-man plaid slippers on his feet. Did he have to change his shoes the minute he got inside the front door in case he brought mud in?

We look a happy little threesome, sitting relaxed in front of the fire. We *needed* that fire during the winter of 1946/1947. It was so cold that all the pipes froze everywhere. The outside lavatory froze up completely. There was no water, not even cold. Harry had to go up the road with a bucket and wait shivering at the standpipe. Biddy stuck it out for a few weeks, but then she packed a big suitcase for her, a little one for me, dismantled my cot, balanced the lot on my pram, and took us to stay with my grandparents in Kingston.

We stayed on, even when it was spring. Harry lived by himself in Bath until the summer, and then left the Admiralty and managed to get a job in the Civil Service in London, even though he'd left school at fourteen. They looked for a place to rent but half of London had been bombed. There were

24

no flats anywhere, so Harry moved in with my grandparents too.

Which of my books starts with the main girl describing all the beds she's ever slept in, including her baby cot? For a little while they live with her step-gran, though it's a terrible squash – and my poor girl has to share a bed with this grandma.

It's *The Bed and Breakfast Star*.

I had to share it with her. There wasn't room in her bedroom for my campbed, you see, and she said she wasn't having it cluttering up her lounge. She liked it when I stopped cluttering up the place too. She was always wanting to whisk me away to bed early. I was generally still awake when she came in. I used to peep when she took her corset off.

She wasn't so little when those corsets were off. She took up a lot of the bed once she was in it. Sometimes I'd end up clutching the edge, hanging on for dear life. And another thing. She snored.

I love Elsa in *The Bed and Breakfast Star*. She's so kind and cheery, though she does tell really awful old jokes that make you groan! I'm not very good at making up jokes myself, so when I was writing the book, I asked all the children I met in schools and libraries if they knew any good jokes, and then I wrote them down in a little notebook, storing them up for Elsa to use. There were a lot of very funny jokes that were unfortunately far too rude to print in a book!

There used to be several bed and breakfast hotels for the homeless in the road where I lived. I used to chat to some of the children in the sweetshop or the video shop. I knew how awful it must be to live in cramped conditions in a hotel, and many of their mums were very depressed. Still, the children themselves seemed lively and full of fun. I decided to write a book about what it's like to be homeless, but from a child's point of view.

The Bed and Breakfast Star has a happy ending, with Elsa and her family living in the very posh luxury Star Hotel – though I don't know how long they'll be able to stay there!

5

38 Fassett Road

We lived at 38 Fassett Road, Kingston, for the next two years. I was probably the only one of us who liked this arrangement. It was much more peaceful living with Ga and Gongon. These were the silly names I called my grandparents before I could talk clearly and I'm afraid they stuck.

It must have been difficult for my grandparents having a volatile couple and a toddler sharing their living room, cluttering up their kitchen, using the only bathroom and lavatory. It must have been agony for my parents not being able to row and make up in private. They couldn't even be alone together in their own bedroom because I was crammed in there with them in my dropside cot.

I didn't have my own bedroom until I was six years old. I didn't really *need* one when I was little. I didn't have many possessions. I had my cot. I had one drawerful of underwear and jumpers in my mother's chest of drawers. I had one end of her wardrobe for my frocks and pleated skirts and winter coats.

I had my toys too, of course, but there weren't

many of them. It was just after the war and no one had any money. I did royally compared with most little girls. My first doll was bigger than me, hand-made by my Uncle Roy. He was in hospital a long time during the war because his whole jaw was shot away and had to be reconstructed. He passed the time doing occupational therapy, making a huge doll for me, and then later one for *his* newly born daughter Rosemary.

I called my doll Mary Jane. She had an alarmingly nid-noddy head and her arms and legs dangled depressingly but I tried hard to love her. She had brown wool curls, a red felt jacket and a green skirt. You could take her clothes off but then she looked like a giant string of sausages so I generally kept them on. Mary Jane never developed much personality, but I remember being astonished on a rare visit to my uncle and aunt's to find that Rosemary's twin doll had exactly the same staring face and woolly hair and dangling body but wore a yellow jacket and a blue skirt. It was as if I'd found a letter box painted yellow, a lamppost painted blue. She was my first doll, my only doll, and I thought all other rag dolls would be identical.

I was given a new doll the next Christmas. I had a doll every single Christmas throughout my childhood – and a book for my birthday. My next doll was Barbara. She was a real shop-bought doll with a cold hard body and eyes that opened and shut if you tipped her upside down. The first day I owned her I tipped her backwards and forwards until she must have been dizzy, and her eyelids went *click click click* like a little clock. Her eyes were brown and her hair was short and brown and curly, rather like mine. She had a frock with matching knickers and little silky white socks and white plastic shoes that did up with a small plastic bobble.

She was a little girl doll, not a baby, but she had her very own pram. Her composition legs were permanently bent in a spread sitting position so she was very happy to be wheeled about. I pushed the pram around my grandma's back garden and up and down the hallway and in and out of her kitchen.

I had twins the following year, Timmy and Theresa, soft dolls with green checked clothes. Timmy had rompers and Theresa a little dress, again with matching knickers. They had little felt shoes, very soft. The twins were soft all over, but compact – very satisfying after large floppy Mary Jane and hard Barbara, though I tried hard to love all my children equally. Some great-auntie gave me Pandora, a quirky little rag doll with a severe hat and waistcoat and a disconcertingly middle-aged face. My pram was getting crowded by this time.

It was hard to cram all five dolls under the covers.

Then tragedy struck. I was pottering with my pram in the front garden, wheeling my family round and round the pretty crocus patch, when the Maloneys' mad dog came bounding in the front gate. The Maloneys were a very large Irish family, all with carrot-coloured hair and a zest for living. They'd been bombed out and temporarily rehoused opposite my grandparents, causing havoc in the quiet suburban street.

The dog barked furiously and then leaped at my pram. I screamed. Biddy and my grandma came running but they were too late. The dog seized hold of Timmy and ran off with him, shaking and savaging him as if he was a huge rat. He dropped him halfway down the street, tiring of the game. Timmy was brought back scalped, his face chewed to pulp and both arms severed. I wanted to keep and tend him and love him more than ever, but Biddy and Ga said I couldn't possibly play with him now. Poor Timmy was thrown in the dustbin.

I kept my children cooped up indoors for a long time after that. I rode my little green trike in the garden but tensed anxiously whenever I heard the Maloneys' dog barking. But it didn't put me off dogs in general. I longed for a puppy but Ga wasn't any fonder of animals than my mother.

I would always pat any friendly dog I found and

make up imaginary dogs when I played Mothers and Fathers. When I read the Famous Five books at six or seven, I didn't envy George her adventures or even her famous picnics with lashings of ginger beer. I just longed for her dog Timmy. Then one day out at the seaside we came across a very lifelike toy Pekinese in a department store. It was a model of the artist Alfred Munnings's dog Black Knight, VIP. I was told this stood for Very Important Person, which seemed an excessive title for a dog, but I wasn't quibbling. I *longed* for this wonderful toy dog but it was hopelessly expensive. Astonishingly, Biddy fumbled in her white summer handbag for her purse. She bought him!

'Is he for *me*?' I whispered.

'Well, who else would it be for, you soppy ha'p'orth,' said Biddy.

'Is he going to be my birthday present or Christmas present?'

'You might as well have him now,' said Biddy.

'Oh, Mummy, really! You're the best mum in the whole world!'

'Yes, of course I am,' said Biddy, laughing. 'Now, let's hope you stop going on and on about getting a wretched dog. You've got one now!'

I walked out of the shop with him under my arm. He stayed permanently tucked there for weeks. Old ladies stopped me in the street and asked to pat my dog and acted surprised when they found out he wasn't real. I told them shyly that his name was Vip.

At last I was able to write school essays about My Pet. Vip slept in my arms every night. Even when I was a teenager, he slept at the end of my bed by my feet, like one of those little marble dogs on a tomb. I still have him, though my mum had a go at restuffing him and he's never been the same since – he's very fat and lumpy now. Even his sweet expression has changed so that now he looks both dopey and bad-tempered. He obviously didn't take kindly to being restuffed.

I still don't have a real dog because I travel about too much, but when I slow down and stay put, I intend to have not one dog, but two – a retired greyhound called Lola and a little black miniature poodle called Rose.

Which of my characters had a doll called Bluebell – and a fantasy Rottweiler for a pretend pet?

It was Tracy Beaker, of course.

My mum came to see me and she'd bought this doll, a doll almost as big as me, with long golden curls and a bright blue lacy dress to match her big blue eyes. I'd never liked dolls all that much but I thought this one was wonderful. I called her Bluebell and I undressed her right down to her frilly white knickers and dressed her up again and brushed her blonde curls and made her blink her big blue eyes, and at night she'd lie in my bed and we'd have these cosy little chats and she'd tell me that Mum was coming back really soon, probably tomorrow.

Poor Tracy. Someone pokes Bluebell's eyes out and she never feels the same about her afterwards. I think it's just as well Tracy doesn't *really* have a Rottweiler.

Tracy Beaker is the most popular character I've ever invented. She'd be so thrilled to know she's had a very popular television series, her own magazine, all sorts of Totally Tracy toys and stationery and T-shirts and pyjamas, a touring musical and now *three* books about her, *The Story of Tracy Beaker*, *The Dare Game* and *Starring Tracy Beaker*.

I've often told the silly story of how I got her name. I was lying in my bath one morning, starting to make up Tracy's story in my head as I soaped myself. I knew I wanted my fierce little girl to be called Tracy. It sounded modern and bouncy and had a bit of attitude. I couldn't find a suitable surname to go with it. Everything sounded silly or awkward. I looked around the bathroom for inspiration. Tracy Flannel? Tracy Soap? Tracy Toothbrush? Tracy Tap? Tracy *Toilet*?

I gave up and got on with washing my hair. I don't have a shower, so I just sluice the shampoo off with an old plastic beaker I keep on the edge of the bath. I picked up the beaker. Aha! *Tracy Beaker!*

6

Hilda Ellen

I had two books when I was at Fassett Road. I
had my birthday-present history book and now
I also had a Margaret Tarrant nursery rhyme book
with rather dark colour plates. The children wore
bonnets and knickerbockers and boots and fell
down hills and got chased by spiders and were
whipped soundly and sent to bed. My mum or my
dad or my grandma must have read them to me
several times because I knew each nursery rhyme
by heart.

I can't imagine my grandad reading to me. He
was a perfectly sweet, kindly man, though his bushy
eyebrows and toothbrush moustache made him
look fierce. He put on a pinstripe suit every
weekday, with a waistcoat and a gold watch on a
fob chain, kept in its own neat pocket, and caught
the train from Surbiton. He spent all day at
'business' in London. He was a carpet salesman in
Hamptons, a big department store. He was
eventually made manager of his department, a very
proud day. He always smelled slightly of carpets,
as if he secretly rolled himself up in his stock.

He returned home at half past six, listened to *The Archers* on the radio, ate his supper and fell asleep in the armchair, pale hands folded over his waistcoat as if guarding his watch. He gave me a sixpence occasionally or offered me a boiled sweet but that was the extent of our relationship. I don't think I ever sat on his lap. I remember once combing his hair playing hairdressers when I was older, but this was unsatisfactory too, as he had very little hair to comb.

He seemed to have very little of anything, including personality, a nine-to-five man who did nothing with his life – yet he had fought in the reeking muddy trenches in the First World War until he was shot and sent home, badly wounded. Maybe he was happy to embrace a totally peaceful, boring, suburban life – no mud, no bullets, no swearing soldiers, just his little hedge-trimmed semi and his wife, and Phil and Grace Archer and old Walter Gabriel on the radio.

My grandma seemed settled too, perhaps because she'd had such a rackety-packety childhood. I loved curling up by her chair as she sewed, getting her to tell me stories about when-she-was-a-little-girl. These weren't silly Diddle-Diddle-Dumpling See-Saw-Marjorie-Daw stories that didn't make sense, like the rhymes in the Margaret Tarrant book. These were gritty tales of an unwanted, unloved child sent from pillar to post – the sort of stories I'd write myself many years later.

My grandma's mother died of cancer when she was only twenty-seven. Ga, Hilda Ellen, was seven, and her brother Leslie was five. Her father, Papa, was a Jack-the-lad businessman, a fierce, feisty little man up to all sorts of schemes. He palmed his children off on different relatives and got on with his life without them. Leslie was packed off to an uncle, and as far as I know, was never reunited with his sister.

Hilda Ellen was sent to two maiden aunts who were very strict, but they taught her to sew beautifully. She loved dolls. She didn't have a proper big china doll – no one wanted to waste any money on giving her presents – but she scavenged for coppers and sometimes dared save her Sunday school donation, and bought tiny china dolls from the local toyshop. You could get one the size of your thumb for a halfpenny but her hair was only painted in a blob on her head. Penny dolls were the size of your finger and had real silky long hair you could arrange with a miniature brush.

All the dolls were stark naked apart from painted socks and shoes. Hilda Ellen raided her aunts' workbox and made them tiny clothes. At first they were just hastily stitched wrap-around dresses and cloaks, but soon she had the skill to make each doll a set of underwear, even ruffled drawers, and over these they wore embroidered dresses and pinafores and coats with hoods to keep their weeny china ears warm.

The dolls were a demanding bunch and wished for more and more outfits. Hilda Ellen got bolder in her search for material. When the dolls wanted to go to a ball, she crawled to the back of the older auntie's wardrobe and cut a great square out of the back of an old blue silk evening frock. The auntie caught Hilda Ellen twirling her dolls down the staircase, looking like a dancing troupe in their blue silk finery. She recognized the material. She wouldn't have worn that evening frock in a month of Sundays but she was still appalled. Hilda Ellen was sent packing.

Papa had taken up with a new lady by this time and didn't want a daughter getting in the way. Hilda Ellen was sent to relatives who ran a pub in Portsmouth. It was a rough pub, always heaving with sailors, not really a suitable home for a delicate little girl, but Hilda Ellen loved it there.

'I didn't have to stay in my room. Well, I didn't *have* a room. I just had a cot and shared with the bar girls. But every evening I helped in the pub, collecting up the glasses. My uncle would often sit me on the counter and get me to sing a song for all the sailors.'

She was given so many pennies she had a whole drawerful of tiny dolls, and she bought her own scraps of silk and velvet and brocade from the remnant stall at the Saturday market.

Then she was given her own big doll! The hairdressing salon along the road had a china doll in the window with very long golden curls of real hair. She sat there to advertise the hairdressing expertise of Mr Bryan, the owner. Hilda Ellen snipped her own hair every now and then, but she often paused outside the salon window, gazing at the beautiful china doll in her cream silk dress, her golden curls hanging right down to her jointed hips.

Mr Bryan didn't have many clients. He was near retiring age. At Christmas he decided to call it a day and close the business. He donated his doll with the long hair to a local charity which was giving a party for all the poor children of Portsmouth. They tied it to the top of the Christmas tree, like a giant fairy.

Hilda Ellen was at the party. She craned her neck, peering up at the wondrous doll. The Mayor of Portsmouth came in dressed as Father Christmas, his gold chain gleaming under his false beard. He started handing out presents from the tree to every child in the room. Hilda Ellen's heart thumped under her muslin bodice.

Maybe Mr Bryan had seen her peering wistfully in his window and murmured a word in the Mayor's ear. Maybe the Mayor truly *was* Father Christmas. Whatever . . . Hilda Ellen was called out, a young lad was sent scampering up a ladder to the top of the tree, and the beautiful doll was put in Hilda Ellen's arms. She clasped her tight, burying her face in that soft golden hair, quivering with happiness.

She called the doll Mabel and loved her passionately. She made her an entire trousseau of elaborate clothes: a sailor suit with a pleated skirt, a velvet dress with tiny pearl buttons and a crochet collar, a winter coat edged in fur, with a fur-trimmed bonnet and a little fur muff to match.

Hilda Ellen was blissfully happy. She wanted to live in Portsmouth for ever but Papa's lady was now his new wife, with a child on the way. When the baby was born, Papa decided they'd save on a nursemaid and bring Hilda Ellen back to make herself useful. She was old enough, wasn't she – ten or eleven at least?

It was a great pity they'd all forgotten exactly how old she was, even Hilda Ellen herself. She'd had a lot of changes of school but she was bright and loved working hard. She shone especially in needlework classes and art, but she was good at all the academic subjects too. Her teachers thought she was definite scholarship material. She sat the exam without a hint of nerves and passed with flying colours, all set to go to a posh girls' high school, her sights fixed on getting into art school later.

There was just the formality of sending in her birth certificate. When Papa eventually found it at the back of a desk drawer, they had a shock. Hilda Ellen had somehow mislaid a year of her life. She was eleven going on twelve. So that was it. She was too old for the scholarship.

It sounds crazy now. I'm sure someone would ensure that this bright, hard-working girl still got a scholarship somehow. Maybe if her father had pushed harder, they'd have made an exception. But people just shrugged their shoulders and said sorry. Hilda Ellen went and lay on her bed, head in her pillow. I don't know whether she wept. I never saw her cry, not even when she was an old lady in terrible pain. She wasn't one to make a fuss, she just got on with things.

She stayed with Papa and her stepmother. She didn't think much of her. She didn't think much of baby Jack either, or his little sister Barbara, who arrived a year or so later. She bathed them and fed them and sang them to sleep every evening while her stepmother cosied up to Papa. Hilda Ellen had to share the nursery with her half-

45

siblings, but she kept Mabel sitting on a high shelf out of harm's way.

She attended the local elementary school until she was thirteen, but then she had to leave to earn her living. She certainly wasn't going to be a full-time nursery maid. She thought she'd found the ideal job. On a material hunt to the Bon Marché department store in south London she saw they were advertising for attractive young girls to work the newly installed elevators. They were very proud of these beautiful brass lifts, considered very glamorous and state-of-the-art for Edwardian times. They'd already employed a little dark girl and kitted her out in a crimson uniform, to be a special lift girl. Hilda Ellen was little and very fair. The Bon Marché management thought they'd found an excellent contrasting pair.

Hilda Ellen went home full of excitement but Papa was shocked at the idea. He'd not cared what she got up to during her childhood but now she was under his roof she had to behave like a lady. Ladies definitely weren't employed as lift girls. Papa thought they were on a par with chorus girls – or worse.

There was no arguing. Hilda Ellen pressed her lips together so hard her mouth disappeared. Perhaps it made Papa think harder about his daughter and what she should do with the rest of her life. She was good at sewing. She'd made all those fancy outfits for that doll of hers, and a few natty bits and bobs for little Jack and Barbara. Perhaps she ought to be properly trained?

He apprenticed her to a milliner. Hilda Ellen stitched away, pins in her pursed mouth, plaiting straw into hats, like some poor princess in a fairy story.

Then, in 1914, war broke out. Papa went to buy presents for Jack and Barbara at Christmas and found there were hardly any toys in the shops. All the best dolls and toy animals were made in Germany, only we were of course at war with the Germans now. Papa was ever enterprising. Now was the perfect time to start up his own doll factory. He knew nothing about doll-making but that didn't deter him. It should be simple enough. He just needed to take some doll to pieces to see exactly how it was made.

Hilda Ellen came home after a long stint at the milliner's. She went upstairs to free her soft hair from its pins and brush it into a fluffy cloud round her shoulders. She looked up at the shelf to nod at Mabel and her lovely longer tresses. Mabel wasn't there.

Mabel was dismembered in a workroom, cut up like meat on a butcher's block. Even her beautiful blue glass eyes were poked into the hollow of her severed head.

Hilda Ellen met my grandfather, George Alfred, the next year. She was walking arm in arm with a girlfriend over Blackheath, deliberately slowing down as they went past the soldiers' convalescent home, giggling when the poor bandaged boys lounging in deckchairs in the garden called out compliments.

George Alfred took a shine to little blonde Hilda Ellen. He asked her if she'd care to go out with him. She liked the look of this dark handsome soldier with his arm in a sling. She said yes. She'd have said yes if he'd been pug-ugly and bandaged like a mummy. She couldn't wait to leave home.

This is a difficult question! Which of my books is dedicated to my grandma – and can you give me a reason why I chose that book in particular?

Look in the front of *The Suitcase Kid*. It says:

In memory of Hilda Ellen Smeed

There are *several* reasons why I chose this book for my grandma. It's about Andy, who has to move backwards and forwards after her parents split up, living one week with Mum, one week with Dad, never having her own room, her own space, her own *life*. I thought the young Hilda Ellen had a lot in common with Andy.

I also have Andy becoming very close to an elderly couple, Mr and Mrs Peters. Mrs Peters has arthritis but still manages to sew, just like my grandma. Mrs Peters gives Andy her own sewing box for Christmas.

It's got all these little compartments stuffed with threads and needles and a silver thimble and a tape measure that snaps back into place when you touch the button. The compartment tray lifts out and at the bottom are all sorts of materials from her own scrap bag, soft silks and velvets and different cottons with tiny sprigs of flowers and minute checks and pin-head dots, all perfect for making into dresses for Radish. She's got so many little outfits now she wants me to change her all day long so that she can show them all off.

I've made her a dance-frock that covers her paws, a velvet cloak lined with cotton wool fur, even a little sailor-suit with a big white collar and a white cap with special ear-holes.

7

Telling Stories

I once asked my grandma what was the most important thing that had ever happened to her.

'Buying our house,' she said.

I was surprised at the time. It seemed such a sad thing to say. It was such an *ordinary* house too, a suburban semi – two bedrooms and a box room, with no distinguishing features. But now I can see that she didn't necessarily mean the bricks and mortar and all the dark heavy furniture and the dull Axminster carpets. I think she meant she'd got a home at last.

She had a peaceful life living with my grandfather. I never once heard them quarrel. The very worst thing they would call each other was *Fathead*, and that was said in terms of mild irritation, nothing more. They weren't a demonstrative couple at all. I didn't ever see them kiss or cuddle or even hold hands. I knew they slept in the same bed because I was allowed to jump into it when Gongon got up to make their early morning cup of tea.

I'd cuddle up with my sleepy grandma until Gongon came back with the big wooden tray and two

53

green china cups of tea and the biscuit tin. He'd give the tray to Ga and clamber carefully back into bed, and then we'd sit up and they'd sip their tea and we'd all nibble custard creams from the tin. They kept the same tin throughout my childhood, replenishing it from Woolworths' loose biscuits counter every couple of weeks. It was orange and yellow and black, a sunset scene with dark silhouettes of buildings against the evening sky. Every time I go to an antique fair I look for that particular tin design. It must be out there somewhere!

Then my grandpa would go off to the bathroom to shave with his bristle brush and cut-throat razor, going ever so carefully *round* his trim moustache, while my grandma wriggled into her corsets. I wasn't supposed to watch but of course I peeped at her from under the blankets. I was fascinated by this large, prawn-coloured garment, so different from my mother's silky camiknickers and suspender belt. My mum had brassieres too, stitched into two rigid pyramids. She left one at the end of the bed each night, and when my dad was being rude, he'd poke the ends with his finger, denting them. My grandma's corset didn't seem to allow for two bosoms. It compressed my grandma's chest into one large upholstered cushion.

Ga kept her dressmaker's dummy in the little box room with her treadle sewing machine. I'd play

54

games with the dummy and sometimes hug her. She felt *exactly* like my grandma in her corsets.

Cassandra and Rose in one of my favourite books, *I Capture the Castle* by Dodie Smith, pretend that their dressmaker's dummy is a genteel friend called Miss Blossom. Ga's dummy didn't have one personality; she played multiple parts in the theatre of my imagination. One day she'd be a fairy queen, the day after she'd be a mermaid, then she'd be my sister, or a big monkey, or my very special best friend.

I didn't have many real friends when I was at Fassett Road, though there are photos of me playing with various children who came to tea. We are wheeling my pram, sitting on my trike, squatting in my sandpit by the French windows. I am the Persil child, smiling in my dazzling white sunsuit, my white socks, my white sandals. I got told off if I marked my socks or scuffed my shoes or spilled orange squash down my beautifully ironed dress. I didn't have a proper bath every day. This was a once-a-week ordeal with red carbolic soap and lots of scrubbing, and if I whined when the shampoo went in my eyes, I was given a good shake. I had a daily 'wash-down', shivering on the bathroom mat, and my nails were cleaned and clipped until my fingers tingled.

I was a reasonably well-behaved child, though as my mum said, I had my moments. If I was naughty, I was sent upstairs to bed. If I was being really irritating, I got smacked too. Parents smacked their children without any guilt or remorse in those days. It was a perfectly acceptable thing to do. I never got really *hurt*. My mum just gave me a slap on the back of my legs or on my bottom. My grandma gave me a light tap if she caught me with a finger in a pot of her delicious home-made raspberry jam, or picking holes where her kitchen plaster was peeling. My grandpa didn't get involved enough to smack. I asked Biddy if Harry ever smacked me. I was frequently frightened of him, right up to the day he died in his fifties, but I couldn't remember him hitting me.

'He hit you once when you were little, and it worked a treat,' said Biddy. 'You were standing up in your cot one evening, howling and howling, and you simply wouldn't be quiet. I went up to try to get you to lie down and go to sleep. So did Ga. You simply wouldn't see reason. So Harry went up and he gave you an almighty whack and you shut up straight away.'

If I'd done something really bad, I tried to talk myself out of being blamed. I didn't exactly fib. I simply told stories.

'*I* didn't do it,' I'd say, wide-eyed, shaking my head. 'Gwennie did it.'

I'd sigh and shake my head and apologize for

Gwennie's behaviour. Gwennie was one of the imaginary friends who kept me company during the day. Biddy and Ga found this mildly amusing at first but the novelty soon wore off, and I found myself being punished twice over for Gwennie's misdemeanours.

'You must always always always tell the truth, Jac,' Biddy said solemnly. 'You mustn't *ever* tell fibs.'

Try telling that to a storyteller!

Which girl in one of my books always tries to tell the truth? She lives with her grandparents, just like I did when I was little.

It's Verity in *The Cat Mummy*.

I try very hard to tell the truth. That's what my name Verity means. You look it up. It's Latin for truth.

I can be as naughty as the next person but I try not to tell lies. However . . . it was getting harder and harder with this Mabel-mummy situation.

The Cat Mummy is a very sad book (though there are lots of funny bits too). Many children write to me to tell me about their pets. They're very special to them. They say: 'Dear Jacqueline, I'm nine years old and I love reading your books and I've got a cat called Tiger and a guinea pig called Dandelion. Tiger is stripy and Dandelion loves *eating* dandelions. Oh, and I've got a mum and a dad. I've got a little brother too and he is a *pest*.'

They nearly always mention their pets *before* their parents and brothers and sisters, as if they're much more important. The sad thing is, pets don't live as long as people. I often get the most touching tear-stained letters, telling me that some beloved hamster or white rat has died.

I decided to write a story about a girl whose old cat dies. She feels terrible and wishes she could preserve her in some way. She's just learned about the Ancient Egyptians at school and it gives her a very very weird idea!

8

Shopping

I loved living as an extended family at Fassett Road. I liked all the little routines of my preschool life. We would walk into Kingston every day to go shopping. It was a fifteen-minute brisk trot, a twenty-five-minute stroll. Biddy stuck me in my pushchair to save time. It was a pleasant walk, across a little blue bridge over the Hog's Mill stream, down a long quiet street of Victorian houses, some large, some small, past the big green Fairfield, past the library, until we could see the red brick of the Empire Theatre in the middle of town. (I was taken to see *Babes in the Wood* there when I was little and loved it, though I found it puzzling that the boy Babe was a girl and the Old Dame clearly a man.)

Ga had already developed arthritis and could only walk slowly, so we strolled together, peering at everything along the way. We had our favourite houses. She would always pause in front of a pretty double-fronted house with four blossom trees in the garden. '*That*'s my favourite,' she'd say, so of course it was my favourite too.

I live in that house now. My grandma is long dead, but I've hung her photo on the wall – and a replacement china Mabel sits underneath.

Shopping was very different in those days. I loved going to Sainsbury's, but it wasn't a big supermarket with aisles and open shelves and trolleys. The Kingston Sainsbury's then had beautiful mosaic-tiled walls like an oriental boudoir. You queued at the butter counter and watched some white-overalled wizard take the butter and pat it into place with big wooden paddles. You couldn't afford very much butter so you always had margarine too. They were both so hard you had to butter the end of the loaf and then slice it. There wasn't any such thing as ready-sliced bread in packets then.

Then you queued at the cheese counter until another white-garbed lady sliced off the exact amount of cheese for you with a wire and ticked your ration book. You queued at the bacon counter and watched the bacon boy (who always wore a pencil behind his ear) use the scary bacon slicer, cutting your four rashers of best back bacon into wavy ribbons on greaseproof paper. You could queue for a whole *hour* in Sainsbury's and still come out with precious little in your string shopping bag.

Then we'd go to John Quality's on the corner by the market. It was another grocer's, with big sacks of sugar and nuts and dried fruit spread out on the floor, just the right height for me. I was always a very good girl, but Gwennie sometimes darted her hand into a sack and pulled out a dried plum, just like Little Jack Horner in the nursery-rhyme book at home.

Then we'd trail round the market, maybe queuing for plaice or cod or yellow smoked haddock from the fish stall on a Friday, spending a long time haggling at the fruit stall and the veg stall. You could get bananas and oranges now the war was over, but everything was strictly seasonal and none of us had ever even *heard* of exotic things like kiwi fruit or avocado pears or butternut squash. Fruit meant apples and pears, veg meant cabbage and carrots and cauliflower. The frozen pea hadn't even been invented. We didn't have a fridge or freezer anyway.

The only shop I disliked was the butcher's – it smelled of blood. The meat wasn't cut up in neat cellophaned packets, it was festooned all over the place, great red animal corpses hung on hooks in the wall, chickens still in their feathers, rabbits strung in pairs like stiff fur stoles, their little eyes desperately sad.

I shut my own eyes. I breathed shallowly, trying hard not to moan and make a fuss, because if I'd behaved perfectly, I *might* be taken to Woolworths for a treat. I loved Woolworths. It had its own distinctive smell of sweets and biscuits and scent and floor polish. (When I left home and went to live in Scotland at seventeen, I used to go into the Dundee Woolworths just to breathe in that familiar smell.)

I liked the toy counter best. I'd circle it on tiptoe, trying to see all the penny delights: the glass marbles, the shiny red and blue and green notebooks, the spinning tops, the tin whistles, the skipping ropes with striped handles. I always knew what I wanted most. Woolworths sold tiny dolls, though sadly not the beautiful little china dolls of my grandma's childhood. These were moulded pink plastic – little girls with pink plastic hair and pink plastic dresses, little boys with pink plastic shirts and pink plastic trousers, and lots and lots of pink plastic babies in pink plastic pants. The babies came in different sizes. You could get big penny babies alarmingly larger than their halfpenny brothers and sisters.

I was a deeply sexist small girl. I spurned all the pink plastic boys. I bought the girls and the little babies, playing with them for hours when I got home. I sometimes made them a makeshift home of their own in a shoebox. I took them for trips to the seaside in my sandpit. Best of all, I stood on a stool at the kitchen sink and set them swimming in the washing-up basin. They dived off the taps and went boating in a plastic cup and floated with their little plastic toes in the air.

I was very fond of the water myself. I hadn't yet
been swimming in a proper pool but we'd had
several day trips to Broadstairs and Bognor and
Brighton when I'd had a little paddle. Most days
in the summer Ga took me for a ten-minute walk
to Claremont Gardens, near Surbiton Station,
where there was a paddling pool. She stripped me
down to my knickers and I ran into the pool and
waded happily in and out and round about.

I wasn't supposed to go right under and get my
knickers wet, but even if I was careful, the other
children often splashed and I got soaked. One time
Ga thought my knickers were so sopping wet I'd
be better off without them, so she pulled my dress
on, whipped my knickers off, and walked home with
them clutched in a soggy parcel in her hand. We
encountered Mrs Wilton, her next-door neighbour,
on the way home.

'Look at this saucepot!' said Ga, twitching up
my dress to show my bare bottom.

Then she waved my wet knickers in the air while
she and Mrs Wilton laughed their heads off. I was
mortified. I was worried Mrs Wilton might think
I'd *wet* my knickers and then she'd tell her children,
Lesley and Martin, and they'd think me a terrible
baby.

I liked the trips to the paddling pool, but the

best treat of all was a walk to Peggy Brown's cake shop in Surbiton. There's a health food shop on the site now, but in the long-ago days of my childhood the only health supplements we had were my free orange juice for vitamin C (delicious) and cod liver oil for vitamins A and D (disgusting) and some black malty treacle in a jar that my grandpa licked off a spoon every day.

Our concept of eating for health was a little skewed too: a fried-egg-and-bacon breakfast was considered the only decent way to start the day so long as you were lucky enough to have the right number of coupons; white bread and dripping was a nutritious savoury snack; coffee was made with boiled full-cream milk and a dash of Camp; and as long as you ate your bread and butter first then you always tucked into a cake at tea time.

Ga made proper cooked meals every day. She rolled her own pastry and made wonderful jam with the berries from the back garden, but I can't remember her baking cakes. On ordinary days we had pink and yellow Battenburg cake or sugary bath buns from the baker's near Kingston market – but once a week we went to Peggy Brown's special cake shop.

They were fancy cakes with marzipan and butter cream and little slithers of glacé cherry or green angelica. They had exotic names: Jap cakes, coconut kisses, butterfly wings. There were tarts with three different jams – raspberry, apricot and greengage, like traffic lights. My favourites were little individual lemon tarts with a twirl of meringue on top.

Excellent as they were, the cakes were only incidental. We went to Peggy Brown's to look at the shop windows. The owner had a vast collection of dolls, from large Victorian china dolls as big as a real child down to tiny plastic dolls not very different from my Woolworths girls.

Each season Peggy Brown did a magnificent display: false snow and a tiny Christmas tree in winter; Easter eggs and fluffy bunnies in the spring; real sand and a painted blue sea in summer; red and gold leaves and little squirrels in autumn. Each season every single doll had a new outfit. They had hoods and mufflers and velvet coats, Easter bonnets and party frocks, swimming costumes and tiny buckets and spades, Fair Isle jumpers with matching berets and miniature wellington boots.

Ga and I gazed and gazed. Ga worked out how Peggy Brown had designed the costume, cut the pattern, sewn the seams. I rose up, strode straight through the glass and squatted amongst the dolls. We made a snowman or stroked the rabbits or paddled in the sea or kicked the crackly autumn leaves until Ga gave me a little tug. I'd back out of the glass into the real world and we'd go home and eat our Peggy Brown cakes for tea.

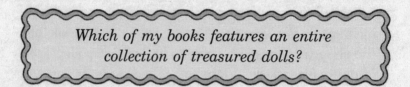

Which of my books features an entire collection of treasured dolls?

68

It's *Lizzie Zipmouth*.

Dolls! Old china dolls in cream frocks and pinafores and little button boots, soft plush dolls with rosy cheeks and curls, baby dolls in long white christening robes, lady dolls with tiny umbrellas and high heels, a Japanese doll in a kimono with a weeny fan, dolls in school uniform and swimming costumes and party frocks, great dolls as big as me sitting in real wicker chairs, middle-sized dolls in row after row on shelves, and tiny dolls no bigger than my thumb standing in their own green painted garden beside a doll's house.

I once had a very touching letter from a little girl of about nine. She loved playing with Barbies but a friend had come to tea and thought her a terrible baby because she still played with dolls. She told everyone at school and now my poor girl was getting horribly teased. I wrote back to tell her that I'd played with dolls right throughout my childhood and that I still had several sitting on my windowsills or lolling on spare sofas.

I put lots of dolls in my books, especially in *Lizzie Zipmouth*, where Lizzie and her scary step-great-gran bond over their love of dolls. It's a bonding thing in my family too. Ga loved dolls, Biddy loved dolls – in fact she's got a collection that outnumbers

Great-Gran's. Hundreds of little glass eyes stare at you when you go into her spare room! I've got all kinds of dolls in my house too, and so has my daughter Emma.

9

Lewisham

We moved when I was nearly four. Jean, one of Biddy's friends, had a brother who rented a small flat in a three-storey house in Lewisham. He was ready to move on now, so Biddy and Harry took his two rooms.

I'm sure they were glad to get their own place. I wasn't as keen. I missed Ga and our daily routines and my treats terribly. It wasn't as if I had a place of *my* own. I still had to share their bedroom. I had my small bed and a rug where I was allowed to line up my dolls, and that was it.

We learned pretty quickly why Jean's brother was so keen to move on. A demented man called Stanley lived on the ground floor. He screamed abuse at his cowed wife. He screamed abuse at us too, and at poor Miss Parker, the retired lady who lived on the top floor. He crouched in his flat, ears cocked, and the moment he heard you coming down the garden path he'd be at his window, purple in the face, screeching.

'Hurry up the steps because of Stanley,' my mum would say when we came back from shopping trips.

She didn't need to tell me twice. I charged up in my Clarks sandals, tripping in my haste.

We couldn't escape him even when we were upstairs in our flat. Stanley would start slamming his own door violently. Not once or twice. Over and over again for a good fifteen minutes, while the whole house shook. Harry was out at work at the Treasury from Monday to Friday. Biddy and I were stuck at home. We went out as much as possible, taking the tram as far as we could afford.

I looked young for my age so Biddy sat me on her lap and pretended I was under three so she didn't have to pay the fare. She let me take a book with me if it was a long journey. I now owned the Margaret Tarrant storybook as well as the nursery rhymes. Margaret Tarrant was very popular in those days and Ga sent me Margaret Tarrant animal postcards every week. I also had *Pookie*, a story about a white rabbit with wings, but all these books were too big and cumbersome to take out. I took a Shelf Animal book instead. They were the same size and format as Beatrix Potter, twee tales about toy animals – Stripy the Zebra, Getup the Giraffe, Woeful the Monkey, Gumpa the Bear and a small, fluffy, teddy-type creature called Little Mut.

I begged Biddy and Harry to read them to me at bed time. Now on the tram I murmured my own versions of the stories as I flipped the pages, looking at the brightly coloured pictures. It looked for all the world as if I was reading. Passengers gazed at me in awe and complimented my mother on my precocity. Biddy smirked, pleased she could take pride in me at last. I usually made her cringe in public. I was still immaculately turned out but I had developed a ferociously needy thumb-sucking habit. I didn't just suck my thumb, I frequently hid my nose in a pocket handkerchief, rubbing the soft cotton with my finger.

'Take that thumb out of your mouth and put that hankie in your pocket! You look tuppence short of a shilling,' Biddy said, again and again.

Sometimes she'd jerk my thumb out impatiently but I stubbornly stuck it straight back. I was missing Ga. Maybe Biddy was too. We were certainly both missing Kingston.

We went up onto Blackheath once, but it seemed too bare and wide and empty compared with the oak woods and red deer of Richmond Park, or the gentle meadows of Home Park, with its flocks of sheep and speckled fallow deer. We went to the Lewisham shops but they weren't a patch on Kingston. There wasn't even one market, whereas we had *three* in Kingston: a big fruit and vegetable market, a little apple and flower market, and on Mondays a huge bustling free-for-all market with ducks and chickens and rabbits, bolts of material, socks and knickers, kiddies' clothes, glittery jewellery, toys, kitchenware and general junk.

Lewisham's big shops didn't compare either. They didn't have a Hides, with wonderful wooden cabinets with labelled drawers, and a money machine that whizzed over your head on a track all round the ceiling like a little runaway train, and then chugged back again with your change. It didn't have Bentalls department store, with its fancy Tudor Rose restaurant where Ga and Gongon took me once for a special treat. Bentalls had a big book department, and toys, and Royal Doulton china ladies, and every season they had a special fashion show, with real mannequins swishing up and down the catwalk. The compère told you their names – Jean and Pam and Suzie and Kay – so you felt as if they were your friends. There was always one older, slightly stouter model, and she got called Mrs Harris. I played in my head that she looked after all the other girls and cooked them their supper at night.

We arrived very late for one fashion show and were stuck right at the back, where I couldn't see a thing. Biddy urged me to burrow forwards, though I felt too shy to barge too far. Then suddenly I was lifted up onto a lovely older girl's lap, where I sat entranced for the rest of the show. She was very fair and very thin, with a silver bangle that slid up and down her delicate arm. She let me try it on and everyone went 'Aaah!' I sensed from the way everyone was staring that she was special.

Biddy was pink with excitement when I was returned to her.

'Do you know who that was? Petula Clark!'

She was a very famous child actress and singer. We listened to her in *Meet the Huggetts* on the radio. She went on to be an internationally acclaimed singer in her adult life. Every time I heard her sing 'Downtown' I'd bore my friends, saying, 'Guess what! I've sat on Petula Clark's lap!'

Which family in one of my books lives in a rented flat above a difficult complaining old lady called Mrs Luft?

It's Marigold and Star and Dolphin in *The Illustrated Mum*.

> 'What a racket!' Mrs Luft was down at the front door sorting through the post. She seemed to be addressing an invisible audience. 'Do they have to be so noisy on the stairs? Up and down, late at night, first thing in the morning. Some people have no consideration.'

Mrs Luft is a positive saint compared with Stanley! I'm sure she feels Marigold and her girls are the worst neighbours in the world. She'd probably be right too, but I have such a soft spot for Marigold and Star and especially Dolphin.

I got the idea for *The Illustrated Mum* in New York! I was there on holiday with my daughter

Emma. We'd had a wonderful day going round the Metropolitan Museum of Art and lots of shops, and now we were sitting down with an ice cream in Central Park, wiggling our sore feet and watching the world go by.

We watched an attractive arty-looking woman wander past. She had the most amazing unusual decorative tattoos. Two little girls were skipping along beside her, in dressing-up clothes and grown-ups' high-heeled silver sandals.

When they were out of earshot, Emma turned to me, smiling.

'They look like characters in one of your books!' she said.

'Maybe I'll write about them one day,' I said – and I did.

Greetings from SUNNY CLACTON

10

Holidays

We had a proper week's holiday by the seaside the first Lewisham summer. We went to Clacton, staying in a hotel called Waverley Hall. This had been carefully chosen (after much peering through brochures) because it wasn't licensed to sell alcohol. My parents thought people who drank so much as a pre-dinner gin and tonic were rabid alcoholics. Waverley Hall boasted many alternative entertainments: a dance held twice a week, a beetle drive and a talent competition.

We have group photos of Waverley Hall guests for year after year of Clacton holidays. When I peer at those fifties families, all the women well permed and posing earnestly for the camera, the men grinning foolishly in their open-necked sports shirts, I feel the adult me would need several stiff gins to do the hokey cokey in their company – but when I was a child, Waverley Hall seemed as glamorous as Buckingham Palace and the evening's entertainment almost overwhelmingly exciting.

Waverley Hall was managed by a charismatic man called Will Tull who struts through my memory singing, 'Let me en-ter-*tain* you!' Every evening there he was, encouraging this stiff congregation of bank clerks and shop managers and secretaries and teachers to run novelty races and sing 'Ten Green Bottles' and join him in his enthusiastic rendition of 'The Music Man'.

'*I am the Music Man and I can p-l-a-y,*' he'd sing.

We'd all yell, '*What can you play?*'

He'd sing, '*I play the . . . trumpet.*'

Then he'd pretend, oompah-oompah-oompah-ing, and we'd all join in too – my mother who couldn't sing a note in tune, my father who was cripplingly shy and self-conscious in public, both oompah-ing at the tops of their voices.

They took dance nights seriously. My dad wore a proper suit and tie and his black patent dancing shoes and my mum wore a sleeveless flowery chiffon frock with a sweetheart neckline. I wore my best embroidered party frock. So long as I behaved myself, I was allowed to stay up for the dance too. I hadn't been taught to waltz or quickstep but I was good at following if someone steered me around, and sometimes my dad let me stand on his shiny shoes and we'd twirl round the ballroom together, stepping in perfect unison.

Will Tull varied dances, announcing Paul Jones swap-your-partner spots and invitation waltzes and Gay Gordons. There was always a conga at the end of the evening. Every single guest stepped and tapped around the ballroom, through the empty dining room, around the kitchens, out into the gardens, across the tennis courts . . . I think if Will Tull had led us down the road, across the esplanade, over the sands and into the sea, we'd have all followed.

The only entertainment I hated was talent night. My dad sensibly steered well clear of this one. My mum did the one and only recitation she knew by heart, 'The Lion and Albert', with a fake northern accent. This was strange, because she normally detested accents of any sort. She was so worried I'd 'pick up' a Lewisham south London twang and drop my aitches like 'ankies that she started sending me to elocution lessons at *four*. Mercifully, there was no 'How now, brown cow' twaddle. We learned poems instead.

I was the littlest and I had a good memory so it was easy for me to shine. My entire elocution class was entered for a public competition. We chanted an interminably long poem about birds. I was the Yellow Hammer. I had to pipe up, 'A little bit of bread and no cheese!' It went down a treat.

Biddy bought me an A. A. Milne poetry book. (I didn't catch up with Winnie-the-Pooh until much later. When I made friends with a child called Cherry whose parents called her Piglet and her sister Pooh, I didn't understand and thought they were very rude nicknames, if not downright insulting.)

I soon learned a lot of the poems and recited 'What is the matter with Mary Jane?' at the talent contest the first year at Waverley Hall. I did it complete with ghastly little actions, hands on hips, shaking my head, pulling faces. It was enough to make a sane person vomit but I got loud applause. Biddy was in seventh heaven. She'd always longed for a child like Shirley Temple. She had my wispy hair permed into a grisly approximation of those abundant curls and encouraged me to perform when I was even shyer than my father.

The second Waverley Hall holiday I knew the whole of 'The King's Breakfast' by heart. Oh dear, I've not looked at it since but I've just gone over it in my head and I still know every awful line.

I was scared of performing it in public in front of everyone. I fidgeted nervously throughout our evening meal, going over the poem again and again in my head. I'd got sunburned on the beach and I felt hot and headachy. I gulped down glass after glass of cold water. A big mistake.

Straight after dinner the child performers in the talent contest were herded off to the little room behind the stage in the ballroom. I didn't get a chance to visit the lavatory. I soon realized

I badly needed to go. I was far too shy to tell anyone. I didn't have enough gumption to go off and find a loo myself. I just sat with my legs crossed, praying.

Will Tull had decided to put me on almost at the end because I'd been such a success the year before. I waited and waited and waited, in agony. Then at long long last it was my turn. I shuffled on stage, stood there with clasped hands, head up, chest out, toes slightly turned out, in perfect elocution class stance.

'"The King's Breakfast" by A. A. Milne,' I announced clearly.

A little ripple of amusement and anticipation passed through the audience. I relaxed. An even worse mistake.

> *The King asked*
> *The Queen, and*
> *The Queen asked*
> *The Dairymaid:*
> *"Could we have some butter for*
> *The Royal slice of bread?"'*

I declared, as I felt a hot trickle seep down my legs into my snowy white socks.

I didn't stop. I didn't run off stage. I carried on reciting as a puddle spread around my feet. I said the last line, bowed, and then shuffled off in soggy despair.

Biddy came and found me and carted me off to get changed. I wept. She told me that no one had even noticed, which was an obvious lie. I'd seen Will Tull follow me on stage with a *bucket and mop*. Biddy switched tack and said everyone simply felt sorry for me. I'd heard the 'aaahs' myself, so knew this was partly true, but I'd also heard the sniggers from the other children. I was sure they'd make my life hell the next morning at breakfast.

'We have to go *home*! Please please please let's go home,' I begged.

Biddy and Harry scoffed at me.

'But they'll all tease me and laugh at me and call me names,' I howled.

'Don't be so silly. They'll have forgotten all about it by tomorrow,' said Biddy.

This seemed to me nonsense. However, no one stared or whispered when we came down to breakfast the next morning. The children didn't breathe a word about it, not even when we were playing in the ping-pong room without adult supervision. I couldn't understand it. Maybe Will Tull had scurried from room to room and implored everyone to be kind, though this seems highly unlikely. Maybe my mum was right and they really had forgotten. Hadn't even noticed. Whatever.

We carried on our Clacton holiday as usual. We sat on the sands all morning, Biddy and Harry in deckchairs, me cross-legged on a towel, reading or colouring or making sand palaces for my pink plastic children. We had our favourite spot, reasonably near the pier so we could stretch our legs and visit the lavatories, but not so near that the strange, dank, rotting-seaweed, under-the-pier smell tainted our squash and sandwiches.

There were amusement arcades on the pier. I didn't care for them particularly, but Harry loved pinball and Biddy proved surprisingly expert on the crane machines. In one week's holiday she could manoeuvre fifty or sixty toy planes and tiny teddies and Poppit bracelets and packets of jacks and yoyos and pen-and-pencil sets out of those machines, enough for several Christmas stockings for friends' children.

There was a theatre at the end of the pier. I didn't like the journey right along the pier to this theatre. I hated it when the beach finished and the sea began. You could see right through the wooden planks to where the water frothed below. My heart thudded at every step, convinced each plank would splinter and break and I would fall right through.

I cheered up when we got to the theatre and watched the summer season variety acts. I liked the dancers in their bright skimpy outfits, kicking their legs and doing the splits. My parents preferred the stand-up comedians, especially Tony Hancock. When *Hancock's Half Hour* started on the radio, they listened eagerly and shushed me if I dared say a single word.

We went to Clacton year after year. We had a lovely time. Or did we? I always got over-excited that first day and had a bilious attack, throwing up throughout the day and half the night. Biddy would sigh at me as if I was being sick on purpose, but Harry was always surprisingly kind and gentle and would hold my forehead and mop me up afterwards. It's so strange, because when I was bright and bouncy he'd frequently snap at me, saying something so cruel that the words can still make me wince now. I was always tense when he was around. I think Biddy was scared of him too at first. She used to cry a lot, but then she learned to shout back and started pleasing herself.

There was always at least one major row on holiday, often more. They'd hiss terrifying insults at each other in our bedroom and not speak at the breakfast table. My tummy would clench and I'd worry that I might be sick again. I'd see other families laughing and joking and being comfortably silly together and wish we were a happy family like that. But perhaps if I'd looked at *us* another day, Biddy and Harry laughing together, reading me a cartoon story out of the newspaper, I'd have thought *we* were that happy family.

In the days before everyone had ordinary cameras, let alone phone and digital cameras, you used to get special seaside photographers. They'd stand on the esplanade and take your photo and then you could come back the next day and buy it for sixpence or a shilling.

There are two very similar such photos taken the Clacton holiday I was six – but they're so very different if you look closely. The first caught us unawares. It's a cloudy day to match our mood. My father looks ominously sulky in his white windcheater, glaring through his glasses. My mother has her plastic raincoat over her arm and she's clutching me by the wrist in case I dart away. I'm looking solemn in my playsuit and cardigan, holding a minute bucket and spade and a small doll. I am wearing my ugly rubber overshoes for playing in the sand. I do not look a prepossessing child.

Biddy berated Harry and me for spoiling that photograph and insisted we pose properly the next day. The sun is out in the second photograph and we look in a matching sunny mood. Harry's whipped off his severe glasses and is in immaculate tennis whites. Biddy's combed her perm and liberally applied her dark red lipstick. I'm wearing my favourite pink flowery frock with a little white collar

89

and dazzlingly white sandals. I've just been bought a new pixie colouring book so I look very pleased. Biddy is holding my hand fondly. Harry has his arm round her. We look the happiest of families.

This is an easy question. In which of my books does a little girl wet herself on stage?

It's *Double Act*, my book about identical twins Ruby and Garnet.

They are jointly reminiscing about the time they played twin sheep in the school Nativity play. Ruby is being mean, teasing Garnet about it, even though she knows it's her most painful and humiliating secret.

She got so worked up and nervous when we had to perform on stage that she wet herself. On stage. In front of everyone. But it didn't really *matter*. I don't know why she still gets all hot and bothered if I happen to bring it up. It was dead appropriate, actually, because that's what real sheep do all the time. They don't hang around the stable with their back legs crossed, holding it in. They go all over the place. Which is what Garnet did. And everyone thought it was ever so funny. Except Garnet.

I longed for brothers and sisters when I was a child. I particularly wanted a twin sister, someone to play with all the time, someone to whisper to at night, someone to cuddle when Biddy and Harry were yelling.

I can see it could have disadvantages though if you have a very bossy dominant twin like Ruby!

Mummy   Daddy   Me

11

School

I can't remember my first day at Lee Manor School. I asked my mother if I cried and she said, shrugging, 'Well, all children cry when they start school, don't they?'

I know I cried over my school dinners. I didn't like meat very much and I hated fat. In those days school dinners were mostly fatty mince, stew with large yellow chunks of fat still on the meat, boiled beef and carrots, the fat tinged pink this time, and occasionally stringy roasts with long slender strips of gristle and fat. Fat fat fat. I tried chewing. I tried swallowing whole. I tried spitting it out into my handkerchief.

'Come along, Jacqueline, eat up your dinner and stop being naughty!'

The world where children could choose their own school dinners was far in the future. I tried hard to eat the fat, tears pouring down my face, and then I'd throw up in the smelly lavatories.

The school dinners made their greasy mark upon each day, but I started to learn to read 'cat' and 'hat' and 'mat' and recite the two times table. I chalked pictures – three round blobs with stick arms and legs and smiles across their stomachs and wobbly printing underneath. *Mummy. Daddy. Me.*

I sang *'Daisies are our silver, buttercups our gold'* and *'Jesus bids us shine with a pure clear light'*. I skipped in the school hall in my vest and knickers. I listened avidly at story time, sitting cross-legged, hands on knees, the way we were taught. I made friends with a little girl who had the two things I wanted most in the world: a baby sister and a tiny Yorkshire terrier. I can't remember my friend's name, or her cute sister's, but the dog was called Rags and I loved him, even though he yapped hysterically when I tried to pat him.

I was making good progress at school, but then I got ill. I had measles badly, and then bronchitis, and then, unbelievably, whooping cough, all in the space of six weeks. I can remember those long hot days, coughing until I was sick, and the even longer nights, wide awake and staring into the darkness. I did my best to *stay* awake too, stretching my eyelids wide open, biting my lip, digging my nails into my fingers so that I'd make long ragged hangnails.

I was too scared to sleep because then the nightmares would start. Men would climb right through my bedroom wall and grab at me. They'd pursue me through the streets and chase me on dodgems at the fair. They'd jump out at me as I ran down long corridors. They'd shove me down stairs, throw me out of windows, topple me off towers. I'd fall and fall and fall and then wake up, heart thudding, head pounding, my nightie rucked up round my waist. I'd pull it down and tuck my legs right up inside and wrap my arms round myself and huddle under the covers.

Biddy had told me to say to myself, 'It's only a silly dream' – but the men weren't running after her, they were out to get *me*. I knew they were real, lurking in the wardrobe. Catch me ever tunnelling through to Narnia. I wouldn't dare so much as open the door.

If it was really late and Biddy and Harry had gone to bed, I could clamber in with them. They'd sleepily protest but mostly put up with me. It was much worse if they were in the other room and I was on my own. I'd wait and wait, trying to count my newly learned numbers, and then I'd call out.

I'd always ask for a glass of water. Biddy came a few times and that was wonderful. She'd tell me off, but not seriously. She'd give me my water, turn my pillow over and settle me down again firmly, giving me a quick kiss on the cheek. But nearly always it was Harry. He could be lovely too, gentle and kind and funny. Or he could be cold and impatient and tell me he was sick of this lark. Or

97

he could yell ferociously for no reason. It was so scary not knowing which mood he'd be in. Other little girls could charm their fathers. They could laugh and tease and joke and their fathers would smile at them fondly. I didn't have a clue how to *do* that. I smiled too anxiously, I begged too cravenly, I froze rigid with my thumb forever in my mouth.

However, Harry was very patient with me during the measles-bronchitis-whooping-cough episode. Maybe he should have gone into nursing, though I don't think that was a career option for a man in those days. He rubbed my back, he held my sick bowl, he gave me drinks of water, and if I was awake when he came home from work, he'd read to me.

He read me 'Tuppenny and Squibbit', a cartoon strip in the *Evening Star*, a London newspaper. Tuppenny was a little girl and Squibbit was half a squirrel and half a rabbit. I longed for a pet like Squibbit. When he was in a very good mood, Harry would pretend to be Squibbit and I'd be Tuppenny and feed him nuts. Then Harry would read *my* little cartoon book about Mary Mouse who lived in a doll's house with a dolly family.

I could read the easy Enid Blyton words myself now. I could stagger through my first Noddy book too, though even at five I found the little nodding man and his big-eared buddy highly irritating. Harry introduced me to the Blyton Faraway Tree books. I found these magical in all senses of the word. I was no longer lying hot and itchy and coughing in my narrow little bed. I was wandering through the Enchanted Wood with Jo, Bessie and Fanny, climbing the Faraway Tree, sliding down Moon-Face's slippery-slip slide, sharing toffee-shock sweets with Silky the fairy and her funny walking clock, climbing the little ladder to the land above. I had a snowball fight with snowmen, I battled red goblins, I tumbled over in Rocking Land, and best of all, I went to the Land of Birthdays and ate wishing cake. I was tempted to wish for a fairy outfit like Bessie with real flying wings, but I always plumped for Fanny's wish, a walking talking doll with her own suitcase of clothes.

It can't have been much fun for my father but he read his way through all three Faraway Tree books – and then went on to read me the first few chapters of *David Copperfield*, a mighty literary leap upwards for both of us. I don't know *why* he chose Dickens. He wasn't a man who read the classics himself – he liked Hammond Innes and Ian Fleming. I listened, enthralled. I expect a lot of it went over my head but I still loved this story of young Davey. I was delighted to discover that children in adult novels were much more complex characters than Jo, Bessie and Fanny, with rich inner lives and fears and fancies. I smiled when Davey was with his mother and dear Peggotty, I nibbled my lips raw when his hateful new stepfather was treating him so cruelly, I breathed great sighs of relief, stretching out under the covers, when they went to Yarmouth. *I* got to know all the Peggotty relations and played with Little Emily. I made up further adventures just for Little Emily and me.

My dad never read on into David's adult life. Perhaps he thought I'd lose all grasp of the story. Perhaps I simply got better. It left a deep impression on me though. I still can't read those early chapters without hearing my father's calm quiet voice saying the words – such a *different* voice from when he was in one of his rages.

When I'd stopped whooping, I was still so weak that Biddy had to borrow a baby's pushchair to wheel me around in. I went back to school eventually but it was hard going. I'd missed so many lessons. There are still black holes in my basic knowledge. They'd learned the alphabet when I was away. To this day I find it hard to remember whether 'f' comes before or after 'h', and what about 'o' and 's', and where does 'q' fit in? I have to sing the alphabet song inside my head to work it out.

I missed the rudiments of maths too. I've never

quite *understood* sums. When I'm calculating, I still frequently use my fingers.

Biddy didn't worry that I'd fallen behind at Lee Manor. We were about to move so I'd be going to a brand-new school. We were going to get our own home at last.

*Which sisters have a father as irritable
and unpredictable as Harry?*

It's Prudence and Grace in *Love Lessons*.

'Oh, Miss Know-It-All! Only you know damn all, even though you think you're so smart. You need to get to grips with maths, even if you're just going to waste your time at art college. Remember that, missy. You thought you could swan off and do your own thing, tell bare-faced lies to your own father, waste everyone's time and money—'

He stopped short, his mouth still working silently though he'd run out of words.

'Bernard? Do calm down – you're getting yourself in such a state. You're making yourself ill!' said Mum, catching hold of his arm.

He brushed her away as if she was some irritating

insect. He focused on me. His face was still purple. Even his eyes were bloodshot with his rage.

Harry wasn't really a bit like Prue's father – but they certainly ranted in a similar manner!

12

Cumberland House

My parents had had their name down for a council flat for years. They'd given up on the whole idea when a letter came. Three new six-storey blocks of flats had been built on Kingston Hill. My parents were offered number twelve, on the first floor of the south block.

Cumberland House looks a bit of an eyesore now, three well-worn square blocks with satellite dishes growing out of the brickwork like giant mushrooms. In 1951 they seemed the height of luxury. There was *central heating*! No more huddling over a smoking fire in the living room and freezing to death in the bedroom, having to dress under the eiderdown in winter. There was a fireplace just for show in the living room. We used it as a centrepiece. The Peter Scott print of wild birds hung above it, with our three painted plaster ducks flying alongside.

We had *constant hot water*. This meant we could have a bath every single day. No waiting for the boiler to heat up and carting tin baths around. We could have a bath first thing in the morning or last thing at night. Biddy could wash our clothes whenever she wanted. Well, she didn't ever *want* to wash them, though she did so diligently. She was a feminist long before the word was invented. When I asked her about washing some PT kit one time, she snapped, 'Why should *I* have to wash it?' I said without thinking, 'Well, it's your job, isn't it?'

I wasn't meaning to be cheeky, but Biddy was outraged. It made me rethink the whole concept of what a mum was supposed to do. Jo and Bessie and Fanny's mum cooked and cleaned and washed the clothes – though David Copperfield's mother lay limply on her chaise longue while the servants did the chores. *My* mum, with her smart clothes and her lipsticks and her cigarettes, wasn't anything like *their* mums.

There was a communal laundry room for each block of flats. There were no washing machines, just big sinks in which you scrubbed the clothes using a wash board, and then you squeezed the water out using a big mangle. Biddy seldom fancied carting our clothes downstairs and chatting to the other women. She washed at our kitchen sink, wringing the clothes out fiercely and spreading them out on the dryer. She ironed everything with elaborate care. She even ironed Harry's socks, spreading them out and ironing up to the heel, and then neatly tucking them into paired balls for the airing cupboard.

106

The best thing of all about Cumberland House was the fact that *it had two bedrooms*! My parents had the biggest bedroom, of course, but I still had a whole room all to myself. I was six years old and I had my own space at last. It wasn't decorated as a little girl's room. I'd read about Ellie's pink and white bedroom in an abridged version of *The Water Babies* and I'd felt as awestruck as sooty Tom, but it didn't occur to me that I could ever have a room like that. We had very little money, and Biddy and Harry weren't the sort of parents who made frilly curtains or wooden furniture.

My bedroom had a built-in wardrobe so I could hang up my favourite dresses in a row: my rainbow party frock; my white dress with the cherry print and little cherry buttons; my blue and green flowery dress with puff sleeves; my pink dress with the fruit pattern and the white collar; my sundress with frills at the shoulders like little wings. There were also the clothes I *didn't* like. I detested my navy pleated skirt, which was stitched onto a white bodice. The pleats stuck out at the front. Biddy was forever telling me to pull my stomach in. I also hated my good Harella coat, fawn with a fancy velvet collar. I was supposed to wear it with a pale brown velour hat. I had to wear both the coat and the hat to my new school and got horribly teased. The boys adopted my velour hat as a new football.

107

I can't say I blamed them.

I had my own proper big bed, brand new, but I had to make do with my parents' old brown eiderdown. It had a gold-thread pattern and it felt silky to the touch, but it was a hideous colour. I had a brown ottoman too, an ugly piece of furniture from Ga's junk room, hard as a rock to sit on, but the seat lifted up like a lid and I could store all my drawings and paper dolls and notebooks inside, plus all my 'sets'. I had a doctors and nurses set, a red plastic case containing various odd instruments and a toy thermometer and stethoscope. I also had a nurse's apron and cap marked with a red cross. I was therefore the doctor *and* the nurse, so all my dolls got first-class medical attention when they were poorly.

My toys all seemed career-orientated. I also had a bus conductor's set with a dinky little ticket holder and a machine to punch the ticket; a small grocery shop with tiny jars of real sweets and little cardboard boxes labelled Daz and Omo and Persil; and a post office set with a rubber stamp and pretend postage. I politely played with these a few times, but if I wanted to play buses or shops, I found it easier *imagining* it. These little props always reminded me that I was simply playing a game. Still, they were useful when the little girl next door, Suzanne, came in to play with me. It gave us something to *do* together. I liked playing with Sue but if I was truthful, I preferred playing by myself.

I had a second-hand chest of drawers. The drawers all stuck so you had to jiggle them around and tug hard at the handles. Once I pulled a handle right off and got severely told off. It might be an old junk-shop piece of furniture but it was all we had.

I kept jumpers and cardigans in one drawer. Biddy hadn't inherited Ga's sewing skills but she liked to knit. She made me jumper after jumper, using her favourite 'rabbit-ears' stitch. Biddy said they looked 'jazzy', and used very bright contrasting colours. They were tight and itchy, and although they were beautifully knitted, Biddy never quite mastered the knack of stitching the sleeves onto the main garment. I always had odd puckers on my shoulders. Sometimes the sleeves were so tight I held my arms out awkwardly to ease the tension. We didn't wear uniform at Latchmere, my new school. I wished we did.

I kept my Viyella nighties and my vests and knickers and socks and pocket handkerchiefs in the bottom drawer, all jumbled together. Biddy wanted to keep them neatly separate, using the two half drawers at the top, but I wanted these for my special things.

I kept tiny books in the right-hand drawer. I had the little illustrated prayer book that had once been

Biddy's. Ga gave it to me one day. I was surprised. My dad had once been a choirboy – I'd even seen a photo of him in a long gown with a white collar, standing with his brother Roy – but to the best of my knowledge Biddy had only set foot in a church twice: once when she was married and once when I was christened.

It was a beautiful pearly white book and I longed to show it off at school. It had my mum's name neatly written in the front – *Biddy Clibbens* – but in the back I found a pencilled parody of the Lord's Prayer. It was just a silly schoolgirl version, not really blasphemous, changing 'daily bread' to 'daily bath' and that sort of thing, but I got terribly worried. We had a fierce scripture teacher at school, who scrubbed our mouths out with carbolic soap if we said rude words and rapped us on the knuckles if we printed God or Jesus without capital letters. I was sure she'd think my mother would burn to a crisp in Hell if she saw her schoolgirl prank. Biddy found me agonizing over her naughty rhyme.

'You silly little prig!' she said, laughing at me, but she got an eraser and rubbed vigorously until there wasn't a trace of it left, simply to stop me worrying.

I worried a great deal. Biddy didn't seem to worry at all. She'd been bright at school and at eleven had passed her exams to go to the girls' grammar school. Ga was so pleased. She'd lost her chance of a proper education but now her daughter could benefit. Biddy had other ideas though. She didn't take lessons very seriously and got distracted by boys. She was happy to leave school at sixteen.

For various reasons *I* left school at sixteen too. Poor Ga. I wish she could have stayed alive to watch her great-granddaughter Emma grow up – at last a bright, focused child who worked diligently, came top in all her exams and is now a senior academic at Cambridge. *And* she can sew!

I kept Biddy's prayer book – without the Lord's Prayer – with my Mary Mouse series and a whole flock of Flower Fairy books by Cicely Mary Barker. I loved these little books and spent hours poring over the carefully painted pictures, making up stories about all the fairies, gently stroking their long shiny hair, sometimes tickling their bare toes. I never bothered reading the odd little rhymes on the facing pages but I learned all the flower names. The sweet-pea picture of the big sister fairy tenderly adjusting the pink bonnet on her little baby sister was my all-time favourite.

I had two storybooks by Cecily Mary Barker too, stories that I loved, more stirring than the Faraway Tree books, more accessible than *David Copperfield*. *The Lord of the Rushie River* was about a sad little ill-treated child called Susan, desperate for her sailor father to come home. She's carried away by her friend the swan, and of course she's reunited with her father at the end of the story. She's worried about her ragged clothes but the swan snatches her a beautiful rainbow-embroidered dress.

I tried to make friends with the swans on the Thames when Harry took me to feed the ducks, but their beaks seemed very forbidding and I didn't like the way they hissed at me. They certainly didn't look as if they'd take me for a ride on their feathery backs and find me a lovely new dress.

The second book was *Groundsel and Necklaces*, a tender little tale about a child called Jenny who ends up with 365 necklaces, one for every day of the year. I read these stories over and over again. I loved stories about sad, spirited little children going through hard times. I already knew I wanted to write that sort of story myself one day. I cared passionately about dresses and treasured my own rainbow party dress with smocking from C & A. I didn't have any jewellery at all at that age but read the page where the necklaces are described over and over again. I never dreamed that one day I might have a *ring* for – well, not every day, but at least every week of the year.

I had my little books in the right-hand drawer. I kept my crayons and paints and pens and pencils in the left. I didn't have proper *sets*, though in my teens I'd buy myself a beautiful Derwent coloured pencil every week with my pocket money until I had the entire range in every single shade. Meanwhile I kept my mix of crayons in a biscuit tin with a picture of a little girl called Janet on the top.

Janet was a very popular child model in those days, her photo in all the women's magazines. She had wispy hair, big eyes and a soulful expression. She was wearing a seersucker frock on my tin and peering slightly cross-eyed through several branches of apple blossom. I'd have Janet on her tin beside me as I drew and crayoned, and so long as I was out of earshot of my parents, I'd chat to her companionably.

I also had a small Reeves paintbox, though I was never entirely successful when it came to watercolour painting. I could control my crayons and get the colours to stay in the lines, but the paint ran away with me. I'd try to create a fairy princess with hair as black as coal, but the black would run into her pale pink face and she'd end up looking like a coal *miner*. I'd start a beautiful mermaid with long golden curls and a shining tail but the blue sea would splash right over her and dye her hair bright green.

I kept my doll's house and my toy farm on the

top of my chest of drawers. I was never really a country girl and didn't play with my farm very much. Maybe this was just as well, as the little cows and sheep and chickens and turkey were all made of lead, and I was exactly the sort of silly child who might have licked them. The farm stayed undisturbed most days, the cows not milked, the sheep not shorn, the eggs uncollected. I was busy next door, playing with my doll's house.

It wasn't especially elaborate, a two-up, two-down 1930s little number with a scarlet roof and green latticed windows, but it was fully furnished. I especially loved my three-piece suite in jade-green plastic. It gave me great pleasure just holding the little armchair and running my thumb up underneath, feeling the strange insides.

I had a proper family of doll's house dolls, dear little creatures with woollen hair and tiny clothes, but they were made like pipe cleaners, and if you tried to bend them to sit on the sofa or climb up the stairs, a leg might snap off suddenly in an alarming fashion. Sometimes I just played that it was *my* house. I'd stand with the front swinging open, my face almost inside the rooms, and I'd act like Alice and shrink myself small.

I didn't have a proper edition of *Alice in Wonderland* with the Tenniel illustrations. My *Alice* had sugar-sweet coloured pictures that didn't fit the story at all. I also had an abridged *Peter Pan* with Mabel Lucie Attwell illustrations. Both stories confused me, and because I read them consecutively when I was about six, they amalgamated oddly in my head, so that Peter flew round Wonderland and Tinkerbell shook pepper at the Duchess and Alice joined up with Wendy to make a little house for the Lost Boys.

I'd have been perfectly happy left to my own devices playing alone all day in my new bedroom – but I had to go to school.

Who had a very small bedroom at her dad's house, with a chest of drawers half painted silver?

It's Floss in my book *Candyfloss*.

It was not much bigger than a cupboard. There was just room for the bed and an old chest of drawers. Dad had started to paint it with some special silver paint, but it was a very small tin and it ran out before he could cover the last drawer. He'd propped a mirror on top of the chest and I'd laid out my brush-and-comb set and my china ballet dancer and my little cherry-red vase from my dressing table at home. They didn't make the chest look much prettier.

'Dad's going to finish painting the chest when he can find some more silver paint,' I said. 'And he's going to put up bookshelves and we're going to get a new duvet – midnight-blue with silver stars – and I'm going to have those luminous stars stuck on the ceiling *and* one of those glitter balls like you get at dances – and fairy lights!'

I always try hard to describe the bedrooms of all my girls. I feel so lucky that I can choose whatever style of bedroom I like now. It's got a very big wardrobe along one wall, and when you open the doors, a little light goes on. I've got a pink velvet Victorian chaise longue by the window. There are specially built bookshelves, a Venetian glass dressing table and big mirrors, and a special shrine of pretty Madonnas and angels and a heart-shaped gold sacred relic with a secret message inside. My fashion mannequin Crystal stands in the corner wearing a beaded black evening frock. She has matching black velvet ribbons in her long fair hair. There's a picture of a doll my daughter Emma drew when she was twelve on the wall. There are more dolls

sitting smiling in odd corners and two droopy knitted animals, one a dog and one an elephant. They are *very* like Dimble and Ellarina in *Candyfloss*.

Ann   Michael

13

Latchmere Infants

It's always a bit of an ordeal starting at a new school, especially in the middle of the term. Everyone else has had a chance to make friends. You're the new girl, the odd one out, the one with the weird clothes, the one who doesn't know the way to the toilets, the one who doesn't know where to sit at dinner time.

I had to stay for school dinners at Latchmere because it was too far away to walk home at lunch time. Biddy didn't want me to go to the nearest school at Kingsnympton, the neighbouring council estate. She got it into her head that the Kingston school *furthest* from our flats was the best one and somehow or other wangled me a place there.

It was a problem getting me to school. We didn't have a car. It would be another ten years before we could afford one. The tandem had fallen to bits. Both my parents now had bikes. Harry cycled twelve miles up to London on his. Biddy attempted the couple of miles to my school with me perched precariously on the back. To my shame I couldn't ride a bike myself. Harry had tried to show me but I didn't seem to

119

have any idea how to steer and kept falling off with a clunk so he got irritated and gave up on me.

I was quite a small child but I was really too big to squat on the back of a bike, so after a few weeks Biddy trusted me to walk to school and back by myself.

'You must look both ways every time you cross a road, do you hear me?' said Biddy.

'Yes, Mummy.'

'There's a traffic lady at the Park Road crossroads – she'll show you across.'

'Yes, Mummy.'

'You do know the way by now, don't you, Jac?'

'Yes, Mummy.'

'And you won't ever talk to any strange men?'

'Yes, Mummy.'

'*What?*'

'I mean, no, Mummy.'

'And absolutely *no daydreaming*!'

'Yes, Mummy. No, Mummy,' I said. No daydreaming! It was as if she was telling me to stop breathing.

It wasn't that unusual to let young children walk to school by themselves in those days. Children in the country would think nothing of walking three or four miles. I liked my half-hour's walk through the quiet suburban streets. I'd make up stories inside my head or talk to imaginary friends. If people started looking at me strangely, I'd realize

I was muttering to myself. I soon perfected a mask expression while inside I was up to all sorts. I already knew I wanted to be a writer. Sometimes I'd pretend to be grown up and a famous author and I'd interview myself. Nowadays it still feels faintly unreal when I'm being interviewed, as if I'm still making it up.

The walk *back* from school was much more worrying. I met up with more children wandering home from their own schools. They were mostly in little gangs. I was on my own. There was one boy in particular who really scared me. He went to the school my mother had spurned. Francis wasn't a rough boy, quite the contrary – he came from a wealthy bohemian family who lived in a huge Victorian house at the bottom of Kingston Hill. Biddy knew the family and turned her nose up at them because the children had tousled hair and colourful crumpled clothes and scuffed sandals. I liked the way they looked, especially Rachel, the thin little girl with a gentle face and spindly plaits.

Francis wasn't gentle though. He glared at me every day, clenching his fists. I scurried out of his way as quickly as possible. Sometimes he'd chase after me, thumping me on my back if he got close enough. I'd arrive home shaky and tearful. I didn't want to tell Biddy. She might go to find Francis and tell him off, and any fool knew that that would make him *really* out to get me.

I pretended I had a stomach ache instead. I had a dodgy stomach at the best of times, and had bad bilious attacks every couple of months, so Biddy took me at my word. Sometimes she'd let me climb on her lap and she'd rub my tummy and I'd feel a lot better – though I had nightmares about Francis at night.

Then one day Francis caught hold of me, said a surprisingly rude word, and then punched me hard in the tummy. I had a *real* stomach ache now. It hurt a lot. My eyes watered but I was determined not to cry in front of him. I just stood there, staring straight back at him. He didn't punch me again. He ducked his head and shuffled off. Rachel looked at me anxiously, her face white. She looked as if she was trying not to cry too.

The next day they were standing waiting for me on the corner. I felt sick with fear, but as I got nearer, I saw Francis wasn't glaring. Rachel was smiling timidly. She held out a crumpled bag of home-made fudge.

'These are for you,' she said.

I took the bag. I had a piece of fudge. I offered the bag back to them. They took a piece too. We stood, teeth clamped shut with fudge. Then we swallowed and nodded goodbye. They went down the hill, I went up the hill. We weren't exactly friends now, but we were no longer enemies.

Francis never punched me again.

I found it hard to make school friends the first few days at Latchmere. I wandered around the playground by myself and crept inside the main door and leaned against the radiators, breathing shallowly because the whole corridor smelled of sour milk. We were all given a small bottle of milk each morning. I hated milk, but you had to drink it right down to the bottom or else you got into serious trouble and were lectured about the starving children in Africa. Then the milk monitor collected all the silver tops up and stored them in huge sacks in a cupboard. They stayed there for months before anyone came to collect them.

The head teacher's office was nearby, and the secretaries' office too. There were two secretaries, the Misses Crow, a pair of stout sisters. They both had hearts of gold, but one was sharp and one was sweet and you knew exactly which one to make for if you'd fallen over and needed a bandage.

Miss Stanbridge, the head, was another stout spinster. She bustled past once or twice while I was drooping by the radiator, my expression probably as sour as the milk. Children weren't supposed to be indoors at play times but she didn't chase me outside. She patted me on the head in a kindly fashion, as if I was a little stray dog, and then marched off purposefully in her great black lace-ups.

My form teacher was *lovely*, dear Mrs Horsley. She wore hand-crocheted jumpers and dirndl skirts and was passionate about country dancing. She was a brilliant storyteller and very kind to all the children in her class, though some of the naughtier boys got a light slap on the backs of their legs if they fidgeted or argued. All teachers hit children then. If you were really really bad, you got the cane in front of everyone, but this rarely happened, especially in the Infants.

Mrs Horsley saw I needed to make friends. I think she had a quiet word with two girls in my class, Hilary and Jane, because they decided to take me under their wing. This was very kind of them but I found them a little oppressive. They were tall, gangly, bespectacled girls, very earnest and upright. They played Mothers and Fathers and wanted me to be the baby. They'd whisper to me in their own voices to be naughty, and then they'd sigh and suck their teeth and go '*Bad* Baby!' and act putting me to bed in disgrace.

This got incredibly boring play time after play time. But then one of the boys started playing with us too – Michael, my first boyfriend. He was a cheery boy with slicked-down hair, rosy cheeks and a big smile. His mother dressed him in sensible long corduroy trousers in the winter. Most of the boys then wore ugly grey short trousers that ended an inch or so above their scabby knees. Sometimes their horrible baggy white underpants showed *below* their trouser hems, a total turn-off. Michael had much more style. I liked him – and he seemed to like me.

'What are you girls playing?' he said, circling us with interest.

'We're playing Mothers and Fathers,' said Jane. 'I'm the mother.'

'Then I'll be the father,' said Michael.

'You can't be. *I'm* the father. I'm tallest,' said Hilary.

'Maybe you can be another baby, like Jacky,' said Jane.

'I don't want to be a baby,' said Michael. 'I'll be a monkey, OK?'

He made screechy monkey noises, waddling around and scratching himself.

I giggled.

'You're Micky the Monkey,' I said. 'You're *my* monkey.'

Mothers and Fathers became much more interesting after that. Sometimes we gave Hilary and Jane the slip and played Baby and Monkey games by ourselves.

It was great having a boyfriend. I didn't really have a proper girlfriend for a while. I knew who I liked the most: Ann, a beautiful child with big brown eyes and long curly hair. She was the youngest of four and had that glossy confidence that comes when you're the family favourite. She wore very frilly white knickers that showed beneath her short flouncy frocks whenever she twirled round. Any other girl would have been teased unmercifully about such fancy underwear, but no one ever picked on Ann. She went to ballet classes and sometimes wore her angora ballet bolero to school.

I wanted an angora bolero too, but Biddy wouldn't knit me one because she said the fluff got everywhere and made a mess. I longed to do ballet, but Biddy was against that idea too. She said she'd have to make costumes for me and she didn't have the time or the patience. Ga's hands were twisted with arthritis now and she couldn't take on any costume-making either.

At the end of the first term at Latchmere there was a Christmas concert. Ann wore a white ballet frock with a real sticking-out skirt, and white ballet shoes and a white satin ribbon tying up her ponytail. She did a snowflake dance without one wobble, the star of the show.

I was proud of her, and a little wistful, but I didn't feel jealous. The only time I felt a real stab of envy was a couple of years later in the Juniors when our teacher decided to give out prizes at the end of term.

There were four prizes, one for English, one for arithmetic, one for handicraft and one for sport. I knew I had no chance winning a sport prize. I was the child picked last for any team because I couldn't ever catch a ball. (I was extremely short-sighted but this wasn't discovered until I was ten, so maybe I simply couldn't *see* the ball.) I certainly wouldn't win a handicraft prize because my cross-stitch purses unravelled and my raffia baskets keeled over lopsidedly. I was a hopeless candidate for arithmetic because I couldn't add up or subtract accurately and was a total duffer when it came to problems. *However*, I was good at English. Very good. I wrote longer stories than anyone else. I was good at reading aloud. I was often picked to read a story to the class if the teacher was called away from the classroom.

I so hoped I'd get chosen for the English prize. I didn't get it. Ann did. It was a book, *The Adventures of the Wishing-Chair* by Enid Blyton. I wished wished wished I'd won that book.

I was almost Ann's best friend at that time. We played pretend games together at lunch time, wonderful rich imaginary adventures. Our favourite was playing that we had a tree house right at the top of a huge oak. It took several minutes of energetic 'climbing' before we were safe in our house each play time. That tree stood so tall and sturdy in my imagination that I actually looked

127

for it in the playground when my daughter started going to Latchmere herself years later.

I furnished our imaginary tree house lavishly. We had a library and an art alcove and a tray for our pretend picnics. Ann went along with this, suggesting stuff herself. It was such a joy playing with someone who could invent too. I still fancied myself as the *chief* instigator of our imaginary games though. I was the girl with the vivid imagination, the girl who was always scribbling stories, the girl who always had her head in a book, the girl who was best at English.

But now Ann was that girl, not me.

I went up to Ann and managed to say, 'Well done!' I asked if I could have a look at her book. She showed it to me proudly. We both stroked the nameplate stuck in the front with the word *Prize* embossed in italic letters and then Ann's name written in bright blue ink.

Ann grinned, still very excited, but a little embarrassed too.

'Clever me!' she said.

She said it lightly, sending herself up. I knew she wasn't being *serious*. But when I told Biddy and Harry about the prize that Ann had won, I twisted the tale a little.

'So the teacher picked Ann instead of you?' said Biddy.

'Yes.'

'I suppose she was ever so pleased?'

'Oh yes, she kept going, *Clever me, clever me.*'

'What a nasty little show-off!' said Biddy.

'Clever me' became a catchphrase in our family after that. I always felt a stab of guilt, because I knew I'd been unfair to Ann.

In one of my books the main girl dreads walking home from school by herself because three girls tease her very spitefully.
Which book is it?

It's *Bad Girls* and it's poor Mandy who's getting picked on.

They were going to get me.

I saw them the moment I turned the corner. They were halfway down, waiting near the bus stop. Melanie, Sarah and Kim. Kim, the worst one of all.

I didn't know what to do. I took a step forward, my sandal sticking to the pavement.

They were nudging each other. They'd spotted me.

I couldn't see that far, even with my glasses, but I knew Kim would have that great big smile on her face.

I stood still. I looked over my shoulder. Perhaps I could run back to school? I'd hung around for ages already. Maybe they'd locked the playground gates? But perhaps one of the teachers would still be there? I could pretend I had a stomach ache or something and then maybe I'd get a lift in their car?

I'm very glad I didn't encounter a girl like Kim at Latchmere. Goodness knows how I'd have dealt with her. It's so horrible when you're being bullied. I wanted to write about that particularly mean name-calling teasing that girls are so good at. I've had so many moving letters since from children who have experienced something similar. I'm always so touched if they feel *Bad Girls* has helped them cope.

14

Hospital

I wasn't a particularly robust child. I had my famous bilious attacks, brought on by excitement, anxiety, fatty meat, whatever. Biddy was brisk on such occasions, perhaps thinking I was sick out of sheer cussedness.

'You always pick your moments!' she said, exasperated.

Certainly I chose the only time they left me with Miss Parker at Lewisham to throw up over myself, my bed, the carpet and most of poor Miss Parker. I was frequently sick the first night of a holiday. I was once sick the last two days of a foreign holiday on a coach driving all the way back from the Costa Brava. It was hell for me throwing up repeatedly into carrier bags. It must have been pretty terrible for my fellow passengers too.

Most children are sick once or twice and that's it. I was a little drama queen, being sick at least twenty times over twenty-four hours. I'd not be able to eat or do anything but lie on a sofa with a book sipping Lucozade the next day.

I also had head colds that dragged on for weeks.

I'd sniffle and snort unattractively and then start coughing like a sea-lion. Biddy's remedy was Vick, a smelly menthol ointment in a dark blue jar. She ladled it onto my chest so that my vests and nighties reeked of it, and worst of all, she rubbed it all round my sore nose, even *up* it, so that my eyes streamed. It felt revolting and it meant I couldn't snuffle into my cuddle hankie at night. I couldn't even suck my thumb: my nose was so sealed with Vick and snot that I had to breathe through my mouth.

I'd just be getting better, only coughing when I ran fast, when I'd start to feel that ominous prickling in my nose and the whole cycle would start all over.

Biddy took me to the doctor. He peered down my throat.

'Good God, she's got tonsils the size of plums! We'll whip them out – and her adenoids too – then she'll be right as rain.'

It was the fashion to remove children's tonsils in those days. You didn't argue about it. I was booked in at Kingston hospital for a week. Biddy was to take me there, just five minutes walk down Kingston Hill. She was told when to come and collect me, but there was to be no visiting at all during the week.

'We find it unsettles the children if they have visits from their parents,' the matron said firmly.

You *certainly* didn't argue with matrons. It seems so sad now that little children were delivered into this scary place, dragged off by strangers to have bits snipped out of them, and then left alone without a cuddle for days. At least I was six, old enough to understand what was going on.

It was quite exciting at first, almost like Christmas or a holiday. Biddy bought me a new Viyella nightie, white with little roses, and because she knew it was pointless trying to part me from my cuddle hankie, she bought me a new snow-white cotton handkerchief specially for the hospital.

She also bought me a brand-new doll. I'd only ever had dolls for Christmas or birthday before so I couldn't believe my luck. She was a beautiful blonde doll with silky plaits and a soft smiley face. She had a red checked frock, white socks and red shoes. I knew at once she had to be called Rosalind.

My favourite children's book at that time was a wonderfully imaginative fantasy story called *Adventures with Rosalind* by Charlotte Austen. It was about a little boy called Kenneth who was given an amazing picture book with a blonde little girl on the front. She steps out of the picture and takes Kenneth on many magical adventures in different lands. Rosalind was a courageous and cheerful little girl, an ideal friend for adventures. I hoped my Rosalind doll would be the perfect companion for me during my big hospital adventure.

I was in a ward with ten or twelve other children. It was comforting because we were all in this new weird scary world together. I chatted shyly with Muriel, the little girl in the next bed, and let her hold and admire Rosalind. We pulled faces at each other when we had our first trayful of hospital food. We giggled at the antics of the boys in the beds opposite.

It was the nights that were the worst. The ward seemed to grow enormously. It was so dark I couldn't even see my hand in front of my face. There was a little pool of light right up at one end where the night nurse sat at her desk, but there was no way of telling whether she'd be cross or not if she knew I was awake.

I mislaid my new cuddle hankie. The night nurse must have heard me scrabbling around feeling for it. She stood up and walked down the dark ward towards me, her sensible shoes squeaking on the polished floor. I lay still, my heart thudding. She came and shone her torch right in my face but I squeezed my eyes shut, huddled in a ball, pretending to be fast asleep. She hovered over me, but eventually turned and squeaked back down the ward again. I didn't dare carry on searching for my hankie. I clutched Rosalind tight instead and rubbed my nose against her checked skirt.

I wasn't allowed any breakfast the day of my operation. I wasn't even allowed to keep my new Viyella nightie on. I had to wear a strange operation gown, which was only *half* a nightie, with no proper back to it whatsoever, so that my bottom showed if I turned round. I was worried I might need to go to the toilet. I didn't want the boys laughing at me.

I was put on a trolley and given a ride to the operating theatre. I'd hoped Rosalind might be allowed to go with me, but she was left behind on my bed. I tried to imagine she was running after me, jumping up onto the trolley, swinging her legs and laughing. Then we were in this new eerie room full of alien beings in masks and gowns. One of them held me down while another put an evil-smelling rubber mask over my face. I struggled and they told me to calm down like a good sensible girl and start counting, one, two, three . . . It seemed the maddest time in the world to start an arithmetic lesson but I obediently mumbled, 'Four, five, six . . .'

And then I was asleep, and when I woke up, I was back in my bed with Rosalind tucked up beside me, and a raw pain at the back of my throat.

They let each child have ice cream for the first meal after their operation. Ice cream was an enormous treat then. You had ice cream with jelly at birthday parties and you *might* be allowed an ice-cream cone once or twice on your summer holiday, but that was your lot. The hospital ice cream was meagre, a slither of Wall's vanilla, but I swallowed it down eagerly, in spite of the pain.

I had a little parcel from home too. Biddy might not be allowed to see me but she sent me a Margaret Tarrant card every morning, and there was a present too, a little book of *Toy Tales* with big printing and lots of pictures. It was a bit babyish when I could cope with hundreds of pages of *Adventures with Rosalind*, but I knew it was the thought that counted. I was surprised that none of the other children got presents or cards or letters. Everyone thought it must be my birthday. They said I was very lucky and my mum and dad must love me very much.

I don't think any of my fictional girls has to have her tonsils out in my books. However, there are a few hospital scenes, some very dramatic and sad. There are also more routine visits. Which of my characters ends up in hospital with a broken arm?

I wonder if you picked Mandy from *Bad Girls*? She *does* hurt her arm and end up in hospital, but it's just a bad sprain. But Em in *Clean Break* breaks her arm running after her beloved stepfather.

'Em, darling! It's all right, I'm here. Does your arm hurt really badly?' said Dad. 'The nurse has just come, pet, they're ready to plaster you up.'

I clung to Dad, scared that it might be very painful. It *did* hurt when they gently but firmly straightened my arm out.

'There we go. We'll have you right as rain in no time,' said the young doctor, smiling at me. 'There's no complications. It's a nice clean break.'

I winced at those two words.

People often ask me if any of the characters in my books are real. Mostly I make it all up, but just occasionally it's fun to write about someone I really know. I've always said I don't put myself in my books but the novelist Jenna Williams in *Clean Break* is very similar to me. Nick's drawn her looking exactly like me too – apart from one tiny detail. I wonder if anyone can spot what it is?

15

Pretend Friends

Junior school was very different from the Infants. I was still at Latchmere, in an adjacent but identical red-brick building, the classrooms built round a quadrangle of grass. They were mostly the same children in my class but somehow *I* wasn't the same. I wasn't little Jacky-no-friends, the odd girl. I was suddenly inexplicably popular, with the girls, with the boys, even with the teachers.

I wasn't the new girl any more. She was a girl called Cherry, an exotic name in those days of Susans and Elizabeths and Janes. She was nicknamed Cherry Blossom Boot Polish and mildly teased. We became friendly because she lived a few streets away and we walked to school together.

I was sad to miss out on my imaginary conversations on the way to school, but it was companionable having Cherry to walk back home with. We'd take our time. We'd run up the old air-raid shelter in Park Road and slide right down. We'd climb little trees on the bombsite and walk along the planks crossing the trenches where new houses were being built. We'd visit the sweetshop on the way home and buy sherbet fountains and gob stoppers and my favourite flying saucers, cheap pastel papery sweets that exploded in your mouth into sharp lemony powder.

I'd occasionally go home with Cherry. Her mother was sometimes out, as she worked as a hospital almoner. They had a big piano in the living room. The whole family was musical. Cherry played the recorder and the violin. Her parents were keen amateur Gilbert and Sullivan performers.

'Gilbert and Sullivan!' said Biddy, sniffing.

She had a job now too, but it was just part time in a cake shop. Cherry's mum tried to be friendly with my mum, but Biddy wasn't having any. She felt they put on airs and considered themselves a cut above us. I wasn't allowed to invite Cherry back. I wasn't allowed to have *anyone* in to play, not unless Biddy was there. She didn't get home till quarter to six now, but I had a key to let myself in.

Lots of the children in my class had similar keys. They wore them on strings round their necks under their vests. People called them latchkey kids. I thought *I* was a latchkey kid but Biddy soon put me right.

'*You're* not a latchkey kid! As if I'd let you go out with a grubby piece of string round your neck! You have a proper real leather shoulder purse for *your* key!'

I had to wear the purse slung across my chest. It banged against my hip when I ran and it was always a worry when I had to take it off for PT but I had to put up with it.

I didn't mind letting myself in at all, though there was always an anxious moment reaching and trying to turn the key in the stiff lock, jiggling it this way and that before it would turn. But then I was in and the flat was mine. It wasn't empty. It was full of my imaginary friends.

I wasn't allowed to cook anything on the stove in case I burned myself, but I could help myself to bread and jam or chocolate biscuits or a hunk of cheese and a tomato – sometimes all three snacks if I was particularly starving. Then I was free to play with my friends. Sometimes they were book friends. I had a new favourite book now, *Nancy and Plum* by Betty MacDonald. Nancy was a shy, dreamy girl of ten with long red plaits, Plum was a bold, adventurous little girl of eight with stubby fair plaits. They were orphans, badly treated by horrible Mrs Monday, but they ran away and were eventually adopted by a gentle kindly farmer and his wife.

I read *Nancy and Plum* over and over again. I loved the parts where they imagined elaborate dolls for their Christmas presents or discussed their favourite books with the library lady. Nancy and Plum became my secret best friends and we played together all over the flat. Whenever I went on a bus or a coach ride, Nancy and Plum came too. They weren't cramped up on the bus with me, they ran along outside, jumping over hedges, running across roofs, leaping over rivers, always keeping up with me.

When Nancy and Plum were having a well-earned rest, I'd play with some of my *own* characters. I didn't always make them up entirely. I had a gift book of poetry called *A Book of the Seasons* with Eve Garnett illustrations. I thought her wispy-haired, delicate little children quite wonderful. I'd trace them carefully, talking to each child, giving her a name, encouraging her to talk back to me. There were three children standing in a country churchyard who were my particular favourites, especially the biggest girl with long hair, but I also loved a little girl with untidy short hair and a checked frock and plimsolls, sitting in a gutter by the gasworks.

Eve Garnett drew her children in so many different settings. I loved the drawings of children in window seats. This seemed a delightful idea, though I'd have got vertigo if I'd tried to perch on a seat in our living-room window, looking down on the very busy main road outside. I loved the Garnett bedrooms too, especially the little truckle beds with patchwork quilts. I copied these quilts for my own pictures and carefully coloured in each tiny patch.

I'd sometimes play with my dolls, my big dolls or my little doll's house dolls – but perhaps the best games of all were with my paper dolls. I don't mean the conventional dolls you buy in a book, with dresses with little white tags for you to cut out. I *had* several books like that: Woolworths sold several sorts – Baby Peggy and Little Betsy and Dolly Dimples. I scissored my fingers raw snipping out their little frocks and hats and dinky handbags and tiny toy teddies, but once every little outfit was cut out, white tags intact, I didn't really fancy *playing* with them. I could dress them up in each natty outfit, but if I tried to walk them along the carpet or skate them across the kitchen lino, their clothes fell off all over the place. Besides, they all seemed too young and sweet and simpering for any of *my* games.

My favourite paper dolls came out of fashion books. In those days many women made their own clothes, not just my grandma. Every department store had a big haberdashery and material department, with a table where you could consult fashion pattern catalogues – Style, Butterick, Simplicity and Vogue. At the end of every season each big hefty book was replaced with an updated version but you could buy the old catalogues for sixpence. Vogue cost a shilling because their designs were more stylish, but I didn't like them because their ladies weren't drawn very realistically, and they looked too posh and haughty.

I loved the Style fashion books. Their ladies were wonderfully drawn and individualized, with elaborate hairstyles and intelligent expressions. They were usually drawn separately, with their arms and legs well-displayed. It was highly irritating finding a perfect paper lady with half her arm hidden behind a paper friend. She'd have to suffer a terrible amputation when I cut her out.

I cut out incredibly carefully, snipping out any white space showing through a bent elbow, gently guiding my sharp scissors around each long curl, every outspread finger, both elegant high heels.

I'd invent their personalities as I cut out each lady. It was such an absorbing ritual I was lost to the world. I remember one day in the summer holidays, when Biddy was out at work and Harry was *off* work for some reason, sitting at the living-room table with his horse-racing form books and his *Sporting Life*, working out which bets he was going to put on. He seemed as absorbed in his world as I was in mine. I forgot all about him until he suddenly shouted, 'For Christ's sake, do you have to keep snip-snip-snipping?'

I jumped so violently I nearly snipped straight through my finger. I cut out my paper ladies in my bedroom after that, even when I was alone in the flat. I spread each lady out on my carpet. I cut out girls too, especially the ones with long hair, though plaits were an exceptionally fiddly job. I seldom paired them up as mothers and daughters. They were simply big girls and little girls, living in orphanages or hostels or my own kind of invented commune. There would be a couple of men too, but they were usually rather silly-looking specimens in striped pyjamas. No one sewed men's suits from scratch, not even my grandma, so you only got nightclothes and the occasional comical underwear. I certainly didn't want any grinning goofy fools in white underpants down to their knees and socks with suspenders hanging round *my* ladies.

I didn't bother with the boys either, though there were more of them in short trousers. I did have a soft spot for the babies though, and cut out the prettiest. Then I could spend hours at a time whispering my games. My favourite of all my paper girls was a bold, long-haired lady called Carola, in a lacy black bra and a half-slip. She was a naughty girl and got up to all sorts of adventures. I'd carry her everywhere with me, tucking her carefully inside my book.

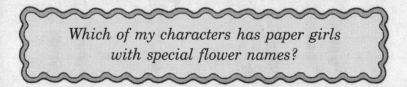

Which of my characters has paper girls with special flower names?

149

It's April in *Dustbin Baby*.

I carefully cut out long lanky models with skinny arms and legs, my tongue sticking out as I rounded each spiky wrist and bony ankle, occasionally performing unwitting amputations as I went.

Sylvia found me an old exercise book and a stick of Pritt but I didn't want to make a scrapbook. I wanted to keep my paper girls free. They weren't called Naomi and Kate and Elle and Natasha. They were my girls now, so I called them Rose and Violet and Daffodil and Bluebell.

I seem overly fond of the name Bluebell. It's also the name of Tracy Beaker's doll and Dixie's toy budgerigar. Sorry I keep repeating myself!

16

Mandy

I was taken to the cinema regularly. I didn't go to the children's Saturday morning pictures – Biddy thought that was too rowdy. I watched proper adult films, though the very first time I went I disgraced myself. This was at the Odeon in Surbiton, when I was three and still living at Fassett Road. All five of us – Biddy, Harry, Ga, Gongon and me – went to see some slapstick comedy. I didn't do a lot of laughing.

I thought it was all really happening before my very eyes (remember, we didn't have television in those days). I found it very worrying that these silly men were sometimes so big that their whole heads filled the screen. I couldn't work out where the rest of their bodies were. I knew I didn't want these giants coming anywhere near me. Then they shrank back small again. They were running away, pursued by even scarier men with hatchets. They dodged in and out of traffic in a demented fashion, then ran into a tall block of flats, going up and down lifts, charging along corridors, through rooms to the windows. They climbed right outside, wobbling on the edge. The camera switched so you saw things from their point of view, looking down down down, the cars below like little ants. The audience *laughed*. I screamed.

I had to be carted out of the cinema by Biddy and Harry, still screaming. They were cross because they'd wasted two one-and-ninepenny tickets.

'Why did you have to make such a fuss?' said Biddy.

'The man was going to fall!' I wailed.

'It wasn't *real*,' said Harry.

It took me a while to grasp this, which was odd seeing as I lived in my own imaginary world so much. However, I grew to love going to the cinema, though I never liked slapstick comedy, and I still hate it whenever there's a mad chase in any film.

We saw *Genevieve* together, and all three of us found that very funny indeed. Biddy said she thought Kay Kendall was beautiful. I thought this strange, because Kay Kendall had short dark hair. I didn't think you could possibly be beautiful unless you had blonde fairy-princess hair way past your shoulders.

Harry quite liked musicals but Biddy couldn't stand anything with singing, so Harry and I went to see *Carousel* and *South Pacific* together. I thought both films wondrously tragic. I don't think I understood a lot of the story but I loved all the romantic parts and all the special songs.

When Harry was in a very good mood, he'd sing as he got dressed in the morning – silly songs like 'Mairzie Doats an Doazie Doats' and 'She Wears Red Feathers and a Hooly-Hooly Skirt', and occasionally a rude Colonel Bogey song about Hitler. But now he'd la-la-la the *Carousel* roundabout theme tune while whirling around himself, or he'd prance about in his vest and pants singing, '*I'm going to wash that man right out of my hair.*'

I can't remember who took me to see *Mandy*. It was such an intense experience that the cinema could have crumbled around me and I wouldn't have noticed. I was *in* that film, suffering alongside Mandy. She was a little deaf girl who was sent away to a special boarding school to try to learn how to speak. There was a big sub-plot about her quarrelling parents and the developing relationship between Mandy's mother and the head teacher of the school, but that didn't interest me. I just watched Mandy, this small sad little girl with big soulful eyes and dark wispy plaits. I cried when she cried. When she mouthed 'Man-dee' at the end of the film, I whispered it with her.

I wanted to be Mandy's friend in the film and make her plasticine necklaces and play ball with her and comfort her when she couldn't sleep at night. I was old enough now to understand that the film wasn't real. Mandy was played by a child actress, Mandy Miller. I thought she was wonderfully gifted. Biddy showed me a photo in the *Sunday Mirror* of the real Mandy at the premiere of her film, and I realized she was much more glamorous in real life. She still had the spindly plaits, but instead of the pleated skirt and tartan windcheater she wore in the film, she was wearing a sophisticated silk party frock with puffed sleeves and a broderie anglaise collar and velvet ribbon at the neck and waist. She was even wearing *white gloves*.

I had a third Mandy in my head from then on, not the deaf child in the film, not the real actress. I had *my* Mandy, an imaginary friend with big eyes and dark plaits, and we were inseparable for years.

Biddy took me to see every Mandy Miller film that came out, though I wasn't allowed to see *Background* because it had an over-twelve rating, probably because it was about divorce. People thought so differently about divorce in those days. They frequently *whispered* the word. It was considered shameful, barely socially acceptable. It was the reason why so many incompatible couples stayed together. They didn't want to go through the public disgrace of a divorce. I thought this odd even then. In fact I used to pray my own parents *would* divorce because there were so many screaming fights now. Sometimes I was caught up in a quarrel too, both of them yelling at me, appealing to me, while I begged not to have to take sides. Sometimes I simply listened from my bedroom while they argued endlessly, whipping each other with cruel words, then slapping and shoving, hurting and hating.

Perhaps this was another reason why Mandy's films meant so much to me. She was in one or two child-centred fun films like *Raising a Riot* (about a family living in a windmill), but most of Mandy's films were about unhappy, anxious children living tense lives. My favourite Mandy film was *Dance Little Lady*, a colourful melodrama about a beautiful ballet dancer, her unscrupulous impresario husband and their only daughter, played by Mandy. The ballet dancer has a fall and can't work, the impresario loses interest in her, they fight bitterly – but they both love their little girl, a budding ballet dancer herself. Mandy does a proper dance in the film, her hair tied back with a satin ribbon, wearing an amazing cream, pink and turquoise beribboned tutu with white fishnet tights and pink ballet shoes.

There were no videos or DVDs in those days, of course, but I rewound that dance scene again and again inside my head. The film had a very dramatic ending. The father is in charge of Mandy one weekend but leaves her alone in their lodging house. There's a fire, Mandy is in peril, but the father comes rushing back and rescues her. She clings to him in her white nightie on the rooftop, the flames licking nearer and nearer. He manages to throw her to safety before he's engulfed by the flames himself. I thought it the most thrilling film ever, though I think I'd have severe reservations about it if I ever saw it again!

It might seem odd that I remember Mandy's films so vividly when I only saw most of them once – but I had a fantastic *aide-mémoire*. I kept my own scrapbook of any Mandy Miller photos I saw in newspapers or magazines, but these were just tiny blurred images. I also had a little attaché case bursting with big glossy Mandy photos, some of them 'stills' from her films, some specially taken publicity photos. Biddy looked at the photo copyright names in the papers, found out the right addresses and took me up to London with her to the film companies and press offices.

I was still a very shy child. I'd be paralysed with embarrassment when Biddy blagged her way through reception and then begged for Mandy Miller photos.

'It's for the kiddie, you see,' she'd say, nodding at me. 'She's mad about Mandy.'

I'd hang my head and blush scarlet, but nine times out of ten they'd soften and let us have several photos. Sometimes Biddy had to pay, but mostly we got them for nothing. Biddy would wrap them in tissue paper and carry them carefully on the tube and train in her shopping bag. When we got home, I could spread out my new photos and relive each film, frequently inventing new scenes, completely different new plots and characters to suit myself.

I used the film photos for most of my imaginary scenarios because Mandy looked sad or anxious or tragic and that gave me more scope. I felt more in touch with that Mandy. The Mandy photographed in her own home was a different girl entirely, a blessed child leading an idyllic life. I treasured a series of photos taken at her birthday party. Mandy's wearing a beautiful smocked Liberty frock, lighting the candles on her cake while her mother and her big sister and her friends smile at her.

Biddy didn't make birthday cakes. She *did* make lovely fairy cakes with lemon-flavoured icing and a walnut stuck on top. I liked them very much but they weren't quite the same as real birthday cake with icing and butter cream and special candles. I didn't have birthday parties either. Biddy said the flat was too small and she didn't have time to prepare for them as she went out to work. I was partly relieved because I'd have been horribly shy and scared that we wouldn't pass muster as a normal happy family, but I still felt a pang whenever I looked at the photo of Mandy's party.

At about the same time – she's wearing the same checked hair ribbons – there's a set of photos taken in her back garden. Mandy's playing in her tent and climbing a tree with a friend, and then she's swinging dangerously upside down from a branch, her plaits flying.

I didn't have my own garden – but I could play out in The Jungle, the huge overgrown wilderness behind the flats. I was very much a girl for playing *in*, but sometimes I went down to The Jungle with Sue, the little girl next door. We were both meek girls whose mothers fancied themselves a cut above the other residents. We were sent out to play in clean checked summer frocks, little white socks and polished sandals. We had enough sense to steer well away from the tough gangs, who would pull our hair, tug our skirts up to mock our white knickers and then push us into the nettles.

They had a rope attached to one of the tallest trees so you could swing like Tarzan. We swung too, timidly, and we both climbed the fir tree with the easiest branches, all the way to the top. One slip and we'd have broken our necks. It was just as well our mums never found out what we were up to.

Mandy had a white poodle, and there was a lovely photo of her giving him a big hug. I decided poodles were my favourite dogs too. I had a little black china poodle on my windowsill at home, and a kind old lady at Waverley Hall won a white furry poodle at bingo on Clacton Pier and gave it to me. I was overwhelmed, though this poodle quickly developed alopecia. His fur fell out, leaving ugly yellow glue stains, and then one of his glass eyes loosened and dangled out of his head, so Biddy put him in the dustbin.

When I got my Vip, I decided I loved Pekes most of all, but I've changed my mind now. I can't wait to have my little black miniature poodle.

Much to my joy, Mandy seemed a bookish girl. She was photographed several times with books spread all around her. My all-time favourite photograph of her shows her sitting up in bed in her flowery nightie, holding a gilt-embellished copy of *Peter and Wendy* by J. M. Barrie. I hope she's somehow hung onto that book. I've got a first edition of it myself, bought in my twenties for ten shillings – that's 50p in today's money. A first edition in a dust wrapper was recently auctioned for £3000!

I didn't know anything about the value of books as a child, but I did know the price of every doll, and I was seriously impressed that Mandy was photographed holding an Elizabeth doll. This was a special doll brought out to commemorate the Queen's Coronation in 1953. She wasn't a grown-up doll with a crown; she was a child doll with blonde curls and a cotton frock with a tight white plastic belt to match her neat white plastic shoes.

I longed for an Elizabeth doll but they were nearly three pounds – much too expensive. Biddy took me to see several shelves of them in Hamleys and they all smiled down at me, fanning their fingers in regal waves.

> *Which of my characters gets taken to Hamleys toyshop and longs to be given a special doll?*

It's Dolphin in *The Illustrated Mum*.

We went to Hamleys in Oxford Street afterwards, a special huge toy shop. Micky took us to look at the dolls though even he could see that Star was past that stage. I knew I should be too old for dolls too but I ached with longing as I looked at all the specially designed dolls locked away in glass cases. They had beautiful gentle faces and long long long hair. My fingers itched to comb it. They had wonderful romantic outfits too, hand-sewn smocked dresses and ruched pinafores and perfect little leather boots.

I leaned my forehead on the cold glass and stared at them all, making up names for each one and inventing their personalities. They all reached out for me with their long white fingers. They looked so real I was sure they couldn't be cold and stiff to touch. I chose the one I liked the very best. She had long blonde curls and blue eyes and a dress and pinafore outfit the pink and blue of hyacinths, with pink silky socks and blue shoes fastened with little pearl buttons. I called her Natasha and knew she and I could be best friends for ever . . .

Children often ask me which is my favourite out of all my books. I tend to chop and change a little but I frequently choose *The Illustrated Mum*. I never re-read my books once they're published – I'd find it awkward and embarrassing and want to change things – but I've watched the beautiful television film of *The Illustrated Mum* several times, and I always end up in tears.

1953 CORONATION 1953

17

The Coronation

The Queen's Coronation was an enormous big deal in the 1950s. We thought differently about royalty then. They were like mysterious powerful gods with gold crowns permanently perched on their heads. Each school had a poster of the royal family in the hall entrance. The national anthem was frequently thumped out on the school piano while we all stood up straight, and woe betide you if you messed around or got the giggles. If you so much as sneezed during *'happy and glorious'*, you could get the cane. They didn't just play 'God Save the Queen' in schools. It was played at almost every public event, even at every cinema show down the Regal or the Odeon.

The country was in a state of feverish excitement before the Coronation. People plotted for weeks to work out how they could camp overnight on the route and catch a glimpse of Elizabeth in her gold carriage. There were little replicas of this gold carriage everywhere, complete with weeny horses. I hinted and hinted but didn't get lucky. My only Coronation memorabilia were the silver spoon and the blue china commemorative mug given free to every school child – and Harry broke my mug a week later. I expect the spoon might still be rattling about at the back of my mother's cutlery drawer somewhere. Maybe I'll try to reclaim it.

We didn't go up to London to see the Coronation. Biddy and Harry didn't see the point so I didn't get to wave my little Union Jack flag. However, we did *see* the Queen getting crowned. We got our first television so we could watch, along with hundreds of thousands of families all over the country. It was the talking point everywhere – who was forking out for an eleven-inch Bush television to see the Coronation. It was the first huge national event that the population could see simultaneously. We didn't have to rush to the cinema the next week and watch Pathé News. We could peep right inside Westminster Abbey and see the Archbishop of Canterbury place the crown on Elizabeth's head from the comfort of our own utility armchairs.

Biddy invited Ga and Gongon. The five of us watched the Coronation, with commentary by Richard Dimbleby – brother of the lady who declared I was an ultra-clean well-kept baby. We felt he was practically our best friend. We listened to his hushed, reverent tones, describing the scene we could see for ourselves in blurred black and white miniature.

We all knew it was a momentous occasion. It was also very very very boring. After half an hour of squatting on my little leatherette pouffe I sloped off to play with my paper dolls. I was reminded that this was a once-in-a-lifetime event and I should pay attention, but Biddy's telling-off was half-hearted. She was yawning and fidgeting herself. We weren't especially royalist in my family, though we'd read Crawfie's account of her life as a governess to little Lilibet and Margaret Rose, serialized in some women's magazine. Even so, Biddy bought a tea caddy with a picture of the newly crowned Queen looking very glamorous, and when full-colour souvenir books of the Coronation appeared in Woolworths, Biddy bought one. I leafed through the pages listlessly, but I liked the new Queen's crown and sceptre and orb – I was always a girl for flashy jewels.

We also went together to see a children's film called *John and Julie* later that year, about a little girl who runs away to see the Queen's Coronation. I thought the girl playing Julie was quite sweet, but not a patch on my Mandy.

Biddy kept the newspapers with the coverage of the Coronation in case they might be valuable one day. Maybe she's still got them. I wish she'd kept all my *Girl* comics instead!

There's certainly no mention of the Queen's Coronation in any of my books! I don't think there's anything about the royal family either. So OK, who lives in the Royal Hotel?

It's Elsa in *The Bed and Breakfast Star*.

We went to stay at the Royal Hotel. The Royal sounds very grand, doesn't it? And when we got down one end of the street and got our first glimpse of the Royal right at the other end, I thought it looked very grand too. I started to get excited. I'd never stayed in a great big posh hotel before. Maybe we'd all have our own rooms with satellite telly and people would make our beds and serve us our breakfasts from silver trays. As if we were Royalty staying in the Royal.

Maybe if Elsa achieves her big ambition to be a comedian, she might *just* be asked to take part in a Royal Variety Performance in front of the Queen.

18

Papers and Comics

We were a family with a hefty newspaper bill. Biddy liked the *Daily Mail* and Harry had the *Telegraph* and the *Sporting Life* and the *Racing Post*. Harry's biggest hobby was horse racing. He went to race meetings occasionally, and every Saturday afternoon he crouched in his armchair, fists clenched, watching the racing on our new television. He'd shout excitedly if his horse looked as if it had a chance – 'Come on, come on!' – jigging up and down as if he was riding the horse himself.

I don't know how much he won or lost, he never told us. He didn't put flamboyantly large amounts of money on any horse. Later on, when we had a telephone, I heard him place each-way bets for a few shillings, but he was a steady punter, betting every day there was a race on.

He kept every racing paper and form book and studied them religiously, jotting down numbers and marking likely names. He squashed his suits and trousers up into a tiny corner of his wardrobe so that he could store all this information inside.

He also bought a London evening paper on his

way home from work. There were three to choose from in those days. Newspaper sellers used to shout, '*Star*, *News* and *Stan-daaaard!*' over and over again. Harry bought the *Star*, the paper with the strip cartoon 'Tuppenny and Squibbit'.

I had my own comics too. I started off with a twee little baby comic called *Chick's Own*, where the hard words were hy-phe-na-ted, but soon I progressed to the much more rufty-tufty *Beano*. I liked the Bash Street Kids because the humour was imaginative and anarchic, but I'd have liked it to be a bit more girly. I read *Schoolfriend* and occasionally *Girls' Crystal*, but they were plain black-and-white comics. The most magical comic of all was *Girl*, well worth fourpence-halfpenny out of my shilling pocket money.

It was delivered every week. I was so entranced by some of the serial stories that I could barely wait for the next episode. I didn't really care for dark-haired schoolgirl Wendy and her blonde friend Jinx on the front cover, but I was a particular fan of Belle of the Ballet inside the comic. I talked about her enthusiastically to my teacher Mrs Symons and she gently corrected my pronunciation. Up till that moment I'd been calling her Belly of the Ballette.

The best serial was on the back page. Every week there were inspiring stories about special women, written by the Reverend Chad Varah. Sometimes these heroines were well known, like Florence

Nightingale, the Lady with the Lamp. Sometimes they were long-ago historical figures like Princess Adelaide, a particular favourite. Sometimes they were religious, like Mary Slessor, the mill girl from Dundee who became a missionary. Sometimes they ticked every single box, like Joan of Arc. I'd seen her picture in my nursery history book but I had no idea what happened to her. The last Joan of Arc picture strip was such a shock. The illustration of Joan standing in yellow flames, clutching her wooden cross, her eyes raised piously, made me shake with a complicated mixture of excitement, horror and pity.

I started to be stirred by current sad stories in the newspapers too. On Sundays Biddy liked to take the *Mirror* and the *News of the World* so she could have a good juicy read over her fried breakfast in bed. One summer they serialized Ruth Ellis's story while she was locked up in Holloway, the women's prison. I read over Biddy's shoulder. She tutted over Ruth's blonde hair and pencilled eyebrows and dark lips. 'She's obviously just a good-time girl. Look at that peroxide hair! Talk about common!'

I thought she looked glamorous and Ruth had always been one of my favourite names. I loved the story of Ruth and Naomi in Scripture at school, and there was another Ruth in a current favourite book, *The Tanglewood's Secret* by Patricia St John. It had made a big impression on me because a boy in that book had climbed a tree, fallen and died. It had all been very sad, and Ruth and I had been very upset. This new true story about a real Ruth was about death too. She'd shot her boyfriend. I couldn't help sympathizing a little because it sounded as if he'd been horrible to her. But now she'd been tracked down and convicted of murder, and in a few weeks' time she was going to be hanged.

I hadn't really taken on board what capital punishment meant until then. It seemed a crazy idea. If society was so shocked that Ruth Ellis had killed someone, why was it right that *she* should be killed too, and in such an obscene and ritualistic way? I couldn't believe that anyone could legally drag a healthy person from their cell, put a noose around their neck and then hang them.

I didn't think they would ever go through with it. I thought it was just a threat to frighten her. I thought she'd get a last-minute reprieve.

She didn't. They went ahead with the whole grisly procedure. They hanged her at nine o'clock in the morning.

One of my books has wonderful illustrations set out at the beginning of each chapter, lots of little pictures in a strip, like the most imaginative and beautiful drawn comic. Which is it?

It's *Candyfloss*.

I'm so very lucky having Nick Sharratt illustrate
my books. I think they're all brilliant illustrations
but maybe *Candyfloss* is my favourite. We had fun
with the very last page, putting in lots of familiar
faces. See how many of the children you recognize!

19

Health

I started to brood about death after reading about Ruth Ellis. I hadn't really had anyone close to me die. Harry's mother had died when I was a baby. His father had died a few years later, but I hardly knew him. Maybe Ga and Gongon were next on the Grim Reaper's list. They weren't a robust couple. Gongon had a heart attack one Christmas when I was a child. He wasn't rushed to hospital. He stayed upstairs in bed and everyone tiptoed round, whispering and looking worried.

He made a full recovery but he was treated like an invalid after that. He retired early from work and sat in his armchair and sucked sadly on his pipe like an ancient old man when he must only have been in his fifties.

My grandmother wasn't in much of a position to wait on him hand and foot. Ga suffered from cripplingly painful arthritis. She changes quickly in the family photo album from a little blonde woman with a curvy figure to a fat old lady in longish skirts and granny shoes. Maybe her steroid treatments made her put on weight. She ate exactly the same as my grandfather and yet he was matchstick-thin.

Once a month she went up to a London hospital and tried every treatment going. She even had gold injections for a while. I hoped her teeth and fingernails might suddenly gleam gold, but there was no external evidence of this treatment whatsoever and I don't think it helped much internally either. She was in constant severe pain. Sometimes she could hardly get out of her armchair, and her face would screw up in agony, but she never once cried.

Her poor hands were so badly affected that her fingers became claws and she couldn't sew any more. Many years later, when I had my daughter Emma, Ga struggled desperately, her lips clamped together, and knitted her little dresses and cardigans and tiny woollen buttoned shoes, and crocheted an enormous soft white shawl. *I* want to cry when I think of all that painful effort.

She had a new hip put in and there was talk of new knees, but there was a limit to what they could do. Her feet swelled with bunions and in her later years she could barely walk.

But neither grandparent died when I was young. Biddy and Harry stayed reasonably healthy too. Biddy had frequent heavy colds like me. (I had *just* as many colds after my tonsils had been pulled out.)

They always went to her chest and made her cough, but this was probably because she smoked so much. Her chic red packets of Du Maurier cigarettes were part of her, like her Max Factor Crème Puff powder and her Coty L'Aimant perfume. She smoked like a chimney, she sucked clove sweets and pear drops and humbugs, she ate Mars bars constantly, childishly chewing along the top, saving the toffee part till last. She wouldn't walk for more than two minutes in her high heels and determinedly took no exercise whatsoever – and yet she's still going strong now, in her mid-eighties.

Harry never smoked and didn't have a sweet tooth. He had odd tastes in food. He'd eat peanuts from the shell, cracking them into newspaper in the evenings as he watched television. He'd construct his own odd little teas of beetroot and St Ivel cheese. He rarely cooked, but he had his own particular specialities, like very good tinned-salmon fishcakes. He ate healthily, if weirdly, and he took masses of exercise, cycling all the way up to London and back every day. He frequently went for long walks and he was also a very active member of the local tennis club. He seemed fit as a fiddle – but his heart started playing up and he died when he was only fifty-seven.

Maybe it was because of all his temper tantrums. When he was in full rant, his face would go an ugly

181

red and the veins would stand out on his forehead. We could never tell when one of these terrifying temper fits would start up. Sometimes they came out of nowhere. Other times Biddy seemed to go out of her way to provoke him.

'He's got a terrible inferiority complex, that's why he gets into these states,' she said.

She didn't see why she should try to make a fuss of him and boost his confidence.

'I'm not going to *pretend*,' she said, outraged at the idea. 'It's not my way. If I think he's useless, I'll say so.'

She did, repeatedly. When she got a job as a book-keeper at Prince Machines and they had a firm's dance, she insisted that Harry go with her. Surprisingly, he agreed, but the evening wasn't a success.

'He just sat there like a lemon, wouldn't say a word,' Biddy raged. 'He wouldn't even dance with anyone, not even when this woman begged him. I was so embarrassed!'

'For God's sake, she was *drunk*,' said Harry. 'And it wasn't a dance – she wanted me to join in these damn daft party games.'

Biddy had started playing her own private game with a man called Ron who worked at Prince Machines. Surely that was part of the reason for all the rows? Yet they never seemed to argue about him. Ron was almost like part of our family – *Uncle* Ron to me. When I was old enough to be left on Saturday evenings, Biddy *and* Harry went out with Uncle Ron. They mostly went to pubs, which was the strangest thing of all, because they were both still teetotal. Maybe they sipped bitter lemons all evening.

We even had a joint holiday together, with Uncle Ron's wife Grace, who understandably didn't seem keen on this weird situation.

I plucked up courage recently to ask Biddy if Harry realized what was going on under his nose.

'I don't know,' she said impatiently. 'We didn't ever discuss it.'

I always knew about Uncle Ron – and several other uncles – and I certainly wasn't going to blab to my dad, but I did think it horribly unfair to him. I didn't *like* my dad and he could be incredibly alarming and unkind, but I always felt sorry for him. It wasn't until he got ill that I realized there were not one but two 'aunties' lurking in the background, both of whom came to his funeral.

They both told me – separately – how much my dad had loved me and been proud of me. I was astonished. I couldn't remember him saying anything of the sort to me. In fact several times he'd told me he couldn't stand me.

Perhaps they were just being kind and felt it was the polite thing to say at funerals.

Yet sometimes he acted like he really *did* love me, even if he never said so. That's what's so puzzling about writing a true story. If I was making my story up, I'd invent a consistent father, good or bad. Real people change so. Harry might have been a bad father to me in many ways, but he lived long enough to be a wonderful caring grandfather to Emma, patiently playing with her for hours, never once losing his temper.

Harry could sometimes be gentle and imaginative with me too. He had a passion for the countryside and as soon as we moved to Cumberland House he'd pore over maps and go for bike rides round the Surrey lanes. When I was on holiday from school, he'd take a day off from work and take me for a long country outing. We'd walk the Pilgrim's Way, stand beside the deep green Silent Pool and struggle up the slippery chalk paths of Box Hill. We'd pick blackberries or hazelnuts, or buy bags of tomatoes to supplement our cheese sandwich picnics.

I was a weedy little girl but I could walk seven or eight miles in my sturdy Clarks sandals. Harry was generally at his best on these occasions. He'd let me chatter and he'd sometimes join in my imaginary games in a desultory fashion. We watched an adaptation of Robert Louis Stevenson's *Kidnapped* on the television and played we were Davie and Alan wandering through the woods. Well, I played, and Harry trudged along, nodding every now and then. Sometimes he'd tell me the name of his favourite racehorse and I'd gallop along beside him, pretending to be winning my race.

We sometimes took the train to Guildford. Before setting out for the surrounding fields and hills Harry would take me to the big second-hand bookshop at the top of the town. It was a huge dark muddle of a shop with long corridors and sudden steps up and down and a series of connecting rooms, but if you negotiated this labyrinth properly, you found a whole room of children's books.

Harry had a happy knack of finding me a book I'd like. He was a member of the Westminster Public Library near his office at the Treasury, and he sometimes borrowed a book for me. He brought home *Marianne Dreams* by Catherine Storr, a magical book about two sick children who draw themselves into a nightmare world of their imagination. It had a profound effect on me. I was very careful not to draw anything too scary with my best Venus HB pencil after that, just in case.

He also brought me an adult book, *The River* by Rumer Godden, about a family of children in India. I was only eight or nine. I found it hard to get into the first few pages, but when I got used to Rumer's strange style, I *adored* it. I particularly identified with Harriet, the intense literary child-narrator. Biddy had considered calling me Harriet, as an amalgamation of Harry and her own real first name, Margaret. She'd decided against this idea because she thought Harriet such a plain old-fashioned name. I was a plain old-fashioned child and *longed* to be called Harriet. I didn't care for the name Jacqueline at all, especially the way Biddy said it when she was cross with me – '*Jacqueline!*' Still, the other name under consideration had apparently been Babette, so maybe I got off lightly.

Two sisters in one of my books have a grandma with very bad arthritis. Can you remember who they are?

They're Ruby and Garnet, the identical twins in *Double Act*.

Gran's arthritis got worse. She'd always had funny fingers and a bad hip and a naughty knee. But soon she got so she'd screw up her face when she got up or sat down, and her fingers welled sideways and she couldn't make them work.

That's Garnet doing the talking. I found it an interesting challenge swapping from one twin to the other, so that they both get to write their story. Sometimes people don't realize that there are *two* illustrators for *Double Act*. Nick Sharratt does all the Ruby drawings, and Nick's friend Sue Heap does all the Garnet drawings. They have similar styles. It's fun flicking through the book quickly, deciding which picture was drawn by Nick and which by Sue.

20

Biddy

Biddy was very happy to go out to work. Harry only gave her a meagre amount for housekeeping and she hated being dependent on him. She worked at Roberts the cake shop first. I thoroughly enjoyed all the extra bath buns and currant slices and apple puffs.

Then she got a job as a playground lady in Kingsnympton Juniors, though this was the very school she'd turned down for me. Biddy was strict with me and expected me to know my place and to say please and thank-you. I must never interrupt. I must never say 'What?' if I didn't hear her. I had to rattle through 'I'm sorry, what did you say?' I certainly mustn't say 'Pardon' because that was common. 'Toilet' was common too. We said 'lav' in our family, and we used genteel euphemisms for what we did *in* the lav. It must have been a terrible trial for Biddy to be surrounded by ordinary, lively, cheeky council estate kids. That job didn't last long.

She tried taking the newspapers round to all the patients in Kingston Hospital. This was a job she loved, especially going round the men's wards chatting them all up. She took me with her in the summer holidays. I wasn't allowed on the wards, but I'd wait outside in the hospital gardens. I'd have a book with me, and I'd take a handful of my favourite paper girls and sit swinging my legs on a bench, carefully fanning my girls out on my lap. Sometimes a nurse or a cleaner would come and have a little chat with me. One elderly lady was especially kind and gave me the odd sweet or two. Biddy had drummed it into me never to take sweets from strangers but I knew the old lady was just being friendly.

These were part-time jobs. Biddy branched out and got a full-time job at Prince Machines when I was eight. She stayed there the longest of all her jobs, probably because of Uncle Ron. Then she worked in an office up in London, behind the scenes in Bentalls department store, and then in the finance office of Kingston Polytechnic. She even worked as a cocktail barmaid for one evening but gave up because she didn't have a clue what any of the drinks were. Eventually she set herself up in a small way as an antique dealer. She traded in Richmond for years, and then kept a small stall in the local antique centre well into her eighties. Even now she bids over-enthusiastically on eBay.

In the days of my childhood she had no spare cash whatsoever, but she managed to be inventive with her money. We never ate out as a family but Biddy and I had secret treat lunches together. We went to Joe Lyons in Kingston after a Saturday shop. We always had tomato soup, fish and chips, and strawberry mousse. She also took me to Winifred's, a small café on Kingston Hill that specialized in home-cooked food: steak-and-kidney pies, or sausage and mash, or a roast and three veg. They had proper puddings too, like baked jam roll with custard, much appreciated by the elderly male clientele.

I remember reading a *Woman's Companion* one day while we were waiting to be served. I was only eight or nine, but it was one of my favourite journals, a lowbrow story magazine with a pale red cover. I particularly liked the problem page, though there were sometimes words I didn't understand.

'Mummy,' I piped up, 'what are periods?'

I knew by the embarrassed coughs and rustles all around me that I'd somehow spoken out of turn.

'I'll tell you later,' Biddy hissed – and fair enough, she did.

We had our jaunts up to London to look at the dolls and beg for Mandy photos. We also went to the big C & A clothes shop in Oxford Street to look at the party dresses. I hankered after the flouncy satin dresses – bright pinks and harsh blues and stinging yellows – but Biddy thought these *very* common. She chose for me a little white dress with delicate stripes and multi-coloured smocking and a lace collar. I still preferred the tarty satin numbers, but I loved my demure pretty frock and called it my rainbow dress.

I *didn't* love the trying-on process. Biddy was always in a hurry, and if there was a long queue for the changing room, she pulled off my coat and tugged my dress over my head, leaving me utterly exposed in my vest and knickers. I protested bitterly, scarlet-faced.

'Don't be so silly,' said Biddy. 'Who on earth would want to look at *you*?'

She was forever putting me in my place and reminding me not to get above myself. If I got over-excited at a dance or a party and joined in noisily with all the other children, Biddy would seize hold of me and hiss in my ear, 'Stop showing off!' Yet this was the same mother who wanted me to turn into Shirley Temple and be the all-singing, all-dancing little trouper at a talent show.

She had no patience with my moans and groans but she could be a very concerned mother at times. When I was seven or eight, I developed a constant cough that wouldn't go away even when she'd spooned a whole bottle of Veno's down me. She was always worried about my chest since my bout of bronchitis so she carted me off to the doctor.

He didn't find anything seriously wrong with me. I think now it was probably a nervous cough, an anxious reaction to the tension at home. The doctor advised Sea Air as if I was a Victorian consumptive.

'Sea Air!' said Biddy.

We lived seventy miles from the seaside and we didn't have a car. But she took it on board valiantly. She somehow managed to find the money to take me on Saturday coach trips to Brighton right the way through the winter. We mooched round the antique shops in The Lanes and had a cup of tea and a bun in a café and walked up and down the pier and shivered in deckchairs while I breathed in the Sea Air. It worked a treat.

You certainly didn't go to Biddy for tea and sympathy, but she was brilliant at getting things done. She was almost too good when it came to school projects. I remember a nature project when we were told to collect examples of different leaves. This was a simple enough project. I could easily gather up a handful of leaves on my way home from school. But when I casually mentioned it to Biddy, she snapped into action. She dispatched Harry and me to Richmond Park on Sunday morning and instructed us to find at least twenty different samples. We did as we were told. Biddy spread leaves, berries, nuts – goodness knows what else – all over the living-room table. It was our job to identify each example with an inadequate I-Spy spotters' guide, *her* job to mount them magnificently on special white board. She labelled them in her exquisitely neat handwriting, then covered the finished work of art with protective cellophane.

My arms ached horribly carrying this confection like a splendid over-sized tray on the half-hour walk to school. The other children claimed – justifiably – that I'd cheated. The teacher seemed under-impressed with Biddy's showy display. I had enough sense to lie like crazy when I got back home, telling Biddy that I'd been highly praised and given top marks for my project.

She particularly excelled at Christmas presents. She had no truck with Father Christmas, not seeing why he should get the kudos when she'd done all the hard work and spent the money. I didn't feel at all deprived. I didn't care for Father Christmas either. I hated having to queue up to have my photo taken with this overly jolly old gent in Bentalls department store at Christmas. Once he'd peered myopically at my short-cropped hair and given me a blue-wrapped present for a boy.

We didn't go in for stockings at Cumberland House. Biddy organized a special Christmas bumper *box* stuffed with goodies wrapped in bright tissue paper. There might be a Puffin paperback – *Ballet Shoes* or *The Secret Garden* or *The Children Who Lived in a Barn*. There would definitely be a shiny sheath of Mandy photos. I'd hold them carefully and very lightly trace her glossy plaits, smiling back at her. There could be crayons or a silver biro, and red and blue notebooks from Woolworths with the times tables and curious weights and measures printed on the back. I never encountered these rods, poles and pecks in my arithmetic lessons, and didn't want to either. There would be something 'nobby' – Biddy's favourite word of approval for a novelty item like an elephant pencil sharpener or two magnetic Scottie dogs that clung together crazily.

These were all extras. I always had a Main Present too. Hard-up though she was, Biddy never fobbed me off with clothes or necessities like a school satchel or a new eiderdown. My Main Present was a doll, right up until I got to double figures.

They were always very special dolls too. Sometimes I knew about them already. Once I saw a teenage rag doll with a daffodil-yellow ponytail and turquoise jeans in a shop window in Kingston and I ached to possess her. Biddy didn't think much of rag dolls but she could see just how much I wanted her. We'd go to look at her every week. I went on and on wanting her. Then one Saturday she wasn't there any more.

'Oh *dear*,' said Biddy, shaking her head – but she could never fool me.

I pretended to be distraught – and probably didn't fool her either. I waited until I was on my own in the flat, then hauled one of the living-room chairs into my parents' bedroom, opened Biddy's wardrobe door, and clambered up. There on the top shelf was a navy parcel, long but soft when I poked. It was the teenage rag doll, safely bought and hidden away.

I'd go and whisper to her at every opportunity, imagining her so fiercely she seemed to wriggle out of her wrapping paper, slide out from the pile of Biddy's scarves and hats, and climb all the way down her quilted dressing gown to play with me. My imagination embellished her a little too extravagantly. When I opened her up at long last on Christmas Day, her bland sewn face with dot eyes and a red crescent-moon smile seemed crude and ordinary. How could *she* be my amazing teenage friend?

Another Christmas I had a more sophisticated teenage doll, a very glamorous Italian doll with long brown hair and big brown eyes with fluttering eyelashes. She wore a stylish suedette jacket and little denim jeans and tiny strappy sandals with heels. When I undressed her, I was tremendously impressed to see she had real bosoms. This was a world before Barbie. She must have been one of the first properly modelled teenage dolls. I was totally in awe of her.

I had been reading in Biddy's *Sunday Mirror* about Princess Ira, a fifteen-year-old precociously beautiful Italian girl who was involved with a much older man. I called my doll Ira and she flaunted herself all round my bedroom, posing and wiggling and chatting up imaginary unsuitable boyfriends. I shuffled after her, changing her outfits like a devoted handmaid.

I had one real china doll from Biddy. She saved up ten shillings (fifty pence, but a fortune to us in those days) and bought her from an antique shop in Kingston. She wasn't quite a Mabel. She had limp mousy hair and had clearly knocked around a little. She was missing a few fingers and she had a chip on her nose but she still had a very sweet expression. I loved her, and her Victorian clothes fascinated me – all those layers of petticoats and then frilly drawers, but she was difficult to *play* with. She was large and unwieldy and yet terrifyingly fragile. I could move her arms and legs but they creaked ominously. I brushed her real hair but it came out in alarming handfuls, and soon I could see her white cloth scalp through her thinning hair.

I *wish* Biddy had been fiercer with me and made me keep her in pristine condition. She'd be happy living in my Victorian house. I'd never let some

197

silly little girl undress her down to her drawers and comb her soft hair. She never really came alive for me. I can't even remember her name.

The best Christmas dolls ever were my Old Cottage twins. Old Cottage dolls were very special. I'd mist up the special glass display case peeping at them in Hamleys. They were quite small but wondrously detailed: hand-made little dolls with soft felt skin, somehow wired inside so they could stand and stride and sit down. One Old Cottage doll in little jodhpurs and black leather boots could even leap up on her toy horse and gallop. The dolls were dressed in a variety of costumes. You could choose an old-fashioned crinoline doll, an Easter bonnet girl, even a fairy in a silver dress and wings. I preferred the Old Cottage girls in ordinary everyday clothes – gingham dresses with little white socks and felt shoes. Every doll had a slightly different face and they all had different hairstyles. Some were dark, some were fair; some had curls, but most had little plaits, carefully tied.

Biddy knew which I'd like best. She chose a blonde girl with plaits and a dark girl with plaits, one in a blue flowery dress, one in red checks. Then she handed them over to Ga. She must have been stitching in secret for weeks and weeks. When I opened my box on Christmas morning, it was a wondrous treasure chest. I unwrapped my Old

Cottage twins and fell passionately in love with them at first sight. Then I opened a large wicker basket and discovered their *clothes*. Ga had made them little camel winter coats trimmed with fur, pink party dresses, soft little white nighties and tiny tartan dressing gowns, and a school uniform each – a navy blazer with an embroidered badge, a white shirt with a proper little tie, a pleated tunic, even two small felt school satchels.

I was in a daze of delight all Christmas Day. I could hardly bear to put my girls down so that I could eat up my turkey and Christmas pudding. I'd give anything to have those little dolls now with their lovingly stitched extensive wardrobe.

There's a Christmas scene at the start and end of one of my books. Which do you think it is?

It's *Clean Break*.

I was getting too big to believe in Santa but he still wanted to please me. I found a little orange journal with its own key; a tiny red heart soap; a purple gel pen; cherry bobbles for my hair; a tiny tin of violet sweets; a Jenna Williams bookmark; and a small pot of silver glitter nail varnish.

But Em thinks it's going to be the best Christmas ever, especially when her stepdad gives her a real emerald ring – but it all goes horribly wrong. She has a tough time throughout the next year, but it's Christmas Eve again in the last chapter. Someone comes knocking at the door and it looks as if this really *will* be a wonderful Christmas.

21

Books

Whenever I read writers' autobiographies, I always love that early chapter when they write about their favourite children's books. I was a total book-a-day girl, the most frequent borrower from Kingston Public Library. I think I spent half my childhood in the library. It meant so much to me to borrow books every week. It gives me such joy now to know that *I*'m currently the most borrowed author in British libraries.

In those other autobiographies people mention maybe six favourites, or select their top ten fiction characters. I can't choose! I feel as if I'm juggling my way through thousands of books, standing in a stadium jam-packed with fiction characters. They're all waving at me and mouthing, *Pick me! Pick me!*

I'll pick Enid Blyton first. She wasn't ever my favourite author but she got me *reading*. I pored over Pookie the white rabbit and the Shelf Animal books, but I couldn't work out what each word said. Then I went to school in Lewisham and learned that the c-a-t sat on the m-a-t, but I didn't really call that reading because it was so slow and laborious and there wasn't a real story.

I can't remember the magic moment when it all came together and I stopped stabbing the words with my finger and muttering each sound. I could suddenly just *do* it. Harry had read me all three Faraway Tree books and now I read them too. I spent months and months reading all the Enid Blytons I could find in the library. I didn't have to think about it. I didn't have to struggle with a single word. I didn't have to strain to understand what was going on. I could just let my eyes glide over the comfortably big print and experience all her different worlds.

Unlike most children, I didn't care for the Blyton mystery stories. I found the Secret Sevens and the Famous Fives boring. None of the children seemed to have much personality apart from George. I always like to read about fierce tomboy girls, though I was mostly a meek girly-girl myself.

I *did* rather enjoy some of the Adventure books. I owned a second-hand copy of *The Mountain of Adventure*. Somewhere in this book – presumably up the mountain – the children discovered a cave behind a waterfall and set up some sort of camp there. It seemed an incredibly romantic concept to me. I'd crawl under the living-room table with a doll or two and pretend the checked tablecloth was the waterfall. There was another underground cave in the book, filled with medieval religious figurines studded with jewels. I found this an awe-inspiring chapter too. We weren't a religious family and I'd certainly never been in a Catholic church, but somehow I'd seen a statue of a Madonna holding baby Jesus. I thought she was beautiful. The idea of a whole heavenly host of Madonnas cradling a nursery of Holy Infants was captivating. I imagined them taller than me, with real sapphires for eyes and solid gold haloes on their heads like celestial hats.

Even so, I preferred Blyton in more everyday mode. She wrote a book I particularly liked called *Hollow Tree House* about two children who run away and hide in – where else? – a hollow tree. I longed passionately for my own tree house, and planned, down to the finest detail, the things I would keep there (my favourite books, my Woolworths notebooks, my drawing book and tin of crayons, my Mandy photos), as if I thought I could conjure a sturdy tree growing out of our concrete balcony. There were plenty in the wilderness behind the flats, but I had no way of claiming personal ownership and no one to build me my house. Still, I was good at imaginary tree houses. Ann and I shared one in the playground at Latchmere, so it was not too difficult to pretend one for my own personal use at home.

I liked Enid Blyton's St Clare's school stories too. I had no desire whatsoever to go to boarding school myself. I was appalled at the idea of being in the company of other children all the time, with no opportunities whatsoever for private imaginary games, but it was fun to read about such a strangely different environment. The twins themselves were a little dull, but I liked Carlotta, the dashing circus girl, and Claudine, the naughty French girl – both apparently based on *real* girls.

I knew this because I'd solemnly read Enid Blyton's *The Story of My Life*. Some of the chapters were a bit of a struggle because I was still only about six or seven, but I found some passages riveting. I was interested to learn that little girl Enid had nightmares too, and she gave sensible practical tips on how to cope with them. She wrote about her own imaginary worlds. It was such a relief to realize that someone else had a weird vivid inner life like my own. It was fascinating learning about her writing routine. In those days children didn't know very much about their favourite authors. Sometimes they had baffling names like Richmal Crompton or P. L. Travers so you didn't even know whether they were men or women.

So Enid Blyton got me reading fluently and

reinforced my desire to write, though I knew right from a very early age that I wanted to write very different sort of books. I wanted to write books that didn't seem to exist yet – books about realistic children who had difficult parents and all sorts of secrets and problems; easy-to-read books that still made you think hard; books with funny bits that made you laugh out loud, though sometimes the story was so sad it made you cry too.

I took to reading adult books *about* children, like Catherine Cookson's series about a tough little Tyneside girl called Mary Ann. She came from a very poor family and her beloved dad was a drunk, forever letting them down. Mary Ann was a devout Catholic and popped into the church the way other kids bobbed into the chip shop. She had Mary, Joseph and Jesus as her own personal ultra-good imaginary friends.

I envied Mary Ann and wished I was a Catholic too, especially if it meant saying prayers to beautiful statues of Mary. I'm not a Catholic, I'm still not at all religious, but gentle Madonnas – plaster, china, glass and wood – grace many corners of my house.

The only book written for children that struck me in any way as realistic was *The Family from One End Street* by Eve Garnett. It's a story about a poor family. Dad's a dustman, Mum's a washerwoman, and there are seven children. I wasn't so interested in reading about the boys but I loved the two oldest sisters, Lily Rose and Kate. Lily Rose was lumpy and helpful and took her responsibilities as a big sister seriously. She helped Mum with her ironing but had a terrible accident with the hot iron on a green artificial-silk petticoat. Kate was thin and clever and passed her exams to go to grammar school. She was so proud of her smart new uniform that she insisted on wearing it on a day trip to the seaside – a *big* mistake.

These girls seemed real to me, and they looked real too in Eve Garnett's drawings. They had straggly hair that stuck out at odd angles, their dresses had saggy hems and they wore plimsolls instead of shoes, just like most of the children I knew. Not me though. Biddy would have died if *I*'d looked like a child from a council estate. She had my hair viciously permed so that I looked as if I'd been plugged into an electric light socket.

She struggled to buy me new clothes every year. She wasn't having her daughter a Second-hand Rose with a telltale line around the coat hem where it had been let down. She *certainly* wasn't going to let me run around in plimsolls. I had Clarks strapover shoes in winter and brown sandals in the summer to wear to school, and strappy black patent shoes and snow-white sandals for best. No child was better shod. If my shoe heels ever got worn down, Harry would squat in the kitchen with a little cobbler's last and tap in 'Blakies' to make them last longer.

My favourite children's book at that time – well, maybe first equal with *Adventures with Rosalind*, was *Nancy and Plum* by Betty MacDonald. I read it so many times I knew long passages by heart. I suffered with them at Mrs Monday's orphanage, hurried anxiously beside them when they ran away, and celebrated when they met up with the kindly Campbells. They adopted Nancy and Plum and gave them lots of hugs and cuddles and chicken pies and beautiful dolls and lovely girly outfits.

I knew perfectly well this wasn't *likely* but I didn't care. I thought *Nancy and Plum* a perfect book. I also enjoyed a story by Betty MacDonald's sister called *Best Friends* – now there's a familiar title. In *this Best Friends* Suzie makes friends with Coco next door and they have fun together and share a tree house. Children's books in the 1950s sprouted veritable forests of tree houses.

I didn't only like books about poor or under-privileged children. I loved all the Mary Poppins books about the solidly middle-class Banks children, with their cook and their boot boy – and of course their magical nanny, Mary Poppins. I borrowed most of the Mary Poppins books from the library, reading them in reverse order and waiting weeks and weeks before I found the first in the series back on the shelf.

I begged Biddy to let me belong to a book club because *Mary Poppins in the Park* was the introductory book, available for just a few shillings. She gave in, so I got my very own yellow Mary Poppins book. I took it to school and carried it around with me all day. I then received a book club book a month, none of which were so much to my taste – Kitty Barnes, Malcolm Saville, Lorna Hill – all very worthy popular authors but they just didn't do it for me. However, there was one Pamela Brown book among the book club choices and I'd soon read my way along all the Browns on the shelf in the library. I particularly liked her Blue Door series about a group of children who set up their own theatre.

Pamela Brown wrote the first in the series when she was only fifteen, a fact that impressed me greatly. I wondered if any of my stories in my Woolworths exercise books would ever get published. They were mostly family stories about misunderstood children (surprise!), but I also wrote about girls who could fly, sad Victorian tales about poor little beggar children, comical fantasy stories, melodramatic love stories, even a very long retelling of the story of Moses from his sister

Miriam's point of view. I didn't *really* believe I had a chance of seeing my stories in print. It was a daydream, like some little girls long to be actresses or rock stars or fashion models.

In one of my books I pretend there's going to be a special children's television serial based on Enid Blyton's book The Twins at St Clare's. *Who is desperate to get a part in it?*

It's Ruby in *Double Act*. But her twin, poor Garnet, is appalled at the idea.

I can't act.

I don't *want* to act.

I can't go to an audition in London! I can't say a lot of stuff with everyone watching. It'll be even worse than being a sheep. Why won't Ruby understand? She won't listen to me. She's riffling through *The Twins at St Clare's* right this minute, trying to choose which bit we'll act out.

Only I'm not going to act.

I can't can't can't act.

I can't act either, but I had a tiny part in the television serial of *Double Act*. When Yvonne, the producer, asked me if I wanted to take part myself, I thought it would be fun. I thought I knew the perfect part for me. Ruby and Garnet's dad has his own second-hand bookshop. I am famous for my vast collection of books (around 15,000! There are shelves all over my house *and* a special little library at the bottom of my garden). I won't be able to read all my books even if I live to be 500, but I still can't stop buying them. So I thought it would be fun if I played a customer in the Red Bookshop. I thought it might make children chuckle if they spotted me in a dark corner of the bookshop, happily browsing.

Yvonne had other ideas. She wanted me to play the fictional casting director who puts the twins through their paces at the audition. As she's been drawn in the book with short hair, flamboyant jewellery and extraordinary boots, I suppose it's easy to guess why Yvonne saw me in the part. But this meant I had to learn lines. I found this extraordinarily difficult. I just couldn't remember them – even though I *wrote* the lines myself!

I managed to stagger through somehow, but decided I'd definitely stick to my day job – writing – in future!

22

The Boys and Girls Exhibition

I got to meet Pamela Brown when I was nine. They used to hold a special Boys and Girls Exhibition at Olympia and Biddy took me one Saturday. I found it a very overwhelming day. The sheer *noise* of thousands of over-excited children in a vast echoing building made my ears throb. We were pushed and pummelled as we struggled round all the stands. Biddy was a pushy woman too, and occasionally batted a child out of her way. There was a lot of argy-bargy, mostly between mothers desperate to get their own kids to the front of each queue.

I wished Biddy had left me languishing at the back of the most popular stand, George Cansdale and his animals. George Cansdale was an animal expert and had his own programme on children's television. I wasn't as passionately fond of animals as most children, apart from my constant yearning for a dog. I didn't like anything creepy-crawly at all, and kept well away from anything with beaks or sharp claws.

George Cansdale had a whole enclosure of animals with him. All the children at Olympia wanted to stroke the rabbits and guinea pigs and kittens. Biddy shoved me from the back until I was practically catapulted onto George Cansdale's lap. He nodded at me as he sank his hands deep into a strange big coffin-shaped box.

'Hello, little girl. What's your name?' he said, starting to haul something heavy from the box.

'Jacqueline, sir,' I said.

Oh, we were so polite in the fifties. I practically bobbed a curtsey.

'You seem a very sensible little girl, Jacqueline,' said George Cansdale. 'Shall we show the other children just how sensible you are?'

He was still hauling what looked like enormous skeins of khaki wool from the box. Loop after loop. Coil after coil. A snake! An enormous brown snake, with a mean head and a forked tongue flicking in and out.

There was a great gasp, a collective series of *Beano*-comic exclamations: '*Aah!*' '*Ugh!*' '*Eek!*'

I was so shocked I couldn't even scream. I couldn't back away because I had Biddy and hundreds of children pressing hard against me.

'You're not scared of snakes, are you, Jacqueline?' said George Cansdale.

I bared my teeth in a sickly grin.

'Shall we show the other children how sensible you are?' he said, reaching towards me, his arms full of writhing snake.

He wound it round and round and round my neck like a loathsome live scarf.

'There! Look how brave Jacqueline is,' said George Cansdale.

The children oohed and aahed at me. I stood still, the head of the snake an inch away, its tongue going flicker flicker flicker in my face.

'There! Nothing to be frightened of, is there, Jacqueline?' said George Cansdale.

I was way past *fright*. Any second now I was going to wet myself. Mercifully, George Cansdale unwound the snake coil by coil until I was free at last. Biddy gave me a tug and tunnelled us through the crowd to the ladies' toilets.

'Why did you let him put that horrible slimy snake round you?' Biddy said, dabbing anxiously at the velvet collar on my coat.

'It wasn't slimy, it was *warm*,' I said, shuddering. 'Oh, Mum, it felt *awful*.'

'Well, you should have said something, not stood there looking gormless,' said Biddy, but she gave me a quick hug nevertheless.

That should have been enough excitement for one day, but Biddy was determined to get her money's worth. We went to a kind of Mind Body

Spirit section and had our bumps read by a shy man in spectacles still wearing a shabby brown demob suit. I'm surprised Biddy went for this, because his nervous fingers probed deep into our perms as he felt for significant bumps on our heads, wrecking our hairdos. Perhaps she was at a crisis point with Uncle Ron and wanted to see what fate had in store for her.

The Bump Man seemed disconcerted by Biddy's head.

'You're a real Peter Pan,' he said.

This pleased her no end, because she thought this meant she looked young for her age – which she did. He fumbled about in her curls, pressing and prodding, as if her head was a musical instrument and might start playing a tune. He said she was very bright and very determined. Then he ran out of steam and decided to do a bit of handwriting interpretation instead, maybe to reassure her she was getting her money's worth.

Biddy smiled happily. She always took great pride in her beautiful handwriting. The rare times she wrote a letter she always drafted it first and then copied it all out exquisitely in pen. The Bump Man admired her handwriting and said she was exceptionally neat and meticulous, which wasn't really straining his psychic powers.

Then it was my turn. I wrote my own much

shakier signature. We were being mucked about at school. Every year the new teacher had different ideas about handwriting. I was currently in a class where we were all forced to write in very sloping copperplate with blotchy dipping pens and brown school ink. My natural handwriting was little and stood upright, so I was struggling. The Bump Man said my personality was still forming. He felt my head too, not so nervous of me, kneading it as if it was an awkward lump of dough. He asked me various silly questions and I muttered answers in monosyllables.

'She's very shy,' said the Bump Man. 'What do you like doing best, dear?'

'Reading,' I whispered.

'Mm. Yes. You're very dreamy.'

'You're telling me!' said Biddy. 'I sometimes think she's not all there. What do you think she'll be when she grows up?'

'Oh, a teacher, definitely,' he said.

I was bitterly disappointed. I so so so wanted to be a writer. If I couldn't ever get anything published, I wanted to be a hairdresser and create beautiful long hairstyles all day. I didn't want to be a *teacher*. In the 1950s most teachers in primary school were in their forties and fifties, even sixties. Many of the women had their grey hair scraped back in buns. They all wore sensible flat laced shoes. When they sat down, their long-legged pink directoire knickers showed unless they kept their knees clamped together. I didn't want to look like a teacher.

I was glad to see the back of the Bump Man. To cheer me up Biddy took me to the Book Corner. There, sitting on a chair, was the famous children's writer Pamela Brown. We knew it was her because she had a placard saying so right above her head. She looked incredibly smart and glamorous, the exact opposite of a frumpy teacher. She was dressed all in black, wearing a beautifully cut black tailored suit, a tiny black feathery hat on her soft curls, and high-heeled black suede shoes. She wore a string of pearls round her neck, one last elegant touch.

She was sitting bolt upright on her chair, staring straight ahead. I know now the poor woman must have been dying of embarrassment, stuck there all alone, waiting for someone, *anyone*, to approach her, but to me then she seemed like a queen on her throne. I just wanted to gaze at her reverently.

Biddy had other ideas. She prodded me in the back.

'Go and say hello to her then!' she said.

'I can't!' I mouthed.

'Yes you can! It's Pamela Brown. You know, you like her books.'

Of course I knew.

'So *tell* her you like them,' said Biddy.

I was almost as frightened of Pamela Brown as

I was of George Cansdale, but at least she was unlikely to produce a snake from her handbag and wrap it round my neck.

'Hello,' I whispered, approaching her.

'Hello,' said Pamela Brown.

She seemed a little at a loss for words too but she smiled at me very sweetly.

'I like your books,' I confided.

'I'm so pleased,' she said.

We smiled some more and then I backed away, both of us sighing with relief.

Who's got a worst enemy called Moyra who had a gigantic snake called Crusher for a pet?

It's Verity in *The Cat Mummy*.

Do you have any pets? My best friend Sophie has got four kittens called Sporty, Scary, Baby and Posh. My second-best friend Laura has a golden Labrador dog called Dustbin. My sort-of-boyfriend Aaron has got a dog too, a black mongrel called Liquorice Allsorts, though he gets called Licky for short. My worst enemy Moyra has got a boa constrictor snake called Crusher. Well, she says she has. I've never been to her house so I don't know if she's telling fibs.

I've got a very sweet-natured elderly ginger and white cat called Whisky. I wouldn't mind a kitten and I'd love a dog – but I would *hate* to have any kind of snake as a pet!

23

More Books!

I don't apologize for another chapter about books (and it's a long one too). This is a book *about* books. I wouldn't be a writer now if I hadn't been a reader.

I've told you about my two favourite books, *Nancy and Plum* and *Adventures with Rosalind*, but I'm afraid you can't read them for yourself because they're long out of print. I've mentioned Enid Blyton and Eve Garnett and Pamela Brown, but I think my favourite popular contemporary author was Noel Streatfeild.

Her most famous book is *Ballet Shoes*, a lovely story about three adopted sisters, Pauline, Petrova and Posy Fossil, who attend a stage school. Pauline wants to be an actress, Petrova aches to be an airline pilot and Posy is already a brilliant ballet dancer. *I* wanted to be a ballet dancer too. I loved dancing and could pick up little routines quite quickly. I had read enough books about girls longing to be dancers to realize that I had ballet dancer's *feet*. My second toe is longer than my big toe, which means I could go up on my points more easily, and

I have very high arches. I was sure this was a genuine sign that I could be a Belle of the Ballet. I wanted most of all to be a writer, of course, but I didn't see why I couldn't be a ballet dancer too. Ann Taylor did ballet. Mandy did ballet.

'Well, *you're* not doing ballet,' said Biddy. 'I'm not tackling those costumes. It would be a bally nightmare.' She chuckled at her own bad joke.

Biddy had done ballet herself as a small child. She was little and cute with curly hair so she'd been chosen to be in all the concerts, as a fairy, a kitten, a rabbit . . . Ga had made all her costumes.

'We can't ask her to make your costumes now her arthritis is so bad,' Biddy said firmly. 'You wouldn't *like* ballet anyway. You wouldn't be any good at it. *I* wasn't.'

So I never got to try. I practised valiantly by myself for a while. I had a pair of pale pink pull-on bedroom slippers and I pretended these were proper ballet shoes. When Biddy and Harry were at work, I hummed the 'Sugar Plum Fairy' tune and pranced up and down our flat, whirling and twirling round the table and the television, pirouetting down the hall, executing a daring leap up onto Biddy's bed and then sweeping a deep ballerina curtsey to myself in her dressing-table mirror. Perhaps it's just as well I didn't have an audition.

I picked up a lot of tips from *Ballet Shoes* but

most of all I liked it for all the realistic little details of girl life. It was written in the 1930s so it was already dated when I read it twenty years later. I puzzled over the Fossil sisters' poverty when they lived in a huge house on the Cromwell Road and had a cook and a nanny, but I loved it that they were such *real* girls. They quarrelled and larked around and worried about things. I felt they were *my* sisters. I sighed over Pauline becoming swollen-headed when she had her first big part in a play; I suffered agonies with Petrova, forced into acting when she felt such a fool on stage and longed to be with Mr Simpson fixing cars in his garage; I envied Posy as she glided through life, showing off and being insufferably cute. I knew how important it was for the girls to have a smart black velvet frock for their auditions. I loved the necklaces they got for a Christmas present from Great-uncle Matthew. I longed to go too on their seaside holiday to Pevensey. I knew without being told that it was definitely a cut above Clacton.

Noel Streatfeild was a prolific writer, and so I went backwards and forwards to the library, determined to read everything she'd ever written. I owned *Ballet Shoes*. It was one of the early Puffin books, with a bright green cover and Ruth Gervis's pleasing pictures of the three girls in ballet dresses on the front. Those illustrations seemed so much part of the whole book (Ruth Gervis was Noel

Streatfeild's sister) that the modern un-illustrated versions all seem to have an important part lacking. But at least *Ballet Shoes* is still in print. Most of Noel Streatfeild's books have long since disappeared from bookshops and libraries.

I loved *White Boots* and *Tennis Shoes* and *Curtain Up*. I was given *Wintle's Wonders* as a summer holiday present. I remember clutching it to my chest so happily the edges poked me through my thin cotton dress. It was an agreeably chunky book, which meant it might last me several days.

Noel Streatfeild edited a very upmarket magazine for children called the *Elizabethan*, which I subscribed to. Enid Blyton had a magazine too, *Sunny Stories*, but that was very much for younger children. I had to struggle hard with some of the uplifting erudite articles in the *Elizabethan*, which was strange because Noel's books were wonderfully easy to read.

She wrote some fascinating volumes of autobiography, and one biography of *her* favourite children's writer, E. Nesbit.

I loved E. Nesbit too. Biddy gave me *The Story of the Treasure Seekers* when I was seven. It was my first classic but it wasn't too difficult for me as it was written in the first person. You were meant to guess which one of the Bastable children was the narrator. It seemed pretty obvious to me that it was Oswald. I didn't realize this was all part of the joke. Now I think *The Story of the Treasure Seekers* is a very warm and witty book, and it makes me crack up laughing, but as a seven-year-old I took it very seriously indeed. It seemed perfectly possible to me that the children *might* find a fortune. I failed to understand that Albert's uncle frequently helped them out. I had no idea that if you added several spoonfuls of sugar to sherry, it would taste disgusting. I'd had a sip of Ga's Harvey's Bristol Cream at Christmas and thought it was even worse than Gongon's black treacle medicine. *I* thought the taste would be improved with a liberal sprinkling of sugar too.

I wished there were more Bastable *girls*. I liked Alice a lot, and I felt sorry for poor po-faced Dora, especially when she wept and told Oswald she tried so hard to keep her brothers and sister in order because their dying mother had asked her to look after the family. There were occasional Edwardian references that I didn't understand. I sniggered at the boys wearing garments called knickerbockers. But E. Nesbit's writing style was so lively and child-friendly, and the children seemed so real that I felt I was a token Treasure Seeker too, especially as they lived in Lewisham.

I loved *The Railway Children* too, and was particularly fond of Bobbie. I liked it that Mother was a writer and whenever she sold a story, there were buns for tea. (I copied this idea many years later whenever *I* sold a story to a publisher!) There was a special children's serial of *The Railway Children* on television – not the lovely film starring Jenny Agutter, this was many years earlier than that.

I sat in front of our new television set, spellbound. At the end of each episode the television announcer said a few words. She was called Jennifer, a smiley, wavy-haired girl who was only about twelve. She told all the child viewers about a *Railway Children* art competition.

'All you have to do is illustrate your favourite scene,' she said, smiling straight at me, cross-legged on the living-room floor in Cumberland House.

'Mummy, can I do some painting?' I said.

I had to ask permission because Biddy wasn't keen on me having my painting water on the dining table and went through an elaborate performance of covering it over with newpapers, and rolling my sleeves right up to my elbows so my cuffs wouldn't get smudged with wet watercolour.

'Of course you're not doing any painting now. You're due for bed in ten minutes,' said Biddy.

She believed in Early Nights, even though I'd often lie awake for hours.

'But it's for a competition on the television,' I said. *'Please!'*

Biddy considered. I was quite good at painting for my age. Most of the children in the Infants were still at the big-blob combined-head-and-body stage, with stick arms and legs, the sky a blue stripe at the top of the page and the grass a green stripe at the bottom. I'd copied so many pictures out of my books that I had a slightly more sophisticated style, and I liked giving all my faces elaborate features. I was a dab hand at long eyelashes, though I was sometimes too enthusiastic, so my people looked as if two tarantulas had crawled onto each face.

'Have a go then,' said Biddy, relenting.

I was still having a go when Harry came home from work wanting his tea.

'You'll have to wait for once,' said Biddy. 'Jac's painting.'

I dabbled my paintbrush and daubed proudly. I was on my third attempt. I'd tried hard to draw a train for my first picture, but I couldn't work out what they looked like. I didn't have any books with trains in them. I'd seen the little blue *Thomas The Tank Engine* books in W. H. Smith's, but I didn't fancy them as a girly read.

I made a determined attempt at a train, painting it emerald-green, but it looked like a giant caterpillar. I took another piece of paper and tried to draw the train head-on, but I couldn't work out where the wheels went, and I'd used up so much green paint already there was just a dab left in my Reeves paintbox.

'Blow the train,' I muttered. I drew Bobbie and Phyllis and Peter instead, frantically waving red flannel petticoats. I drew them as if *I* was the train, rapidly approaching them. Their faces reflected this, their mouths crimson Os as they screamed.

I got a bit carried away with the high drama of it all, sloshing on the paint so vigorously that it started to run and I had to blot it up hurriedly with my cuddle hankie. The finished painting was a little wrinkly but I still felt it was quite good.

'Put your name and address on the back carefully,' said Biddy. 'And put your age.'

I did as I was told and she sent it off to the television studio at Alexandra Palace the next day.

I won in my age category! It was the only time I won anything as a child. They didn't send my painting back, which was a pity, but they sent a Rowney drawing pad as a prize. I've felt very fond of *The Railway Children* ever since.

I'd read my way through most of the girly children's classics before I was ten. Woolworths used to stock garishly produced, badly printed children's classics for 2s 6d, a third of the price of most modern books. I read *Little Women* over and over again, loving Jo, the tomboy harem-scarem sister who read voraciously and was desperate to

232

be a writer. I also had a soft spot for Beth because she was shy and liked playing with dolls. I loved *What Katy Did* and felt desperately sorry for poor little Elsie, the middle child who wasn't in on Katy and Clover's secrets. I wasn't so interested in Katy after she fell off the swing and endured her long illness. I couldn't stomach saintly Cousin Helen. I enjoyed the Christmas chapter the most, and the detailed descriptions of all the presents.

I read *The Secret Garden* by Frances Hodgson Burnett, thrilled to read about irritable, spoiled children for a change, totally understanding *why* they behaved badly. I liked *A Little Princess* even more. I found Sara Crewe a magical character. I particularly loved the part at the beginning where she finds her doll Emily and there's a detailed description of her trunk of clothes. I shivered in the attic with Sara after her fortune changed, and found the scenes with Becky and Ermengarde very touching. I was charmed that Sara made a pet out of Melchisedec – though if a real rat had scampered across the carpet in my bedroom, I'd have screamed my head off.

I read the beginning of *Jane Eyre* too. Biddy had a little red leatherette copy in the bookcase. I fingered my way through many of these books, but they were mostly dull choices for a child. *Jane Eyre* was in very small print, uncomfortable to read, but I found the first page so riveting I carried on and on. I was there with Jane on the window seat, staring out at the rain. I felt a thrill of recognition when she described poring over the illustrations in Bewick's *History of British Birds*. I trembled when her cousins tormented her. I was horrified when Jane's aunt had the servants haul her off to the terrifying Red Room. I shivered with Jane when she was sent to the freezing cold Lowood boarding school. I burned with humiliation when she was forced to stand in disgrace with the slate saying LIAR! around her neck. I wanted to be friends with clever odd Helen Burns too. I wanted to clasp her in my arms when she was sick and dying.

I read those first few chapters again and again – and Jane joined my increasingly large cast of imaginary friends.

Which girl in my books has Jane Eyre for her imaginary friend?

It's Prue in *Love Lessons*.

For years and years I'd had a private pretend friend, an interesting and imaginative girl my own age called Jane. She started when I read the first few chapters of *Jane Eyre*. She stepped straight out of the pages and into my head. She no longer led her own Victorian life with her horrible aunt and cousins. She shared my life with my demented father.

Jane was better than a real sister. She wasn't babyish and boring like Grace. We discussed books and pored over pictures and painted watercolours together, and we talked endlessly about everything.

I didn't base the character of Prue on myself, even though we shared an imaginary friend *and* both had odd fathers. I was quite good at art, like Prue, and I was also fond of an interesting Polish art teacher at secondary school – but I *didn't* fall in love with him!

24

Television and Radio

How many television channels can you watch on your set at home? How many channels do you think there were when I was a child? One! The dear old BBC – and in those days children's television lasted one hour, from five to six. That was your lot.

I watched Muffin the Mule, a shaky little puppet who trotted across the top of a piano, strings very visible. He nodded and shook his head and did a camp little hoof-prance while his minder, Annette Mills, sang, *'We love Muffin, Muffin the Mule. Dear old Muffin, playing the fool. We love Muffin – everybody sing, WE LOVE MUFFIN THE MULE.'*

Children's television was not sophisticated in those days.

Annette Mills's speciality was performing with puppets. She also did a little weekly show with Prudence Kitten. I *adored* Prudence. She was a black cat glove puppet, ultra girly, who wore flouncy frocks and pinafores. You couldn't get colour television in those days so I always had to guess the colour of Prudence's frocks. She had her own little kitchen and bustled around baking cakes and making cups of tea, especially when her best friend Primrose was coming on a visit.

There was another puppet on children's television called Mr Turnip, an odd little man with a turnip head. He was best buddies with a real man called Humphrey Lestocq. No one could spell his name so viewers were encouraged to call him H.L. when he appeared on his television programme, *Whirligig*.

There was a slapstick comedian specially for children called Mr Pastry, a doddery old man who kept tripping over and making lots of mess. Comedians on adult television weren't necessarily more inspiring, though Biddy and Harry and I laughed at Arthur Askey, especially when he did his 'Busy Bee' song (don't ask!), and Harry had a soft spot for Benny Hill.

Television went wildly upmarket and downmarket, in those days. There was *The Brains Trust*, with its bombastic introductory music and its little quote from Alexander Pope: 'To speak his thought is every human's right.' Even panel games were treated very seriously. We watched *What's My Line?* every week, hosted by Eamonn Andrews (chatty Irishman), with Lady Isobel Barnett (posh dark-haired lady), Barbara Kelly (lively Canadian blonde), David Nixon (bald magician) and Gilbert Harding (grumpy intellectual). Eamonn and David and Gilbert wore full evening dress with bow ties; Lady Isobel and Barbara wore long dresses with straps and sweetheart necklines.

Some of the children's programmes were posh classy affairs too. Huw Wheldon had a talent show for children called *All Your Own*. He seldom chose showy little singers and dancers with ringlets and toothy grins. Huw Wheldon specialized in pale spectacled geeky children with high-pitched voices who played the cello or collected stamps. There was once a glorious troupe of strange children who acted out a mad chess game, singing at the end, *'Ro, ro, rolio, tumpty tumpty tum. Now the battle's over, we'll have lots of fun!'*

ITV started up when I was about eight but Biddy fought not to have it. She said it was common. Maybe we simply couldn't afford a new television set. Everyone at school was talking about all the new programmes, especially *Wagon Train*.

'Silly cowboy rubbish,' said Biddy, sniffing.

Then she weakened, or maybe Harry forked out so he could watch his horse-racing on the new channel. We had a brand-new television with a fourteen-inch screen – and ITV. I *still* wasn't able to join in the *Wagon Train* discussions at school. We watched one episode and Biddy poured scorn on it. It wasn't just silly cowboys, it was *sentimental*. Biddy said it made her want to throw up.

I was sometimes allowed to watch cowboys on children's television: the Lone Ranger with his trusty friend Tonto – or was that his horse? No, that was Silver. You saw him rearing up at the start of the show, the masked Lone Ranger waving on his back. I didn't like cowboys particularly, I just liked the part where they moseyed into town and stomped bow-legged into the saloon bar. I longed to be one of the naughty ladies who ran the saloon. I loved their flouncy ruffled skirts and their fancy high-heeled cowboy boots. There was also Davy Crockett with his furry hat. For a while every small boy wanted one of those hats with a weird tail hanging down the back. They all hid round corners and fired at each other with their toy Davy Crockett guns. He had his own theme tune: '*Davy – Daveee Crockett, King of the Wild Frontier*.'

This was always requested on *Children's Favourites* on a Saturday morning, which was on the radio. Practically every child in the country listened to Uncle Mac and the selection for each Saturday. He rarely played the current favourites in the Hit Parade. These were special *children's* songs, played over and over again throughout the fifties. The lyrics themselves were repetitious:

How much is that doggy in the window?
(Woof, woof!)

The one with the waggly tail.
How much is that doggy in the window?
(Woof, woof!)
I do hope that doggy's for sale.

How about:

There's a tiny house
(There's a tiny house)
By a tiny stream,
(By a tiny stream,)
Where a lovely lass
(Where a lovely lass)
Had a lovely dream,
(Had a lovely dream,)
And her dream came true
Quite unexpectedly
In Gilly Gilly Ossenfeffer Katzenellen
Bogen by the Sea.

That was sung with great gusto by Max Bygraves, who recorded any number of comedy songs. I was very fond of his 'Pink Toothbrush' song, which always made me laugh.

Best of all was 'Nellie the Elephant' – by Mandy Miller! Mandy had made records before. They were *dire* – even I had to admit it, though I still loved playing them on our wind-up gramophone. We owned very few records. Harry liked Mantovani, and we had the soundtrack to *South Pacific*, and the Mandy recordings. Mandy's best effort so far had been singing, *'Oh let the world be full of sunshine, for Mummy, for Daddy and for me.'* She didn't always stay in tune either. But she really came into her own when she made 'Nellie the Elephant'. It was a sweet, funny song with a proper story and she sang it beautifully, putting her heart and soul into it, going, *'Trumpety trump trump trump!'* with great emphasis and expression.

Which of my characters gets to appear in a Children of Courage *documentary on television?*

It's Elsa in *The Bed and Breakfast Star*.

My news interview was repeated later in the year in a special compilation programme called *Children of Courage*. And I got to do another interview with a nice blonde lady with big teeth, and Mum spent some of Mack's betting money on a beautiful new outfit from the Flowerfields Shopping Centre for my special telly appearance.

I've been on television lots of times now. I'm especially proud that I've got a gold Blue Peter badge! I think my favourite time was when *The South Bank Show* did a documentary about me. They didn't just interview me – my daughter Emma's on the programme too, and my dear friend Anne, and there's even a glimpse of my best secondary school friend Chris. Paterson, the jeweller who makes all my wonderful rings, says on the programme that 'Jacky's rock 'n' roll!' I loved that bit.

I've also been on *Desert Island Discs* on the radio, which was great fun. My first choice of music was . . . 'Nellie the Elephant'!

25

Teachers

The head of Latchmere Juniors was a man called Mr Pearson. I have a photo of me standing next to him but I don't think I ever spoke more than a couple of sentences to him. We weren't frightened of him though. He seemed a quiet, kind, gentle man, though every now and then he caned one of the boys in Prayers. I always shut my eyes when this happened. Mr Pearson didn't seem to have much stomach for corporal punishment either, and got it over and done with as briskly as possible.

He spoke earnestly in Prayers, often telling us inspirational true-life stories (like the ones on the back of my *Girl* comic). He had a particular passion for Shackleton and told us such vivid stories about his long trek across the ice that we shivered even in the height of summer.

Mr Pearson was a chess fanatic too and insisted that every child in the Juniors be taught how to play. There was a special chess club, and children were always to be found sitting cross-legged in the playground around a chessboard. I learned to play too but I wasn't very good at it. I didn't have a mathematical mind that could plan ahead. I couldn't apply my mind to plotting potential chess moves. I'd think *castle* and *knight* and I'd be off in a daydream, galloping the little wooden knight through imaginary forests to an enchanted castle. My king would be in check before I knew where I was.

Mr Pearson took us for a lesson when we were in the top class, our equivalent of Year Six. He taught us *codes* – how to invent them and how to crack them. I was better at this. I knew the shape of words, the rhythm of a sentence, and often worked by instinct rather than patient analysis. I should have taken up writing in code. Years later I stupidly confided all sorts of secret things to my diary. Biddy read it and hit the roof – and the floor – and all four walls.

Our form teachers taught us English and arithmetic and PT. We had a special teacher, Miss Audric, who taught us scripture, music and nature study. Most of the teachers were eccentric. Miss Audric was the all-time Queen of Quirkiness. She had bright carrot-coloured hair wound in plaits round her head. On sunny summer days she'd sit in the grass quadrangle, undo her hair and brush it out so that it fell in an orange curtain way past her waist. Then she'd plait it all up again, playing Rapunzel. She wore woollen suits, hand-crocheted, in extraordinary bright colours – emerald green, purple, electric blue. She played the violin and the piano and all different kinds of recorder. She winced when we had difficulty piping our way accurately through 'Little Bird'. She was someone else who believed she had a personal hotline to Jesus. She told us stories about him as if he was a dear friend of hers. We almost believed she'd nipped on a bus to visit her pal when he was sharing out the loaves and fishes and raising Lazurus from the dead.

I always had problems with Jesus' miracles. I could *believe* them, but didn't see how they worked. I thought of those five loaves and two small fishes. I thought of five sandwich loaves. What kind of fish would you find in the sea of Galilee? Cod? If Jesus was holy enough to spread this simple feast around five thousand hungry people, why didn't he pull out all the stops and provide chips to go with the fish, and maybe mushy peas too, and some butter to go on the bread? Then I had problems with Lazurus, resurrected from the tomb, smelling so bad that all the disciples had to put their sleeves over their noses so they didn't breathe in his decaying stench. What happened *next*? Did poor Lazurus have to trail around Palestine with his reek all around him, shunned by everyone? Did he look like the Living Dead from Zombie-land, creatures in an American horror comic I wasn't supposed to read?

I really wanted to know the answers to these and a host of other biblical questions, but I had enough sense not to ask Miss Audric. She was very strict and could quell you with one of her looks. If you got the giggles during one of her squawky violin solos, then Woe Betide You.

Miss Audric had a mad dog that thought it was a wolf. Whenever she took it for walks in Richmond Park, it made a beeline for the deer. The herd scattered as it raced up, teeth bared. Even the mightiest stag would trot off in terror. Miss Audric's dog could probably see off a herd of elephants, let alone timid deer. She brought it to school occasionally and we were all scared stiff of it. I can't remember what it was really called but we all nicknamed it Fang.

Miss Audric decided to take us on a walk in Richmond Park for our nature study lesson. She rounded us all up – more than forty of us – made us form a crocodile, then marched us out of the school and up to the park. This was a brisk half-hour walk in itself. Many of us were flagging by the time we got to the park gates. Still, it was a sunny day and we went whooping and swooping into the ferny wilderness of Richmond Park, dodging around the ancient oak trees.

Miss Audric didn't stop us. We were all escapees

from school now. It was time to go back for the next lesson but Miss Audric didn't care. She strode out in her conker-coloured lace-ups and we skipped after her.

We went past the witch's pond, further into the park than I'd ever been with Harry, up and over the steep hill, across the flat plain where the deer grazed. Miss Audric lectured us on the differences between red deer and fallow deer and taught us about antler formation. Some of the boys raised their arms and pretended to be stags, locking antlers. We were all getting a bit restless now.

'Miss Audric, it's getting very *late*,' Cherry interrupted nervously.

She learned the violin and was Miss Audric's favourite.

'Well, we can all go scurrying straight back to school – *or* we can fill our lungs with this fine fresh air and finish our lovely walk,' said Miss Audric. 'Hands up who wants to keep on walking!'

We were all tired out by this time but none of us was brave enough to keep our hands down. We waved in the air and feigned enthusiasm and we walked on . . . and on . . . and on, all the way to Pen Ponds. We couldn't help perking up then because the two vast ponds shone blue in the sunlight. They had bright yellow sand at the edge, just like the seaside. Seagulls circled overhead and ducks and swans bobbed up and down on little waves.

Miss Audric sat regally on a bench, taking off her shoes *and* her lisle stockings. She undid them decorously, manipulating her suspenders through her crocheted skirt, but it still seemed very bold of her. We kept giving her long pale feet little sideways glances. Miss Audric wriggled her toes, perfectly content.

We begged to go paddling.

'Just get your tootsies wet – and no splashing!' she commanded.

The girls teetered at the edge, obediently only ankle-deep. The boys plunged in up to their scabby knees, holding their trousers up to their groin. There was a *lot* of splashing.

'Behave yourselves!' Miss Audric bellowed, but she still didn't sound cross.

It was as if we were in a fairytale place and Miss Audric was turning into an unlikely wood nymph. She let down her long hair and stretched out in the sunshine. She closed her eyes. She wasn't falling asleep, was she? It was getting very very late. We wouldn't be back for the end of afternoon school at this rate.

Cherry cleared her throat. 'What's the time, Miss Audric?' she said loudly.

We peered at Miss Audric nervously, as if she might turn into a wolf and yell *Dinner time*! She did look annoyed to be woken from her nap, but when she consulted her watch, she seemed a little startled.

'Shoes and socks on, lickety-spit,' she said, rolling up her stockings and fitting them carefully over her feet and up her long pale legs. She didn't seem to mind not having a towel to dry herself. We all had to cope without one too, though it was horrible squeezing soaking wet sandy feet into tight socks and shoes.

'Right, back through the park, quick *march*!' said Miss Audric.

We weren't up to marching now. We could barely crawl. Our wet socks rubbed our feet raw. We were all limping with blisters before we got to the park gates. Miss Audric kept checking her watch now, urging us to hurry up.

'I *can't* hurry!'

'I'm *tired*!'

'My feet are so *sore*.'

'I want to go to the toilet.'

'I want to sit *down*.'

'Yes, let's all sit down for a bit, Miss Audric, *please*.'

'No sitting! We've got to walk – *fast*! I tell you what, we'll sing.' Miss Audric threw back her head. '*I love to go a-wandering* – come on, join in, all of you!'

So we all sang.

'I love to go a-wandering
Along the mountain track,
And as I go, I love to sing,
My knapsack on my back.
Valdereeee, Valderaaaa,
Valderee, Valderaa-ha-ha-ha
My knapsack on my back!

We went a-wandering all the way back through the Kingston streets to school. Mothers were clustered anxiously in the playground. Mr Pearson was standing in the main entrance, arms folded. Miss Audric wasn't cowed. She swept past them like the Pied Piper, leading her limping bunch of children back into school.

Perhaps it was just as well Miss Audric wasn't a form teacher. She might well have abducted her class for a week at a time. Her children would have developed stout legs and stamina and known a great deal about Jesus and music and nature, but reading, writing and arithmetic wouldn't have got a look in.

Our form teachers weren't *quite* as eccentric as Miss Audric, but they were a very weird bunch all the same. The first year of the Juniors we had Mrs Dowling. She was a teacher of the old school – scraped-back bun, pleated skirt, flat lace-ups. She could be scathing at times. I wore a new dress with a flared skirt to school one day, and I couldn't resist twirling round once or twice.

'Thank you for showing us your knickers, Jacqueline,' said Mrs Dowling, and of course everyone sniggered.

We had Mrs Symons in our second year and she was so much sweeter. She was Austrian and had a heavy accent, so we thought, ignorantly, that she was a bit 'funny'. She tried very hard to make every child feel special. She liked my stories and gave me big ticks and the odd gold star, even though my pages were likely to be full of blots and smears. I had trouble with the school dipping pens. My ideas ran away with me and I couldn't write quickly with those horrible scratchy pens because the ink spurted out and spattered the page. The inkwells encouraged the boys to play *Beano*-comic tricks. They'd dunk the tips of girls' plaits in the inkwells and make inky blotting-paper pellets and fire them with their rulers.

When we were nearly at the end of term, Mrs Symons told us that Santa Claus would be coming soon. We were streetwise kids, eight going on nine. We looked at her, eyebrows raised.

'Don't you believe in Santa Claus?' said Mrs Symons, pretending to be shocked. 'You wait and see, my dears.'

On the last day Mrs Symons took the register and then told us she had to go on an errand, but a special visitor would be coming to look after us. She trotted off. Five minutes later a portly gentleman with a long white beard came striding into our classroom in wellington boots, wearing a scarlet robe edged with white cotton wool.

'Hello, children! I'm Santa Claus!' he said, with a pronounced Austrian accent.

Santa Claus was carrying a big sack. He had little wrapped presents for every single child in the class.

I loved dear Mrs Symons – but I loved my next form teacher even more.

I've written a book where a boy character likes playing chess in the playground. Which book is it – and what's the boy's name?

It's *Bad Girls* – and the boy is Mandy's friend Arthur King.

I sat next to Arthur King at lunchtime and then afterwards he tried to teach me how to play chess. It got ever so boring. I wanted to let my mind wander and think about Tanya meeting me from school and how we were going to be friends for ever and ever.

'No, *look*, if you put your queen there I'll be able to take it with my knight,' said Arthur.

I couldn't get worked up about it. The queen didn't have long hair and a flowing dress, the knight didn't have shining armour and a plume in his helmet. They were just twirly pieces of plastic with no personality whatsover.

Mandy gives Arthur rather a hard time at first. I'm glad she makes proper friends with him at the end of the book.

26

Mr Townsend

Mr Townsend took us in the third year. I fell in love the very first day in his class. He stood in front of the blackboard and wrote his name – L. R. Townsend – in beautiful chalk copperplate. L. R. We found out soon enough that these initials stood for Leonard Reginald, dreadful old-codger names, but nothing could make Mr Townsend seem ridiculous. He wasn't a particularly tall man, but he was fit and muscular, with tanned skin and dark-blond curly hair, practically film-star looks, a world away from the usual musty male teacher model.

He smiled at us all and sat on the edge of his desk.

'Hello, everyone. I'm Mr Townsend. By the end of the day I hope I'll know all *your* names.'

We all sat up straight at our desks and smiled back at him.

'Isn't he *lovely*?' Marion whispered.

I sat next to her that year, though we didn't really have much in common. Marion was a very blonde girl with a very pink face. She looked squeaky clean, as if she'd just had a good scrub in her bath. She was squeaky clean inside too. She went to church twice on Sundays, knew her Scripture off by heart and prayed to Jesus every night. Marion had a special smug holy expression when she said the word Jesus.

I knew even on that first day that Marion and I weren't always going to see eye to eye, but at least we were united in our love for Mr Townsend. There wasn't a single child who didn't adore him. The boys loved him because he was sporty. He still played for a good rugby team and he loved cricket and tennis. He encouraged the athletic boys and coached them enthusiastically, but he didn't shout at the weedy ones who ran knock-kneed and couldn't catch. He was gently sympathetic – but he was no easy pushover. He never let anyone take advantage of his good nature. He never caned any child. He didn't need to. The girls loved him because he was so kind and caring and artistic too. He shyly showed us his watercolour sketchbook. We all tried hard to copy his delicate landscapes with the school primary colour poster paints.

He taught us our lessons, fairly but firmly, but at play times he wasn't just our teacher, he was our friend. He'd throw a ball about with the boys and ruffle their hair and pretend to bop them on the nose. He'd chat to the girls, treating us totally seriously. A little bunch of us would lean against him fondly. Marion once actually climbed on his knee. There was never anything odd or weird about Mr Townsend. We all knew adults who'd try to pat you or cuddle you too close. Mr Townsend was as kindly and gentle and safe as Santa Claus, though he didn't have a silly beard or a habit of going 'Ho ho ho!'

I tried harder in his lessons than I ever had before, simply because I wanted to be top of his class. I didn't have much chance because I was totally useless at arithmetic. I could add and subtract and multiply and divide accurately enough (though I frequently had to work it out on my fingers), but I couldn't do *problems*. You know the sort of thing: *If it takes six men ten days to dig a hole 30 feet by 60 feet how long will it take eight men?* I couldn't concentrate on the logistics. I made up the six men in my head and wondered *why* they were digging this hole of such huge dimensions. Was it the foundations of a house? A swimming pool? A grave for an elephant? What time in the morning did they start digging? Did they have breaks for a cup of tea and a bacon sandwich? Why were the two extra men brought into play? Were they reserve builders, like reserve players in a football match? I'd be off in a daydream and all the other children would be on question three already.

Marion was good at arithmetic. It was her

second-best subject (she shone at scripture). When we had an arithmetic test, I edged a little closer to her at our shared desk. She hunched over her page as she wrote down her sums, guarding her work with her hand, but as she turned the page, I could sometimes get a glimpse of her neat answers.

She saw me writing down an answer at the end of my untidy workings out and frowned. 'You copied that off me!' she whispered.

My mouth went dry. I suppose I *had* copied. Copycats were deeply despised.

'No I didn't,' I said.

'That's a fib!' said Marion.

'No, I didn't copy, I *didn't*,' I lied.

I was getting scared Marion might tell Mr Townsend. I glanced at him anxiously.

Marion saw me looking. 'I'm not a telltale,' she said.

'There's nothing to tell because I didn't copy, so there,' I said.

'I know you did,' said Marion. She paused. 'And *Jesus* knows too!'

I couldn't help looking up to see if I could spot Jesus peering all the way down from Heaven, sucking his teeth and shaking his head at me. But at least Mr Townsend didn't know, and I cared about him much more than I did about Marion's Jesus.

I managed to pass muster in all the other

lessons. I shone at English. I liked it best when we could make up stories, but I tried hard when we were told to write factual accounts too. Sometimes I blurred the distinction between the two. Mr Townsend set us the subject 'My Day Out'.

I chewed the top of my pen, deliberating. Marion set to work, scribbling away with her fountain pen, writing about her day out in the country in Daddy's Morris Minor. It was all right for her. We didn't have a car so we didn't have Days Out. We hardly ever went out as a family, Biddy, Harry and me. It wouldn't work – Biddy would nag and bicker, Harry would snap and sulk, I'd pick my hangnails and start pretending.

Well, I could *pretend* a Day Out, couldn't I? I got cracking with a sigh of relief. I decided we'd go for a Day Out in London. I didn't invent a posh car for us. I wanted to be convincing. I took us by train from Kingston railway station. I embellished the journey with a few imaginary treats. I had a *Girl* comic and a packet of Spangles to suck while Mummy and Daddy chatted and laughed and looked out of the window.

I knew what to do with us when we got to Waterloo. We went over the bridge to the Strand. I was proud of my authentic details. I walked us up the Charing Cross Road to Foyles. I knew this was the biggest bookshop in London. I had several

261

books at home with the distinctive green Foyles sticker inside. I described my book-browsing session in loving detail, fantasizing about the different books in the children's section. I decided Mummy would buy me *What Katy Did at School* and Daddy would buy me *Tennis Shoes* by Noel Streatfeild.

Then we went to Hamleys, the big toyshop in Regent Street. I looked at the dolls with Mummy and the toy trains with Daddy, and they bought me a tiny teapot no bigger than my thumbnail for my doll's house. Then we had lunch at Lyons Corner House, the only restaurant I knew in London.

I had another gnaw of my pen, deliberating over our afternoon. I decided we'd go to the zoo. I'd been there once when I was five to see baby Brumus, the polar bear, so this pretend time we went to see Brumus grown up, and the monkeys and the lions and the giraffes. I had a ride on a camel and an elephant. This wasn't fantasy – children really could have special rides on the animals in those days. It had actually been very uncomfortable on that baby Brumus visit. I'd been placed between the camel's humps and I was scared I might slip sideways. You sat on a special seat for the elephant ride, but I'd been strapped in with a lot of over-excited boys who kept poking me, and they all shrieked with laughter and said rude things when the elephant relieved itself.

I walked us all round the zoo, Biddy and Harry and I all licking Wall's ice-cream wafers. Biddy wasn't a woman who'd willingly walk to the end of the road in her tiny size-three heels, and she actively disliked most animals, so my imaginative powers were stretched to the limit.

I let us all have a sit down and *another* slap-up meal in Lyons. Our Day Out wasn't over yet. I extended it into the evening. I decided to take us to the cinema to see a film called *The Bad Seed*.

Biddy and Harry had actually seen this film when it was on in Kingston. I'd longed to see it. I'd seen stills from the film in *Picturegoer*, a magazine I bought every now and then in case it had photos of Mandy. *The Bad Seed* starred another child film star, Patty McCormack. My heart still belonged to Mandy, but I did fall in love with Patty McCormack's wonderful ash-blonde hair, styled in a fringe at the front and then two long beautiful plaits. She looked incredibly sweet and innocent and childish, with her neat hair and checked frock and little red tap shoes. It was a thrilling shock to read a paragraph about this new film and find that Patty played a child murderer.

I begged Biddy to take me to see the film but she said it wasn't suitable. After she'd seen it herself I made her tell me all about this little girl

Rhoda, who drowned a boy in her class because he beat her in a spelling test. He was in a pond and he struggled hard to haul himself out, but Rhoda took off her tap shoe and *hammered his fingers* so he had to let go. This appalled and impressed me. Ann was the only girl I knew who wore tap shoes, and she was a sweet kind girl and one of my friends – but I decided not to argue with her all the same.

I wrote about Biddy and Harry and me going to see *The Bad Seed*. I recounted the plot at length. I'd listened avidly to Biddy. Every now and then I embellished or invented, as always.

'We all agreed it was the best film we'd ever seen. It was the end of a perfect day out,' I wrote, finishing just as the bell went.

'You've written *heaps*,' said Marion, comparing her sparse page and a half with my six, seven, *eight* pages.

I shrugged modestly. I might be rubbish at maths, but I could certainly write.

I hoped Mr Townsend would like my composition. When Biddy asked me if I'd had a good day at school, I told her I'd written the longest composition ever.

'What was the subject?' Biddy asked, as she peeled the potatoes for our favourite treat supper, roast pork chops.

'"My Day Out",' I said, starting to shell the peas for her. I loved doing this and helping myself to the tiny peas in the flat pods – but I always jumped if I found a maggot.

'Mm,' said Biddy absent-mindedly, slicing the potatoes and arranging them in the roasting tin. 'So what did you write about? Did you tell about the time I got you all the Mandy photos in Wardour Street?'

'No, I forgot. I did put about looking at the dolls in Hamleys though,' I said.

'Did you say I bought you those Old Cottage dolls?'

'Well, no, you didn't buy them with me on a day out – they were my Christmas present,' I said.

Biddy raised her eyebrows at me and shoved the roasting tin in the oven. She started shelling peas too.

'You could have juggled with the facts a little to make a good story,' she said. 'You *love* your dolls. And they cost a fortune.'

'Yes, well, I put a lot else. I said you gave me lots of treats – and we all went to *The Bad Seed* in the evening,' I said.

Biddy jumped as if she'd found a maggot as big as a snake. 'You said I took you to *The Bad Seed*!' she said.

'You and me and Daddy,' I said.

'But we *didn't* take you!'

265

'Yes, I know, but I was juggling with the facts to make a good story,' I said, echoing her exactly.

This was not a wise plan. She thought I was being deliberately cheeky and gave me a good shake.

'How on *earth* could you put such a stupid thing? As if I'd ever take you to a film like that. Did you say what it was *about*?'

'Yes, I told the whole story,' I said, my head juddering. 'All about Rhoda and the little boy and the tap shoes and how she killed him.'

'You stupid *idiot*!' said Biddy. 'What sort of mother will he think me, taking you to a film like that! Have you handed this composition in?'

'Yes, at the end of the lesson.'

'Then he's probably marking it right this minute,' said Biddy. 'Well, you must go and tell him first thing tomorrow morning that it was a pack of lies.'

'I can't do that!' I said, starting to cry.

'If you don't tell him, I'll come to the school and tell him myself,' said Biddy, and I knew she meant it.

I spent a sleepless night worrying about it. Mr Townsend would be so hurt and shocked when he found out I was a liar. He'd never like me again. He'd be fondest of saintly Marion, who would never ever lie.

I went to school early, feeling sick. I didn't tell Cherry why I was so quiet. I didn't try to play with Ann. I didn't bicker with Marion. I didn't giggle with any of the boys. I just stood in a corner, head bowed, fists clenched, as if I was already wearing a placard round my neck proclaiming me a LIAR.

Mr Townsend strode in cheerily, swinging his briefcase. He sat down at his desk, opened up his case and pulled out our green English notebooks.

My stomach lurched. I wondered if I ought to make a dash for the toilets. Mr Townsend looked up and saw me gulping like a goldfish.

'Are you all right, Jacky?' he said.

'Yes. No. I don't know,' I mumbled. I took a deep breath. 'Have you marked our English compositions yet, Mr Townsend?'

'Yes, I have.' He beckoned me closer. 'I thought yours was particularly interesting, Jacky. Well done.'

Any other time I'd have spread my wings and flown round the classroom at such sweet praise. But now I felt I was falling. I was going down down down through the parquet flooring, through all the layers of earth we'd learned about in geography, until I tumbled into Hell itself, where I belonged.

'I've got to tell you something awful, Mr Townsend,' I whispered.

'And what's that?' he said, his head on one side.

'It wasn't *true*, my Day Out,' I said. 'We didn't

go to London and we didn't go to Foyles and Hamleys and Lyons Corner House and London Zoo.'

'Didn't you?' said Mr Townsend.

'It was all lies. And . . . and . . . and I definitely didn't go to *The Bad Seed*. Mummy says she'd never take me to a film like that. I just made it all up.'

'Very convincingly,' said Mr Townsend.

He didn't sound too shocked or horrified. He looked as if he was trying not to laugh!

'So did you believe it all?' I asked.

'Well, not quite all of it,' said Mr Townsend. 'I rather think *The Bad Seed* is X-certificated. I don't suppose they'd have let a nine-year-old go into the cinema.'

'Oh,' I said. 'Mr Townsend, are you cross with me for telling lies?'

'I don't think you were really lying, Jacky. You were just making things up. There's a big difference. You've got a very vivid imagination.'

I took the deepest breath in all the world. 'Do you think I might be able to write stories one day?' I asked.

'I'm sure you will,' said Mr Townsend solemnly.

I wanted to throw my arms round his neck and kiss him.

A week or so later Mr Townsend suggested we all might like to start a special project for English.

'I'm going to give each of you your own notebook,' he said.

He patted a pile of brand-new green exercise books. School stationery was in short supply. We were taught to fill in every single line in our exercise books, even using up the fuzzy backing to the covers. We had to keep dipping our scratchy school pens far down into a thick gravy of congealed ink before we were allowed to top up our inkwells. Now we were being given a whole new notebook each. It was a sign that Mr Townsend was taking this special project seriously.

'What is our project going to be on, Mr Townsend?' Julian asked eagerly.

He was the class swot, a highly intelligent, sweet, tufty-haired boy who waved his arm all the time in the-classroom, asking endless questions and knowing all the answers.

'I think I will let you all choose individual projects, Julian,' said Mr Townsend. 'I want you to write about whatever interests you most. Maybe a special sport, a hobby, a period of history, a type of animal, a favourite country – whatever you like.'

'Could I possibly do astronomy, sir?' said Julian.

A few children groaned. Other teachers would have groaned too and mocked Julian's pedantic politeness, but not Mr Townsend.

'I think that would be an excellent choice,' he said.

The rest of 3A had less esoteric choices.

'Bags I do football!'

'No, I'm doing football.'

'Me too.'

'Can I do rugby?'

'Can I write about my dog?'

'I want to write about France – we've been there for our holidays.'

'I want to write about birds. I've spotted heaps in my I-Spy book.'

'Can I write about Gilbert and Sullivan?' asked Cherry.

'You what?'

'Who are they?'

'Are they your boyfriends?'

'They wrote operettas. Mum and Dad sing in them and they're ever so funny,' said Cherry.

There were sniggers.

'Funny ha ha, or funny peculiar?' said Jock, screwing his finger into the side of his head to indicate loopiness.

'No, no, they *are* funny,' said Mr Townsend. '*I've* sung in *The Pirates of Penzance*, Cherry.'

This instantly gave Gilbert and Sullivan a total seal of approval.

'Please may I write about ballet?' Ann asked.

'I wonder if I could write about Jesus?' Marion asked. 'What are you going to write about, Jacky?'

'Maybe . . . maybe I could write a story?' I said.

'No, it's a *project*. You can't write an ordinary old story,' said Marion.

'Yes I can,' I said. 'Well, I don't just want to write a *story*.'

I went up to Mr Townsend's desk, not wanting to shout it out in front of all the others.

'Please could I write a novel for my project, Mr Townsend?' I said.

He hadn't mocked Julian or Cherry. He didn't mock me either.

'I think that's a brilliant idea, Jacky,' he said.

I danced back to my seat and nodded my head at Marion. 'Did you hear that? Mr Townsend said it was an excellent idea,' I said.

'He's just being kind,' said Marion. 'Anyway, you can't write a whole novel.'

'Yes I can,' I said.

I couldn't, of course. I wrote twenty-one sides, and that included a Contents page, but it was divided into seven chapters and it *seemed* like a whole novel to me.

I decided to write about a large family. I very much wanted to be a member of a large family. It was too intense when it was just Biddy and Harry and me. I decided this was going to be about a poor family with problems. I was irritated by the smug, safe, middle-class world of most of my children's books. The fathers were doctors and vicars, the mothers baked cakes and arranged flowers, the children went to posh schools and rode on ponies and had picnics and played jolly games.

I only knew one book about poor people, and that was *The Family from One End Street*. The family were called the Ruggles. I wanted to use a similar semi-comic name. I liked listening to a comedy series on the radio called *Meet the Huggetts*. I decided to call my family the Maggots. I called my first chapter 'Meet the Maggots'. My dad was called Alf and was a bus driver. I drew him with a pipe and a moustache to make it clear he was a man. I wasn't very good at drawing males.

My mum was called Daisy. She didn't go out to work, she just (!) looked after her seven children. She had a bun and worry lines across her forehead. She was particularly worried about her eldest, fifteen-year-old Marilyn, as she was 'dead keen on boys. And boys were dead keen on her too.' She was a pretty blonde. I drew her with ornate earrings. Pierced ears were considered 'fast' on young girls in the 1950s. I wanted Marilyn to be *very* fast.

Then there was Marlene. She was twelve and brainy. She'd passed her scholarship to the grammar school (as I was expected to do next year).

I wrote: 'Her interest is books. You can't drag her out of them.' Poor Marlene wasn't a beauty like her sister. She had a mousy ponytail and had to wear National Health glasses. I'd just started to wear glasses myself. Biddy was enormously proud of the fact that she'd paid for special fancy glasses with upswept frames. She wasn't having her daughter wearing little round pink National Health specs, thank you very much.

The third sister was called Mandy. She was ten and had big brown eyes and dark plaits and was desperate to be an actress. No prizes for guessing who I based *her* on!

Then I branched out and invented nine-year-old boy twins. There were boy twins in *The Family from One End Street* so I was obviously copying. I called my twins Marmaduke and Montague. Daisy had obvious aspirations for her first sons. Then she went on to have Melvyn, a shy, sensitive little boy who was mercilessly teased by five-year-old Marigold, the baby of the family. She was a fiesty little girl with abundant blonde curls and a misleading angelic expression.

I gave each child their own chapter, inventing little domestic scenarios, still shamelessly copying when I ran out of original ideas. Marilyn decided to dye her hair to please her boyfriend Sid and ended up with bright green locks – something very similar happened to Anne of Green Gables. The twins discovered stolen treasure as if they were reserve members of Enid Blyton's Famous Five.

'The Maggots' was *not* a particularly startling or stylish story, sadly – but I can nowadays claim, jokingly, that I wrote my first novel at the age of nine.

Who wrote a story about 'Night-time' at school and tried very hard – but her teacher said that it was very rambling, and she had a warped imagination?

It was Tracy Beaker in the second book about her,
The Dare Game.

> Last week we had to write a story about 'Night-time'
> and I thought it an unusually cool subject so I wrote
> eight and a half pages about this girl out late at night
> and it's seriously spooky and then this crazy guy jumps
> out at her and almost murders her but she escapes
> by jumping in the river and then she swims right into
> this bloated corpse and *then* when she staggers onto
> the bank there's this strange flickering
> light coming from the nearby
> graveyard and it's an evil occult
> sect wanting to sacrifice an
> innocent young girl and she's
> *just* what they're looking for . . .

Tracy thinks she's written a masterpiece but her
teacher, Mrs Bagley, isn't particularly appreciative.
She tells Tracy she has a very warped imagination.
I'm sure my Mr Townsend would have encouraged
Tracy! It's tough that she has Mrs Vomit Bagley for
her teacher. They are *never* going to see eye to eye.

27

Mr Branson

Mr Branson took the top Juniors. We nicknamed him Brandy Balls. We weren't being particularly rude. Brandy Balls were reddish aniseed sweets, very popular in the 1950s. Even so, no child ever called Mr Branson Brandy Balls to his face. We didn't even call him Mr Branson. He was *Sir*, and we stood up when he came into the room, we stood up when he spoke to us, we stood up when we needed to speak to him, we stood up and stayed standing up, hands on head, if we'd been disobedient.

He wasn't a dear gentle friend to us like Mr Townsend. He was a teacher. I can't remember him caning any of the boys but we were all frequently terrified of him. He had a habit of whacking you across the knuckles with a ruler if he felt you needed to get a move on with your writing. If you settled into a little daydream, he'd aim his sharpened chalk at you with surprising accuracy, so that it really stung. If you were ever unwise enough to yawn, you had to run round the playground five times to get some oxygen into your lungs. He urged you to go 'Faster! *Faster!*' until your lungs weren't just freshly oxygenated, they were in danger of total collapse.

We might not have called him nicknames to his face but he had plenty for us, mostly unpleasant. I managed to be Top Girl some of the time, in spite of my lamentable maths, so I think he quite liked me. In fond moods he'd call me Jacky Daydream, almost a term of endearment for Mr Branson. He could also be cruel though. He frequently called me Four Eyes, a nickname I hated, as I was very self-conscious about wearing my new glasses. He also called me Sly Boots because when he stood over me in class, I was so intimidated I didn't dare look up at him.

'You're sly, Jacky, that's what it is. I can't stand people who won't look me in the eye.'

I did my best to meet his fierce bloodshot gaze, my eyelids twitching behind my awful fancy glasses.

I got off easily. He was particularly hateful to the slow and the stuttering, proclaiming them morons and imitating their stammer. He was worst of all to Julian, the most intelligent boy in the class – no, the whole *school*, including the teachers. Mr Townsend had encouraged Julian to ask questions. Mr Branson sighed heavily whenever Julian waved his hand. He'd imitate Julian's voice and encourage the rest of us to laugh at him. He'd call Julian Brainy Bonce or the Professor or His Lordship. Julian continued valiantly waving his hand in class no matter how many times Mr Branson belittled him.

He was unspeakably unkind – and yet he was a brilliant teacher, particularly in English. He was very keen on extending our vocabulary. He'd hand out tattered orange textbooks every week in a special vocabulary lesson. There would be twenty questions and we had to guess the twenty esoteric, extraordinary words on the blackboard in his neat teacher's writing. Then came the best part of the lesson. He'd make up a story incorporating all twenty words, always a bizarre, funny fantasy story that had us laughing our heads off – and effortlessly remembering the definition of every single word.

Mr Branson encouraged us to tell stories too. He asked what we'd been reading and got us to recount the plot. He often picked me to say what I was currently reading, though he pooh-poohed my girly choices. One day I told him I'd been reading *The Prince and the Pauper*. He looked surprised, even impressed. This definitely wasn't a girly book. It was a long, hard, difficult book by Mark Twain. I hadn't actually read the *book*. I'd read a comic-strip version, a Children's Illustrated Classic, luridly coloured and simplified. Still, it gave me a grasp of the story, so I started telling it at great length, embellishing as I went. The bell for play time went long before I was done.

'We'll have the rest after play time,' said Mr Branson.

So after the break I went and stood in front of the class again.

'*The Prince and the Pauper* – part two!' I said.

They all laughed, but seemed keen for me to continue.

The best lesson of all was the last lesson on Friday afternoons. Mr Branson would read aloud to us. He scorned Namby-Pamby Blyton and all her contemporaries. Mr Branson read us boys' tales of derring-do, late-Victorian adventure stories. I usually hated that sort of story, but Mr Branson was so brilliant at reading aloud that the boys in the book ran through our classroom, seizing our hands and whirling us away with them. We climbed mountains, we jumped across ice floes, we swung on creepers through the jungle. When the bell went for the end of afternoon lessons, our heads jerked with the shock of shooting back to the stuffy classroom. We all *groaned* because it was going-home time!

Mr Branson had high expectations of us. He prepared us with regimental precision for our eleven plus exam. There were two non-fee-paying grammar schools in Kingston – Tiffins Boys and Tiffins Girls – but the catchment area was huge and it was very difficult to pass highly enough to get a place. Mr Branson took pride in the fact that he prodded a handful of his class through the exam. If we failed, we were personally insulting him and his teaching ability. It made taking the eleven plus even more scary.

It loomed over us the moment we started in our top year. SATs tests are like little pimples compared with the huge boil of the 1950s eleven plus. None of us came from the sort of homes where private education was a possibility. The eleven plus was our one chance to get to a grammer school and stay on to do all the right exams and go into one of the professions. If you failed the eleven plus, you went to a secondary modern school and left at fifteen and started work straight away. You *worked* and therefore you stayed working class. Biddy and Harry and I hovered precariously between working class and lower middle class. Harry was a civil servant, we said 'lav' instead of 'toilet', we never dropped our aitches or said 'ain't'. I knew I had to live up to our aspirations.

Biddy didn't promise an incredible present if I passed the eleven plus. Most of my girlfriends had been promised a Pink Witch bike if they passed.

'I think that's just putting pressure on the poor kids,' Biddy said. 'I'd never do that to you, Jac. You just do your best, dear.'

281

She knew I'd try hard whether I was bribed or not. And I didn't want a Pink Witch bike. I couldn't ride *any* bike, pink or not.

Very few of the characters in my books ride bikes. I can only think of one girl. Who is it, and which book does she appear in?

It's Treasure in my book *Secrets*.

There was a girl cycling round and round too, doing fantastic wheelie tricks on a BMX. She looked every bit as tough as the boys, her hair tousled, a big red scar on her forehead, her face pale and pinched. She was so skinny in her tight jeans and tiny matted fleece. I stared at her enviously.

She saw me staring. She stuck her tongue out at me. I waggled mine back at her.

Then she grinned. I grinned. It was just as if we knew each other.

I wanted to write about the friendship between two very different girls. Poor Treasure is going through a very tough time – but India isn't any happier, even though she lives in a big posh house and has any number of wonderful things. India is passionate about *The Diary of Anne Frank*. I read it when I was about India's age and thought it the most amazing, moving book too. I used to have a photo of Anne Frank on my bedside table.

498+355=

219+77=

66-24=

303+720=

98+45=

432-91=

1209+272=

28

The Eleven Plus

I had a filthy cold the day I took my eleven plus. One of those head-filled-with-fog colds, when you can't breathe, you can't hear, you can't taste, you certainly can't *think*. I was boiling hot and yet I kept shivering, especially when I was sitting there at my desk, ready to open the exam booklet. I knew I wouldn't have a hope in hell with the arithmetic part. I felt as if those eight mythical men were digging a hole in my head, shoving their spades up my nostrils, tunnelling under my eyes, shovelling in my ears.

I knew copying was out of the question. I wouldn't just risk the wrath and sorrow of Marion and her best friend, Jesus. We'd all been told very sternly indeed that anyone caught copying would be drummed out of the exam, the school, the town of Kingston, England, the World, the entire Universe – left to flounder in Space, with every passing alien pointing their three green fingers and hissing, *'Cheat!'*

'Open your paper and begin!' said Mr Branson. 'And read the questions *properly*.'

I read the questions. I re-read the questions. I read them till my eyes blurred. Pens were scratching all around me. I'd never felt so frightened in my life. I didn't know the answer to a single problem. I could do the simple adding up and taking away at the beginning. Well, I thought I could. When I picked up my pen at last and tried to write in my first few answers, the figures started wriggling around on the page, doing little whirring dances, and wouldn't keep still long enough for me to count them up. I couldn't calculate in my bunged-up head. I had to use my ten fingers, like an infant. I *felt* like an infant. I badly wanted to suck my thumb and rub my hankie over my sore nose, but if Mr Branson saw me sucking my thumb, he'd surely snip it off with his scissors like the long-legged Scissor Man in *Struwwelpeter*. I did try to have a quick nuzzle into my hankie, but it was soggy and disgusting with constant nose-blowing, no use at all.

I could manage the English, just about, but the intelligence test was almost as impenetrable as the arithmetic. The word games were fine, but the number sequences were meaningless and I couldn't cope with any questions starting: *A is to B as C is to?* Indeed! What did they mean? What did *any* of it mean?

I struggled on, snuffling and sighing, until at long last Mr Branson announced, 'Time's up! Put your pens *down*.'

My pen was slippy with sweat. I blew my nose over

and over again while everyone babbled around me.

'It was OK, wasn't it?' said my new friend Christine.

'It wasn't *too* bad,' said Marion.

'I liked that poem in the English part,' said Ann.

'My pen went all blotchy – do you think it matters?' said Cherry.

The boys were all boasting that it was easy-peasy, except Julian, who modestly kept quiet.

I kept quiet too.

'How did *you* get on, Jacky?'

'I thought it was horrible,' I sniffed.

'Oh, rubbish. You're one of the cleverest. I bet you'll come out top,' said Cherry.

'No I won't! I couldn't do half of the arithmetic,' I said.

'Neither could I,' said Christine comfortingly. 'But you'll have done all right, just you wait and see.'

Well, I waited. We all had to wait months until the results came through. Then Mr Branson stood at the front of the class with the large dreaded envelope. He opened it up with elaborate ceremony and then scanned it quickly. We sat up straight, hearts thumping. He took our class register and went down the long list of our names, ticking several. Every so often his hand hovered in the air and he made his mouth an O, hissing with horror.

He had the register at such an angle that we had no way of knowing whether he was up in the As or down in the Ws. We just had to sit there, sweating.

Mr Branson cleared his throat.

'Well, well, well,' he said. 'A lot of shocks and surprises here. Well done, *some* of you. The rest of you should be thoroughly ashamed. Very well, Four A, pin back your ears. I will now go through the register and tell you whether you have – or have not – passed your eleven-plus examination.'

He paused. We waited. I was Jacqueline Aitken then, the first child on the register.

'Jacky Aitken . . . you have *not* passed your eleven plus,' said Mr Branson.

I sat still, the edge of the desk pressing into my chest. Mr Branson glared at me, and then worked his way down the register. I couldn't concentrate. I heard Robert had passed, Raymond had passed, Julian of course had passed – but I didn't catch any of the girls' names. I was too concerned with my own terrible failure.

I wanted to cry, but there was no way in the world I was going to let Mr Branson see me weeping. I even managed to meet his eye.

I could face up to him but I didn't know how I was going to face Biddy and Harry. Biddy had said all the right things. She had tried not to put too much pressure on me. She'd told me simply to do my best. But I hadn't done my best, I'd done my worst. I'd failed. *She* hadn't failed. She'd passed her eleven plus and gone to Tiffins Girls.

Harry had been sent to a technical school so he was particularly keen for me to have a grammar school education. He'd tried tutoring me at home, working our way through intelligence tests and those terrible men-digging-holes problems. He'd start with his kind voice and he'd promise he wouldn't get cross. He said if there was anything at all I didn't understand, I had only to say and he'd go over it again for me. He'd go over it – again and again and again – and I'd struggle to take it all in, but the words started to lose all their sense and the figures were meaningless marks on the page.

'You're not *listening*, Jac!' Harry would say.

'I am. I am. You said you wouldn't get cross.'

'I'm *not* cross,' Harry insisted, sighing irritably.

He'd say it all again, s-l-o-w-l-y, as if that would somehow make a difference. I'd be just as baffled, and make silly mistakes, until Harry would suddenly lose it.

'*Are you a MORON?*' he'd shriek, his fist thumping the page.

I felt I *was* a moron where maths was concerned, but no one seemed to understand that I wasn't one *deliberately*. Harry spent hours and hours trying to coach me even though it had now proved a total waste of time.

I had to tell them as soon as possible to get it over with. I couldn't ring them. Mobiles weren't invented. We didn't even have an ordinary land line at home. Harry possibly had one in the London office but I didn't know the number. I didn't know Biddy's number either, but I knew where her office was. I decided to miss my school dinner and run the two miles to her work to tell her the terrible news.

Poor Biddy. There she was, having a cup of tea and writing beautiful entries in the big accounts book when I burst in on her. Her pen wavered, her tea spilled, but she didn't care. She thought I'd passed. Surely that was the only reason I'd run such a long way at dinner time.

'Oh, Jac!' she said, holding out her arms, her whole face lit up with joy at the thought of her daughter going to grammar school.

'No, no – I've *failed*!'

She was valiant. She kept right on smiling and gave me the hug.

'Never mind,' she said. 'Never you mind. There now.' She paused. 'Did you get given a second chance?'

In those days they let all borderline eleven plus failures sit a further exam in the summer, and those who passed had their pick of the secondary schools. You couldn't get into Tiffins, but it still wasn't to be sniffed at.

I'd been in such a state I hadn't taken it in. I *had* been given a second chance. I went along to sit the exam a couple of months later. Ironically, we were all sent to Tiffins to do the paper. It was more scary not being in our own environment. No one told us where the lavatories were, so we all fidgeted desperately in our seats as time went by. I can't remember any men digging holes this time. Perhaps we only had to do an intelligence test. Anyway – this time I passed.

The twins in Double Act *sit an entrance exam to go to the boarding school Marnock Heights. Which twin passes, Ruby or Garnet?*

It's Garnet – although everyone expected Ruby
to pass.

We couldn't believe it. We thought Miss Jeffreys had
got us mixed up.

'She means me,' said Ruby. 'She must mean me.'

'Yes, it can't be me,' I said. 'Ruby will have got
the scholarship.'

'No,' said Dad. 'It's definitely Garnet.'

'Let me see the letter!' Ruby demanded.

Dad didn't want either of us to see it.

'It's addressed to me,' he said. 'And it's plain what
it says. There's no mix-up.'

'She's just got our names round the wrong way,'
Ruby insisted. 'It's always happening.'

'Not this time,' said Rose.

'Look, it's absolutely not fair if she's read the letter
too, when it's got nothing to do with her. She's not
our mother,' said Ruby.

'No, but I'm your father, and I want you to calm
down, Ruby, and we'll talk all this over carefully.'

'Not till you show me the letter!'

'I'd show both the girls the letter,' said Rose.
'They're not little kids. I think they should see what
it says.'

So Dad showed us.

It was like a smack in the face.

Not for me. For Ruby.

Poor Ruby – and poor Garnet too! I hate the next bit, when Ruby refuses to have anything to do with Garnet. I'm glad they make friends again just before Garnet goes off to boarding school. I've often wondered what happens next!

29
Fat Pat

I still had imaginary friends when I was in the last year of Latchmere but I had many real friends too. I still walked to and from school with Cherry but I didn't play with her so much. I didn't play with Ann any more either. She had a new best friend, a tall rangy girl called Glynis. They were always going off together and playing their own elaborate secret games. Ann was prettier than ever, her hair long and glossy and tied with bright satin bows. She wore wonderful short floral dresses with smocking and frilled sleeves. She had frills all over – when she ran, you caught a glimpse of her white frilly knickers. She was the girl we all wanted to be.

Poor Pat was the girl we all shunned. She was the fat girl, Fat Pat, Chubby Cheeks, Lardy Mardy, Greedy Guts, Two-Ton Tessie, Elephant Bum. She wore sensible loose dresses to hide her bulk. It must have been torture for her to have to take off her dress publicly and do PT in her vest and vast knickers. If she'd been half her size she'd have been considered pretty. She had very pink cheeks and long blonde straight hair, almost white. Her plaits were always incredibly neat, never a hair out of place, her ribbons tied up all day long.

She had the most beautifully neat handwriting too. She'd lie half across her page, her chubby hand moving slowly, her pink tongue peeping out between her lips – so much effort to make those smooth, even, blue letters on the page.

I don't think she had any friends. She wasn't particularly teased in the playground. She was simply shunned.

I shunned her too in front of the others, but if we happened to fetch up together – before school in the classroom, walking down the corridor, in the girls' toilets – I'd make a few hesitant overtures.

'I hope old Brandy Balls isn't in a bad mood today!'

'Can you work out how to do those problems? I haven't got a clue!'

'Hurray, it's raining! No PT! I do hope we can do country dancing instead.'

She'd smile at me and murmur something in reply. One day, when I found her combing the tails of her sleek plaits in the cloakroom, I said, 'You're so lucky to have such lovely long hair.'

I said it because I genuinely thought she had lovely hair. I was also trying to be kind, because Pat rarely got compliments. Her cheeks went a little pinker. She smiled at me and said nothing, but there

These photographs were taken on the launch day of the wonderful *Daydreams and Diaries* exhibition at Seven Stories – National Centre for Children's Books, in Newcastle-Upon-Tyne. The exhibition was all about my early life and my career as a writer. There were special sections about Nick Sharratt, my lovely fans, and my writing habits. There wasn't enough room for all of my books to feature, because I've written so many! So I chose a selection for the exhibition to focus on: *The Story of Tracy Beaker*, *Best Friends*, *My Sister Jodie*, *Cliffhanger*, *The Illustrated Mum*, *The Suitcase Kid* and the *Hetty Feather* series.

LATCHMERE

Report on: J. Aitken.   Form 3.

Terms Endings: 1956   EXAM   MARKS
                                                OUT OF

ENGLISH Reading   Very Good   9   10

         Spelling   Good   17½   20

         Written work
                     Very Good   55   60

ARITHMETIC Mental   Good   20½   25

            Written
                     Very Good   58½   65

                                  160½   180

ART & Handwork: Good

P.T. & Games: Average ability

GENERAL: Jacqueline has worked very hard this year. She should do well in Form 4.

_____   _____
Head   Class

LATCHMERE

Report on: Jacqueline Aitken   Form: 4

Term ending: July 26th 1957.

English: Reading: 49/50

         Spelling: 22/25

         Written work:
            Formal 47/50   Very good
            Composition 47/50

Arithmetic: Mental: 21/25

            Written:
            Mechanical 50/50   Excellent
            Problem 47/50   progress

Art & Handwork:
            Good

P.T. & Games: Exam total 283/300
            Good   Class form   3 | 48

General: _____ Has made excellent headway and achieved results of the highest ____ and throughout. A happy, cheerful ____ able member of

---

These are some of my school report cards from Latchmere Infant School. I was very good at reading, and not so good at games! One of them was written by Mr Townsend, my favourite teacher. I tried my hand at my very first book — *Meet the Maggotts* — as part of a project for Mr Townsend.

I always loved dolls growing up — and I still do now! One magical Christmas, I was given two beautiful Old Cottage Dolls, complete with lots of handmade clothes. I adored them and am very sad to have lost them now. This is a fairy version of an Old Cottage Doll I found in an antique fair, and bought to remind me of the ones I had as a child.

This is another little doll I bought as an adult. It dates right the way back to the Victorian times — so it could almost have belonged to my own Hetty Feather!

I'm so lucky to still have this! *Meet the Maggotts* was written when I was nine. It was about a family with seven children, and was partly inspired by one of my favourite books at the time, *The Family at One End Street* by Eve Garnett. One of the characters was called Marigold. I still liked that name when I grew up, and used it in another story – *The Illustrated Mum*.

THE MAGGOTTS.

BY

JACQUELINE AITKEN.

Two pages from my real diary, when I was twelve! Do you think my writing has changed very much? You can see that, even then, I liked writing all about 'real life', rather than fantasy stories.

EMMA'S OWN

ILL BOOK

I wrote this little book for my daughter, Emma, when she was four. She absolutely loved playing nurses and hospitals.

HOSPITAL

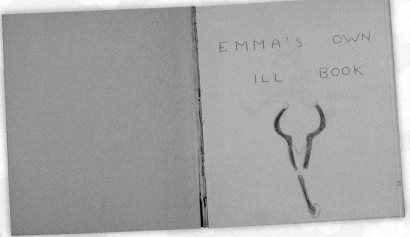

Here's a nurse. She looks after you if you have to go into hospital. Can you see her fob watch?

Hospitals are places where ill people are made better.

Doctors come and examine you and tell the nurses the way to make you better.

They give you medicine and pills, and help you to wash and feed yourself.

Nurses often have time to play games and tell stories even though they're busy people.

Olivia is playing the piano and Octavia is singing and little Odette is listening. They are wearing their very best party dresses. Odette has a string of coral round her neck and two gold bangles and a garnet ring. She's standing a little stiffly because she's scared of crushing her dress.

This is a page from a book I made as a Christmas present for Emma. I drew all the pictures for Emma to colour in herself, and made up a little story about each of the characters.

Nippers

Jacqueline Wilson
Ricky's Birthday

Pictures by Margaret Belsky

Ricky's Birthday was a very special book for me – it was the first of my stories to be published. It was a very simple book for children just starting to read.

Liz's present was wax crayons.
"If I gave you goldfish, they'd burst,"
said Liz. "Feeding them all the time!
So I got you these instead."
"There's red, green, yellow, blue.
Even orange!" said Ricky.
He found a paper bag and did a picture
of Goldy and Mouldy with the orange.

14

Gran's present was a huge bag
of peppermints.
Ricky sucked four at a time.
"You look as if you've got mumps,"
said Gran. "That's it. Enjoy them."

15

The original Radish Rabbit was a toy
belonging to Emma. When Emma
was very young, I would write little
stories involving Radish, complete with
illustrations. Radish later appeared in
my book The Suitcase Kid.

Typed page (with handwritten annotations):

(The first eight pages are set out in a special format, as if Tracy is actually filling in all the details)

My Book About Me

ABOUT ME

My name is Tracy Beaker.

?? I am 10 years 2 months old.

My birthday is on 8th ~~September~~ May. ~~And~~ It's not fair, because that dopey Peter Ingham has his birthday then too, so we just got the one cake between us. And I had to hold the knife to cut the cake together. Which meant we only had half a wish each.

Wishing is for babies anyway. They don't come true.

I was born at ~~Kingston Hospital.~~ Some hospital somewhere. I looked cute when I was a little baby but I bet I yelled a lot.

I am _____ cms tall. I don't know. I've tried measuring with a ruler but it keeps wobbling about and I can't reach properly.

I don't want to get any of the other children to help me.

This is my private book.

I weigh _____ kgs. I don't know that either. Jenny has got scales in her bathroom but they're _____ stones and pounds. I don't _____ them. Let's just say I'm little.

_____ to have green eyes.

Handwritten page:

I'm Tracy Beaker. This is a book all about ME.
I'd read it if I were you. It's the most incredible
dynamic heart-rending story. Honest. And
I bet some great movie magnate reads ~~me~~ it and
turns it into a film and I'll star in my own
story. ~~I suppose~~ I'd better let ~~my friend~~ Peter have a small part too.
But not Louise or Justine. No way! I can
write the script if ~~I~~ ~~go~~ she likes.
Sam is ... But if you want to know who
she is you'd better read this book. There's some
funny bits and some sad bits and some
sad bits and I think it's the best book ever.
But then I would do. Seeing as I ~~think~~ helped
write it.

Perhaps my most famous book of all is *The Story of Tracy Beaker*. This was the first book of mine that Nick Sharratt illustrated, so I didn't have any idea at all what the pictures would look like, and described Tracy in detailed pencil notes along the side of the typescript. In this early version of the story, Tracy had different coloured eyes — green, not black!

Tracy's stories were turned into a very successful TV programme. This is me with Dani Harmer, the actress who was cast to play Tracy, on the set of the first series.

This was the original manuscript for *Best Friends*. I like writing my books by hand to start with, especially in beautiful notebooks like this one.

RLD PUBLISHERS LTD

REN'S AND YOUNG ADULT BOOKS

direct tel: 0181 231 6629   direct fax no: 0181 231 6737
e-mail: childrens.editorial@transworld-publishers.co.uk

22 December 1998

Dear Jacky

Three things, as discussed on the phone today!

1. sample temporary tattoo, which it has been suggested we use to promote THE ILLUSTRATED MUM. Let me know if you're still happy about this once you've seen them (tried them out?!) I should just say that this is not definite yet - just a suggestion.

2. photocopy of the BURIED ALIVE section that will appear in the World Book Day BOOK OF BOOKS. Let me know if you have any comments.

3. a copy of JELLY ROLL for you to read. I haven't read it yet, but I hope you enjoy it (although from the back cover blurb, perhaps 'enjoy' is not the right word...!)

Have a lovely Christmas!

With best wishes

Annie x

Annie Eaton
Editorial Director, Fiction

CORGI · BANTAM · BLACK SWAN · ANCHOR · BANTAM PRESS · PARTRIDGE PRESS · DOUBLEDAY · EXPERT · CHILDREN'S BOOKS (BANTAM, CORGI & DOUBLEDAY)
61~63 UXBRIDGE ROAD LONDON W5 5SA ENGLAND TEL +44(0)181 579 2652   FAX +44(0)181 579 5479
E-MAIL INFO@TRANSWORLD-PUBLISHERS.CO.UK
TRANSWORLD PUBLISHERS LIMITED · INCORPORATED IN ENGLAND NO. 9833831

This is a letter my editor wrote to me after I'd finished writing *The Illustrated Mum*, but before it was published.

18th March 2009

Dear Jacky,

Thank you so much for Hetty Feather. We are all delighted by the story and think you've done a wonderful job of combining absolutely fascinating historical details with your characteristic voice.

We do have a few notes we'd like to pass on – but all fairly minor things. I'm also enclosing the notes I've had from Annette at the Foundling Museum. She thought the story was terrific and said it will be marvellous in attracting more visitors to the museum. I think her notes are generally easy fixes if you want to do them but she was also fine about any artistic license you wanted to take with the finer details for the sake of the story.

✓ P1. I wondered if it might be useful to put London, 1876 at the start of the chapter to set the scene?
✓ P3. I felt it might help here to give a little more of a sense of why she might have been given away? Perhaps Hetty could speculate?
✓ P82. Possibly add 'soap' after 'carbolic' in case kids don't know what carbolic is?
P6. How is Hetty's name chosen? Is it related to anything?
P14. Why does Jem take to Hetty? Think it might be nice to make clearer that he likes her because of some specific trait of hers.
P30. 'we had almost forgotten her' but then they ask about her on p32.
P42. Father's comments about the Hospital sound a little scripted
P43. I wondered if Mother should react here to what Hetty says?
P47. I felt it might be good to make it slightly clearer to the reader that Jem is playing with Hetty when he suggests marriage.
P82. Gideon didn't follow them, he went to the tree.
P90. How would Hetty look after Gideon when they are separated at the Hospital?
P97. I felt it was a little unlikely that Gideon wouldn't guess what was happening after seeing what happened to Saul. Maybe need to make clear that he can't believe they'd do that to him?
P99. I think Hetty and Jem sometimes come across a little too much like lovers, which feels a little odd. Wonder if you could tone down this exchange so it's a little more brotherly?
107 P118. Not quite sure why the girls giggle at the jam?
P146. I'm probably being a bit over-sensitive, but wondered if it was OK for the boy to actually put his hand down Hetty's breeches?

P155. This sense of Hetty as a storyteller comes a little out of the blue – maybe mention a little more when she's playing with Jem?
P167. Where did Hetty hide her gazettes?
P197. This feels quite late for a description of Matron Bottomly – could we have it when we first meet her instead?
P227. I thought this seemed a little too mean for Ida (considering the ending), even if she was hurt by Hetty.
P243. Feels a while since Hetty has thought much about Adeline. Maybe good to add something else once she's back at the Hospital about her?
P306. This is the main area that I think needs some work – the ending is lovely and happy but over SO quickly. It's such a shame not to give these two a little more time once reunited. Do you think you could extend it to make this a slower, more expansive scene? It felt really quite abrupt to us.

I felt a Hetty sequel coming along – what happens next?!

So, not too much to do, hopefully! It's a wonderful story and I know your fans are going to love it. It would be great to have any changes back by around 3rd April if possible – let me know if not.

I'm also enclosing some visuals from Nick for the insides of Hetty – the silhouettes are just lovely, I think – and two very rough images for the cover. We don't think we're there yet and Nick is still working on the idea but something that combines elements of the circus with an image of Hetty is what we're going for. We'd like to possibly break out of the boxed-in image, and we're also not sure the silhouettes work on the cover, so Nick was going to look at full images instead. So, still a work in progress but thought you'd like to see where we'd got to. Do let me know what you think!

I'm working on some cover copy at the moment, will send that over next week for you to check.

All best,
Kelly
Kelly x

JONATHAN CAPE
HUTCHINSON
KESTREL BOOKS
DOUBLEDAY
DAVID FICKLING BOOKS
CORGI
RED FOX

61-63 Uxbridge Road, London W5 5SA
Tel 020 8579 2652
Fax 020 8231 6737
www.kidsatrandomhouse.co.uk

A RANDOM HOUSE GROUP COMPANY

This was the original manuscript notebook for *Hetty Feather*, and a letter my editor wrote to me once she had read the first draft. This was my first historical novel, but I'd always been fascinated by the Victorians. The idea for Hetty's story came to me after I'd visited the Foundling Museum in London, and started thinking about how awful it would be for a mother and child to be separated as so many were then.

HETTY FEATHER
One

My name is Hetty Feather. Don't laugh. It's not my real name. My mother chose my proper name. I'm absolutely certain she would have picked a beautiful romantic name for me (though sadly I have not turned out beautiful or ... picture ...).

'My little darling,' she whispered, wrapping me up tightly in a shawl and holding me close close close to her chest, as if she could never bear to let me go. 'My little ... Rosamunde? ... Seraphina? ... Ernestine ...'

I'm so lucky to receive some very thoughtful home-made presents from fans of my books. I loved this special cat doll and its wonderful sparkly coat!

Dear Jacqueline,
Your last card is really beautiful! I really like it and have looked at it f...
are so clever-clever-clever to find it! Now it is time to say happy birthday to you... are ...
forward to christmas? Pablo has got a christmas tree, and everyone in the family has a ...
under it. (Even baby Finlay - his is an ABC book - cute!)   He had not been born when you ... Pablo's
family.
For my birthday, we did watch a high school musical, but my friends and I found it quite silly!
We sang along in funny voices! We also made strange fruity smoothies, painted T-shirts, made a scrapbook
and made a huge mess of my room, and watched St Trinians on the sofa, under a warm duvet. It was
great fun! I got a Little Richard CD (Great to dance to) a lovely soft toy realistic lemur, a tiny teaset, some
puppy notecards, and many other lovely things.

I just finished one speech, and now I have to do another! It is about a non fiction book
(review) and I am doing 'The young Elizabeth' by Jean Plady. I'm not sure whether to use a powerpoint
or not...

I would be useless at a pub quiz! I don't know what any of the latest ...
mount Everest is, etc

We had Scottish country dancing, and it was not nice. There ...
so I had to dance with my friend 'Lucy'! It was SO embarrassing.

Happy Birthday and
Christmas!

Love Anna xxx

[Speech bubble:] On my birthday 7th April and I wish ...

[Speech bubble:] I wish I knew how to say Happy Christmas in Japanese! Do you like my very special rabbit-size kimono? Jacqueline and Trish are thinking of going to Japan next Spring for a holiday - I do hope they take me too!

I get so many lovely letters from you all, and I do my best to reply to as many as I can. I made a special pen friend called Anna several years ago, and we've been writing to each other ever since! These are the letters and cards we wrote at Christmas in 2007. I often decorate my letters to Anna with a little picture of Radish, from *The Suitcase Kid*.

Jacqueline

Merry Christmas
and a Happy New Year
to you and Tracy

Nick

HIC!

Nick likes to draw special Christmas
cards for his friends, so of course he
drew Tracy Beaker on this card for me!

Congratulations Jacky!

Love, Nick

1 0 0 0 0 0 0 1

I've become quite famous for my jewellery,
especially my silver rings. I treat myself to
a new ring for every book I finish writing.
I have quite a collection now! Nick Sharratt
even drew a beautiful illustration of them, to
celebrate ten million of my books being sold.

At the *Daydreams and Diaries* exhibition, there was a wonderful room built to look just like my childhood bedroom. There were lots of my favourite childhood pictures on the walls, as well as displays of some of my childhood diaries, family photos and school reports.

Nick drew quite a lot of the characters for the exhibition, including a new version of himself. On the launch day, he wore the same jumper he wore in his illustration! This cut out was displayed in the 'Sharrattworld' area of the exhibition, where visitors could learn all about Nick and how he illustrates.

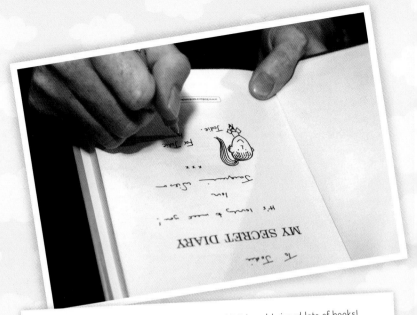

Lots of fans came along to this opening day and Nick and I signed lots of books!

This was taken in the Tracy Beaker set that was specially built as part of the exhibition. The area displayed pieces of Nick's artwork for all the Tracy Beaker stories, my old typewriter, and the first notes and manuscript for the story.

was such a wry and wistful expression on her face. She knew why I was saying it. She felt pleased but patronized. Why should she feel humbly grateful for a crumb of kindness? Why should she be singled out to be the sad girl in the class? She didn't seem to eat more than anyone else. She wasn't lazy. She puffed along heroically after us when we were made to run round and round the playground.

'I can't *help* being fat,' she said. 'It's my metabolism.'

I didn't know what her metabolism was. I imagined it like a night monster, crouching on her chest in the small hours, funnelling double cream and melted chocolate up her nostrils as she slept.

I nodded sympathetically. 'It doesn't matter, being fat,' I said, though we both knew it mattered tremendously.

Pat wasn't taken seriously by anyone at school. She wasn't allowed to be Pat the Person, with her own personality. She was simply Fat Pat, a sad cartoon girl waddling in our midst.

Then she suddenly wasn't in our midst any more. We came back to school after a half-term holiday and she wasn't there. Her seat was empty. Her name wasn't called in register. We didn't really think anything of it. Not until we filed into assembly and saw Mr Pearson standing on the stage, looking very grave.

'I've got some very sad news for you, children. I'm sure you all know Pat in Mr Branson's class. I'm afraid she passed away during the holiday. Our thoughts are with her poor parents. Let us all say a prayer for Pat.'

I shut my eyes and bent my head, utterly stunned. I hadn't really known anyone before who had *died*. Harry's mother had died when I was a baby, Harry's father had died when I was a small child, but they were old to me. Pat was *my* age. She was poor Fat Pat, the girl I chatted to in the toilets, the girl I shamefully ignored in the classroom. But now she'd done something as extraordinary and dramatic and grown up as dying.

I thought of her squashed into a white coffin, her plaits tied with white satin, dressed in a long white nightie. I wondered if her cheeks would still be pink. I thought of her lying in her coffin week after week after week, getting thinner and thinner and thinner until she dieted down to a skeleton. I started to shake. I wished I'd been kinder to her. I wished I'd been her friend all the time. I hadn't properly *known* her so I couldn't really miss her, but it felt as if I did.

I don't think anyone told us what she died *of*. I have a vague feeling it might have been an asthma attack, but I don't remember her ever using an inhaler. Maybe children didn't have them in those days.

We didn't talk about Pat amongst ourselves. I think we all felt guilty. We tried to forget her, but she's there in our form photograph, smiling bravely, as if she was just an ordinary happy-go-lucky member of our class. And now, when I look at that faded black and white photo, I realize she wasn't even *that* fat. I don't need to look at the photo to remember her. I often think about her even now.

I have a very cheery, confident fat boy in three of my books. What is his nickname – and can you think of all three titles?

It's Biscuits, and he appears in *Cliffhanger*, *Buried Alive* and *Best Friends*.

I suppose I'm still a bit greedy, if I'm absolutely honest. Not quite as greedy as Biscuits though. Well, his real name is Billy McVitie, but everyone calls him Biscuits, even the teachers. He's this boy in our class at school and his appetite is astonishing. He can eat an entire packet of chocolate Hob Nobs, munch crunch, munch crunch, in two minutes flat.

Biscuits is so kind and funny and positive – and a *marvellous* friend. He's very supportive of Tim when they're on their adventure holiday in *Cliffhanger*, and they have even more fun on a seaside holiday in *Buried Alive*.

I decided I wanted to find out more about dear old Biscuits, so he popped up again in *Best Friends*.

Gemma gives him a hard time, but *eventually* appreciates him. Biscuits makes brilliant cakes, including a wonderful chocolate biscuit cake. One Christmas my lovely friend and illustrator Nick Sharratt made *me* a fantastic chocolate biscuit cake, very rich and munchy, studded with red glacé cherries. My mouth's watering remembering it!

Ann   Marion   Christine

30

Christine

I made a new friend in Mr Branson's class. She was called Christine, a tall girl with a high forehead and glossy brown hair cut short and clipped back with tortoiseshell hairslides. She went glossy brown all over every summer, effortlessly and evenly tanning, while I went red and blotchy and then peeled.

Christine was six months older than me. She'd been in the class above but now she'd been kept back to repeat a year. She was bright as a button but there were problems at home. I don't think Christine had even sat the eleven plus last year. She couldn't move on to a secondary school because they were all too far away. Christine needed to dash home every lunch time to see her mother.

'My mum's dying,' Christine told me, as soon as we'd made friends.

We huddled up together in the playground, arms round each other, while she told me all about it. Christine told it straight, no soft euphemisms, though the teachers murmured about her mother being 'poorly'.

'She's got cancer,' said Christine. 'She's had it for ages and now it's so bad she can't do anything. She just lies on the sofa downstairs. She's got so thin and she looks so old, not really like my mum any more. But she's still my mum inside, even though she gets muddled and sleepy with all the drugs she has to take.'

'The drugs?' I whispered.

'For the pain. She gets in such awful pain,' said Christine. She said it matter-of-factly, but her eyes watered. 'I give her her dose at lunch time and I take her to the toilet and fix her a drink. She sleeps a bit then, but the drugs wear off. She's often crying by the time I get home. It's the worst pain ever.'

I tried to think what the worst pain ever must be like. I thought of all my tummy upsets, when I sometimes doubled up involuntarily. I imagined that much worse. I wondered how I would cope if it was my mum.

'Isn't there anyone else to help look after her?' I asked, taking Christine's hand.

'There's my dad, but he's out at work in London all day,' said Christine. (He was a civil servant and vaguely knew *my* dad.) 'Anyway, they don't really get on now. Daddy's got this girlfriend. But don't tell anyone.'

I nodded. This was something I understood.

'My mum's got a boyfriend. Don't tell either, OK?'

'I've got a big sister, but she keeps having heaps of rows with my dad and staying out late. She mostly stays round at her boyfriend's house. It's better when she does, it's more peaceful.'

'But it's not fair on you, having to do everything for your poor mum.'

'I don't mind. I *want* to do it. I want to help her,' said Christine.

'What about Patricia?' I said. 'Does she help too?'

She was Christine's sister in the year below, a fair, giggly girl, often acting a little wildly in the playground with her friend Madeleine, letting off steam.

'Patricia tries but she's not that good at making Mummy comfortable. And she gets too upset. She's just a baby,' said Christine, as if there was a lifetime between nine and eleven.

So Christine soldiered on, day after day, nursing her dying mother, doing most of the shopping, the washing, the ironing. She did this willingly, without complaint. The only thing she complained about bitterly was the fact that her mother was dying.

'It's not *fair*,' she said, clinging to me. 'She's so kind and gentle and lovely. Why should she have to die so young? I asked the vicar at our church and he said it's very sad but it's God's will. Well, I think God's a terrible person if he wants to make Mum suffer so much. I *hate* God.'

We stared at each other, both of us shocked at what she'd said. We waited for the thunderbolt to come sizzling out of the sky. Nothing happened.

'I don't blame you,' I said lamely. 'Oh, Christine, it isn't fair at all.'

I held her and rocked her. She cried a little and I cried too. Then we realized we were alone in the playground. Afternoon school had already started.

'Oh, lummy, I've made us late,' said Christine.

'Never mind.'

'Brandy Balls will go barmy.'

'Who cares,' I said, patting her.

We went into the classroom, holding our breath. Mr Branson was writing something on the blackboard. He stopped as we came in. He broke his chalk in two. He aimed one half at me, the other at Christine. He hit both of us on the temple where it hurt most.

'How *dare* you come into my classroom ten minutes late!' he thundered. 'What have you been doing, you idle lazy gossipy girls?'

I clenched my fists. 'I'll tell you what we've been doing!' I shouted back. 'Christine's been crying and I've been trying to comfort her. You *know* her mum's very ill. You know what Christine has to do. How *dare* you call her lazy and idle!'

The class sat statue-still, mouths open. They stared at me. Nobody ever ever ever answered Mr

306

Branson back. I'd obviously gone mental. They stared at Mr Branson, waiting for him to go to the cupboard and get out his cane. I waited too, trembling.

Mr Branson's face was purple. He stood still, making little snorty noises with his nose. A long blue vein throbbed on his forehead. Then he took a deep breath.

'Sit down,' he said.

I sat. Christine sat. Mr Branson took a new piece of chalk and continued writing on the board.

That was *it*! He carried on teaching and then left the classroom at the end of the lesson. I breathed out properly, almost collapsing. I couldn't believe it. I'd shouted at Mr Branson and survived! Perhaps he'd actually felt ashamed, realizing just how hard it was for Christine. But he didn't do anything to make it easier for her.

We didn't either. I was allowed to invite Christine for tea one Friday when her older sister was back at home. Christine and I shut ourselves in my bedroom and I showed her all my dolls, even my special secret paper girls. We got out all my art things and made ourselves cardboard badges with a C entwined with a J design, carefully coloured in Derwent crayon. We pinned our badges on solemnly with safety pins. We fingered all the beads in my shell box, holding the crystals to the light and marvelling at the rainbows. We lay on our tummies and drew portraits of each other.

Then we took a sheet of drawing paper and folded it up into squares to make a 'fortune-teller'. We sat cross-legged, deciding each other's fortune. We were so absorbed in our play we didn't want to stop for tea, so Biddy, with unusual tact, brought our meal in to us. We picnicked on banana sandwiches and cream buns and chocolate fingers and Tizer and then lolled against each other, flicking through old *Girl* comics.

Christine's father came to collect her very late, past my usual bed time. The adults chatted uncomfortably for a minute or so. The fathers exchanged pleasantries about work. Biddy said something about Christine's nice manners. Christine's mother wasn't even mentioned.

She died the day before we took our eleven plus. Christine came to school red-eyed but resolute. She sat the exam along with all of us – and passed.

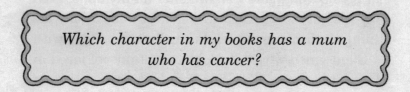

Which character in my books has a mum who has cancer?

It's Lola Rose in the book of the same name.

Mum's fever went down, but she had to stay in hospital a while. Then she was well enough to come home, though she still had to go for her treatment. First the chemotherapy, weeks of it.

All Mum's beautiful long blonde hair started falling out after the second treatment. It was so scary at first. Kendall and I were cuddled up with her in bed in the morning and when she sat up great long locks of her hair stayed on her pillow.

'Oh my God,' Mum gasped. She put her hands to her head, feeling the bald patches. 'This is just like being in a bloody horror movie!'

I wanted to write truthfully about Victoria and her illness. She calls herself Lady Luck – and I do so hope she will be lucky and get completely better. She means so much to Lola Rose and her little brother Kendall. Still, they also have Auntie Barbara to look after them. I *love* Auntie Barbara. I wish I had one!

Jacky and Alan

31

Our Gang

Christine and I were best friends – but we were also part of a gang. There were our two boyfriends, David and Alan. They were best friends too. David was a freckle-faced, rather solemn boy with brown hair and clothes that my mother would call 'nobby'. David's mum had him wearing checked shirts and khaki shorts and baseball boots, clothes we'd consider cool now but were a little odd in the 1950s. Alan wore ordinary grey boy clothes. His sleeves were always rolled up, his collar open, his socks falling down, his sandals scuffed. He had straight fair hair, the sort that has to be smarmed down with water to stop it sticking straight up. He had a cheeky grin and a happy-go-lucky character.

David was my boyfriend; Alan was Christine's. It was all very convenient – though secretly I preferred Alan to David. One play time Christine talked a little wistfully about David.

'Do you really like him then?' I asked.

'Well, yes. As much as Alan. In fact more. But don't worry, Jacky, I know he's *your* boyfriend. I'd never ever try to take him off you.'

'Mm. Christine . . . the thing is, I like Alan. More than David. I wish we could swap.'

'Well . . . can't we?'

We tried to think of a tactful way of putting it to the boys. We didn't want to hurt their feelings. We didn't want them to go off in a huff and take up with two other girls.

'We *can't* tell them,' I said.

'Yes we can,' said Christine.

She was bossier than me and very determined. She caught my hand and pulled me over to the corner of the playground, where Alan and David were swapping cigarette cards with some other boys.

'Hey, Alan and David, Jacky and I want to talk to you,' she said.

They sighed and came over, shuffling their footballers and cricketers into separate packs.

Christine put her arms round their shoulders. 'We like you both very much, but Jacky was just wondering . . .'

'Christine!'

'OK, OK, *we* were wondering, how do you fancy swapping over for a bit? So you can be my boyfriend, David, and Alan, you can be Jacky's boyfriend.'

We waited, while David looked at Alan and Alan looked at David.

'Yep. That's fine,' said Alan.

'Fine with me too,' said David.

Then they went off to bargain for more cigarette cards and Christine and I went off to swap beads, all of us happy.

They weren't *proper* boyfriends, of course. We didn't go out with each other. I didn't go round to play at David's or Alan's and I wouldn't have dreamed of inviting them for one of Biddy's cream-bun teas. Our romances were very low key. We sometimes took turns giving each other 'a film-star kiss', but it was really just a quick peck. We wrote love letters to each other in class, but they were brief to the point of terseness, though for years I treasured a crumpled piece of paper saying, 'Dear Jacky, I love you from Alan.' I was far closer to Christine, to Ann, to Cherry – and to another new friend Eileen.

She wasn't a new girl but she *seemed* new in Mr Branson's class. She'd been away from school for a couple of months in Mr Townsend's class with a badly broken leg. I remembered her as a curly-haired pixie-faced girl, maybe a little babyish for her age. She came into Mr Branson's class transformed. She'd grown several inches. Not just upwards. She had a chest!

She was the first girl in our class to wear a real bra. The boys teased her as soon as they found out and twanged her bra at the back, but Eileen managed to slap them away and keep them in their

313

place. She looked so much older than everyone that she had sudden authority. She swished around the playground in her full patterned skirts, her small waist cinched in with an elasticated belt. She had an air of mystery about her, as if she knew all sorts of secrets. Well, she did. She sat in a corner with Christine and me and told us what it was like to have a period. We knew some of this Facts of Life stuff already, but it was interesting to have Eileen telling us practical details.

We must have been a satisfying audience, Christine and I, with our short haircuts and little white socks and Clarks sandals. Eileen elaborated, telling us things that seemed utterly unlikely – and yet maybe people *really* did this or that? She also told us about some sort of boyfriend she'd met in the summer holidays, Mr Honey. I *hope* he was complete fantasy.

Eileen had a real boyfriend at school now, red-haired Robert, a small, eager boy almost as bright as Julian. Robert seemed an unlikely match for this new sexy Eileen in his short trousers and pullovers and black plimsolls, but they seemed a happy couple for all that. Julian came to play with us too, though he didn't have a girlfriend himself. So this was our gang – Christine, David, Alan, Eileen, Robert, Julian and me.

We started to play together every day. We had our own special club and a badge, and we had to use particular green biros whenever we wrote to each other. We called ourselves the Secret Seven, like the Enid Blyton books, but now we had Eileen with us we didn't act like Blyton children.

Mr Branson always chivied us when he was on playground duty. We liked to sit huddled together against the wall of the boys' toilets – not, I suppose, the most attractive location. Mr Branson would kick the soles of our feet in irritation.

'Come on, you lot, stop flopping there like a bunch of rag dolls. Go and have a run round the playground, get some fresh air into your lungs.'

He'd harangue us until we got up, groaning, and jog-trotted round and round. It wasn't just Mr Branson who picked on us. All the teachers started trying to get us to separate, even our dear Mr Townsend, suggesting skipping for Christine and Eileen and me, football for the boys. We were puzzled at first. Christine and Eileen and I loathed skipping, and felt we were too old to jump up and down chanting:

> 'Nebuchadnezzar, King of the Jews,
> Bought his wife a pair of shoes.
> When the shoes began to wear,
> Nebuchadnezzar began to swear.
> When the swear began to stop,
> Nebuchadnezzar bought a shop.

When the shop began to sell,
Nebuchadnezzar bought a bell.
When the bell began to ring,
Nebuchadnezzar began to sing,
Do ray me fah so la ti dooooooo!

You had to whirl the skipping rope twice as fast for the last part, doing 'bumps' until you tripped. I always tripped as soon as I started bumping because my arms wouldn't whirl round fast enough, but who cared anyway?

The boys were even less keen on football. They were gentle, dreamy boys who didn't want to charge round shouting and kicking. Mr Townsend *knew* this. Why did he suddenly want to break us up and make us start being sporty?

I think the teachers were scared we were growing up too soon. Maybe all this boyfriend/ girlfriend stuff alarmed them, though it was all perfectly innocent. Eileen probably unnerved them, with her knowing look and new figure.

We took to huddling right at the very edge of the playground, behind the canteen, hoping that none of the teachers would spot us there, but if *they* didn't find us, some bossy form monitor would creep round the corner and pounce on us.

Then *I* was made a very special monitor – and all our problems were solved.

*In one of my books there's a girl who talks
with a fake American accent and acts
much older than she really is.
Do you know which book it is?*

It's *Candyfloss*.

'Open your present, Floss. You're such a slowpoke,' said Margot.

She meant *slowcoach*. She's got this irritating habit of talking in a fake American accent and using silly American expressions. She thinks it makes her sound sophisticated but I think she sounds plain stupid.

I could make a l-o-n-g list of reasons why I can't stick Margot. She used to be ordinary – in fact I can barely remember her back in the baby classes – but *this* year she's making out she's all grown up. She's always giggling about boys and sex and pop stars. Judy giggles too. She looks as babyish as me but she's got an older brother who tells her all these really rude jokes. I don't understand most of them. I'm not sure Judy does either.

Floss doesn't like Margot because she's very worried her friend Rhiannon will go off with her.

318

But by the end of *Candyfloss* Floss has found a *much* nicer friend.

Christine Alan Robert Eileen David Julian

32

The Secret!

I wasn't made a form monitor. I was always too dreamy and likely to do something silly. I *certainly* wasn't games monitor material. I was never one of the ultra-helpful children made flower monitor or milk monitor. But Mr Branson had a soft spot for little Jacky Daydream/Four Eyes/Sly Boots, even though I'd dared yell at him in class. On the first of December he made me Christmas card monitor.

Our year was the top year, head of the Juniors, so we had various responsibilities. Every Christmas term a shiny scarlet postbox stood in the entrance hall. All the Juniors posted their Christmas cards into its wide slot. It was a big postbox, carefully constructed out of thick cardboard and given a new coat of paint every few years, but it wasn't big enough to contain everyone's cards. It was my job as Christmas card monitor to bustle along every morning, unlatch the little brass hinges so that the door at the back swung open, and then empty out all yesterday's letters.

The head teacher himself, Mr Pearson, showed

me where I had to sort and store the letters. There were two doors next to his room. I was familiar with the first door. It lead into a dark storeroom where we kept the sacks of milk-bottle tops, saved and recycled. No one washed the tops so the room reeked of sour milk. I hated any kind of milk, even fresh from the cow. If I was ever sent to the storeroom, I held my cardie sleeve over my nose and tried not to breathe in. I wasn't sure I was going to be able to stand being Christmas card monitor if I had to sort them while being gassed by sour milk fumes.

But Mr Pearson was opening the other door. This was my fourth year in the Juniors and I must have seen that door every day, yet I had no idea what was behind it. It was another storeroom, full of trunks and old desks and blackboards and easels. Mr Pearson patted the biggest flat-topped trunk.

'Here you are, Jacky, you can sort the cards into forms on this top. Stack them all neatly now. And then on the last day of term you can come with me when I dress up as Santa Claus and you can be my special Christmas elf delivering all the cards,' he said.

I smiled gratefully, though I didn't exactly go a bundle on being an *elf.* I prayed I wouldn't have to wear a silly costume or false pointy ears.

I went along to collect the posted cards the

second morning. There were only a handful, but I took them out carefully, with due ceremony, opened up the storeroom door and started sorting them in sparse piles on top of the trunk. It only took a minute or so. I ran my finger along the brass studs of the trunk. I wondered what was inside. I collected the cards back into a pile, picked them up and then tried edging the lid open. It didn't budge at first so I thought it must be locked, but when I had one more try with two hands, the lid creaked and then jerked upwards. I lifted it right up and stared awestruck at the contents of the trunk.

Treasure! Gold crowns, silver chains, necklaces, rings, crystal goblets, an entire gold tea-set! I'd read all my Enid Blyton adventure books. What *else* would you expect to find in an old trunk but buried treasure?

It wasn't *real*. The jewels were Rowntrees Fruit Gums, the gold was paint, the silver chocolate wrappers. These were the props from past school plays. I recognized the Three Wise Kings' crowns, the banquet christening plates from *The Sleeping Beauty*. I dug a little deeper. My fingers touched fur, slippery silk, soft velvet. It was all the costumes!

I carefully piled all the fake jewellery and cardboard china onto the floor and pulled out robes and capes and ballgowns galore. I held them up against me, wishing there was a mirror. I found a beautiful long crinoline made of rich purple velvet. I slipped it over my head and then twirled round and round, bumping into boxes in the crowded room.

I played being a Victorian lady, festooning myself with jewellery and giving imperious orders to invisible servants – but for once it wasn't enough to pretend by myself. This find was too marvellous to keep a total secret. I had to share it with Christine.

Back in Mr Branson's class I hooked her silky hair back behind her ear and whispered what I'd found. She looked sceptical at first. She knew my habit of romancing.

'Are you sure you're not making it up, Jacky?'

'You come and see too, tomorrow!'

So Christine hovered behind me the next morning while I undid the letter box and clawed out all the Christmas cards. We waited until the hallway was empty – no teachers, no crying children who'd fallen over in the playground, no mothers waiting to speak to Mr Pearson, and definitely *no* Mr Pearson himself. Then I opened the storeroom door and we scuttled inside.

'See!' I said, lifting the lid of the trunk.

'Oh glory!' said Christine, fingering the crowns, the necklaces, the purple velvet crinoline. 'Oh, Jacky, it's fantastic! This is the best secret *ever*!'

I let her try on the purple velvet dress. I

struggled into a crimson tunic and an ermine-lined cape. I bowed low before her.

'Might I have the honour of a dance, fair Lady Christine?'

'Certainly, my Lord Jack,' said Christine.

We were neither of us quite sure how you did stately dancing, but we twirled a bit and did a lot more bowing and curtseying. Christine climbed up on a chest to pose in a regal fashion, waving a fairy wand. Then she twitched it at the darkest corner, behind a blackboard.

'There's a door at the back, look!'

We clambered over the boxes and chests to get to it. I put my hand on the doorknob, hesitating.

'Maybe it's Mr Pearson's secret room. Perhaps he's in there, cuddled up with Miss Audric!'

We snorted with laughter, clutching each other.

'Open it, go on,' said Christine.

I turned the handle and the door opened. We could dimly see stairs going upwards.

'A secret passage!' said Christine. 'Come on, let's see where it goes.'

Hand in hand, we tiptoed up and up the dark staircase, barely able to catch our breath with the excitement. There was yet another door at the top. We opened it and stepped out into sudden bright daylight. We stood blinking, disorientated, staring at the wooden rail in front of us. There was the

325

hall stage before us, with the school piano – but we were standing way above it now.

'We're up in the gallery!' I said.

I suppose we should have realized sooner, but the gallery was very seldom used. The choir sang there for special concerts, but that was all. We never looked at the gallery because we always faced the stage as we filed in for assembly. But now we were actually up in the gallery, so high we could almost touch the ceiling. It felt as if we'd grown wings and flown there.

Then we heard the clacking of stout heels down below on the parquet floor. We saw Miss Audric's red plaits and her emerald-green woollen suit. We both had a vision of her curled on Mr Pearson's lap like a giant woolly caterpillar. We clamped our hands over our mouths to stifle our giggles.

Miss Audric hitched up her long wool skirt, climbed the steps to the stage and sat at the piano. She waggled her fingers several times as if she was waving at the keys and then she started playing Handel's *Water Music*, ready for us to start coming into the hall for assembly.

'Quick!' I said.

We crept backwards to the door, lifting our feet so our rubber-soled sandals wouldn't squeak on the wooden floor. Then we shot through the door and tumbled down the stairs, laughing wildly, clutching each other.

We slipped inside the storeroom every morning and played dressing up. It was hard coping with such a splendid secret. It fizzed inside us all the time until we felt ready to explode.

'What's *up* with you two?' said Eileen.

'Yes, where do you and Christine keep hiding, Jacky?' said Alan.

'Yeah, you keep sneaking off somewhere before school,' said David.

'Have you found a special secret place?' asked Julian.

'Tell us!' said Robert.

Christine and I looked at each other. We *had* to tell them.

They were desperate to see for themselves but it was too difficult to sneak them all in before school. Besides, everyone arrived at different times, and Eileen and David were often late.

I thought about lunch time. It was quieter in the school entrance then. There was always the risk of running into Mr Pearson – but at twelve thirty the school cook brought him his lunch on a tray and he ate his meal in private in his room.

'OK, here's the plan,' I said. 'We wait five minutes after the bell goes, and then at twelve thirty-five we creep into the school entrance. Mr Pearson will be in his study tucking into his lunch, so he won't be doing any prowling about. But we'll

327

have to be as quiet as mice.'

Julian started squeaking and scuttling on all fours.

'And no messing about, OK! If Mr Pearson catches us, I shall be in *serious* trouble.'

Julian stood up quickly. They all blinked at me seriously. It was a heady moment being able to boss them all around, even Eileen.

They were as good as gold at lunch time. We waited in the playground, Robert checking his Timex watch every few seconds. Then Christine and Eileen and I went off together arm in arm. The boys followed in a little cluster, their cigarette cards splayed in their hands as if they were simply ambling off for a game of swapsies.

We crept into the school entrance, all of us staring fearfully at Mr Pearson's door. Then I took a deep breath, opened the door of the storeroom and shoved them all quickly inside – one, two, three, four, five, six, all seven of us, counting me.

The boys started squealing in triumph when we were all in.

'Ssh! We've got to be *quiet*! Mr Pearson's only just across the hallway!'

'Sorry, Jacky. Come on then, where are these costumes and all this other stuff?'

I swept the piles of Christmas cards out of the way – growing larger day by day – and opened the trunk. The boys weren't *quite* as impressed by the crowns and the jewellery but even they liked the costumes. Eileen adored everything. Christine and I offered her the purple velvet to be polite, but she preferred wrapping herself in long lengths of orange and scarlet and fuschia pink silk so that she glowed like an Indian princess. Robert found a pirate outfit with a patch, Alan was a sailor, David a policeman complete with helmet. Julian scooped up an enormous armful of fur. He stepped inside and became a large lollopy dog with floppy ears.

We played an imaginary game together as if we were still little kids in the Infants. It was as if the costumes liberated us from our real selves. We could be colourful fantasy creatures.

When the bell went for afternoon school, we had to whip all the costumes off quickly and then get out of the storeroom unobserved. Christine went first, taking David with her. Then Eileen and Robert. Then Julian and Alan. I waited a few seconds, looking round the storeroom, enjoying this moment of total happiness. Then I opened the door – and walked straight into Mr Pearson.

He peered at me over his spectacles. 'Jacky? What were you doing in the storeroom? You're only supposed to go in there when you're emptying the postbox.'

I saw Christine and the others standing agonized at the edge of the playground. We were all going to get into terrible trouble unless I kept my head.

I smiled at Mr Pearson. 'Yes, I know, Mr Pearson, but I was in a bit of a hurry this morning and I was scared of being late for Mr Branson so I didn't quite finish sorting yesterday's letters into classes. I thought I'd slip in at lunch time. I'm sorry.'

'That's quite all right, Jacky. I understand,' said Mr Pearson, smiling back at me.

There! I bet you were worried that we'd all be caught and punished, but we got away with it. We spent every lunch time playing in the storeroom until the end of term.

Many many years later I was invited to give a talk about my books at Latchmere. I had a cup of coffee and a chocolate biscuit beforehand in the head teacher's study. I was telling him all about my schooldays, and I mentioned the postbox.

'We still use it!' he said. 'Come with me.'

He took me into the storeroom and there was the red postbox in a corner – and the very same big trunk with the brass studs round the lid . . .

One of the characters in my books wears real Victorian clothes – but she doesn't have a beautiful purple crinoline. She has to wear uniform, stitched by herself. Who is it?

It's Lottie in *The Lottie Project*.

'Do you feel you can manage all this?' she said. 'You look very little.'

'But I am strong, Madam. I will manage,' I said determinedly.

'Very good. You can start on Monday. I will give you the print for your uniform and a bolt of cotton for your apron and caps. I hope you are satisfactory at sewing, Charlotte?'

I blinked at her. 'Charlotte, Madam?' I said foolishly.

'That is your name, it is not?' she said.

'No, Madam, I am called Lottie, Madam. It was the name of Mother's doll when she was small. No one's ever called me Charlotte.'

'Well, I do not think Lottie is a suitable name for a servant. You will be called Charlotte whilst you are working for me.'

I didn't need to do too much research about the Victorians when I was writing *The Lottie Project*. My daughter Emma loved everything Victorian and so I used to read her all sorts of old-fashioned stories. We had a huge 1880s Christmas catalogue and we spent happy hours choosing what we wanted! We also played special Victorian imaginary games. Emma always wanted to be the lady of the house, so I had to be the servant and curtsey to her and do everything she commanded. We wrote long rambling Victorian stories together too. Emma's were better than mine!

33

Bournemouth

The summer I left Latchmere we went on holiday to Bournemouth. We were branching out, staying in a three-star hotel for a whole fortnight.

I'd never been to Bournemouth before. It seemed to take for ever to get there. We still didn't have a car. We struggled with the suitcases on a Green Line bus from Kingston all the way up to London, lugged them down the escalators and onto the underground, and then onto the train to Bournemouth. We flopped down exhausted, and ate our egg sandwiches and Lyons fruit pies and Penguin chocolate biscuits, sharing a bottle of Tizer in plastic cups.

We branched out big-time when we finally arrived at Bournemouth railway station and got in a taxi. It was my very first taxi ride. Biddy and Harry sat bolt upright, their eyes on the meter. I slid around on the leather seat, worrying that there might be a terrible row if it proved too expensive. But it was a paltry sum, so Harry paid it willingly *and* gave the driver a tip.

We were all three impressed by Hinton Firs Hotel. It wasn't particularly *big*, just a perfectly normal family-size hotel, but it had that little extra touch of class. There was a welcome dance that first Saturday, so Biddy tweaked the flounces of her chiffon frock, Harry polished his patent shoes and I squeezed into my best C & A party frock with a sash and a lace collar.

There was no Will Tull urging us to be Music Men and join him in the conga, but there was a proper five-man band playing popular tunes in waltz and quickstep and foxtrot rhythms. There were little tables arranged around the edge of the dance floor so you could toy with a drink all evening. Alcohol! The holiday brochure hadn't mentioned the hotel was licensed! But Hinton Firs was ultra-respectable and we *were* on holiday. Biddy tried her very first Babycham and Harry had half a pint of lemonade shandy. I had orange squash, but Biddy let me have the maraschino cherry from her Babycham. I sucked it eagerly, hoping the drop of perry might make me drunk. Biddy and Harry sat stiffly among all these strangers, maybe hoping to feel drunk too.

Biddy got talking to the family at the next table who'd just arrived too – Mr and Mrs Hilton and their children, Diana and John. I wasn't remotely interested in John, a fair, fidgety boy of nine who pulled silly faces and strutted around with his hands in his pockets. I liked his sister Diana though. She was thirteen, a tall, curvy girl with a high forehead and blonde wavy hair. She wore pale pink lipstick, a blue dress cinched in at the waist, nylons and high heels. She looked years and years older than me. She already had the soft English rose looks that made men turn and stare at her. There weren't any other teenage girls staying in the hotel – so Diana made friends with me.

We chatted, sucking squash through straws, while our parents shuffled round the dance floor and John capered with the other boys in a corner. She told me all about her school and her friends at home and the boy she sometimes spoke to at her church youth club. I told her about Latchmere and Christine and said proudly that I had a boyfriend called Alan.

Then the band took a break to have a quick pint and someone started playing rock 'n' roll records – Tommy Steele and Bill Haley.

'Come on, Jacky, let's jive!' said Diana.

'I can't! I don't know how,' I said, blushing. 'I'll look silly.'

'No you won't,' said Diana. She nodded at John and the other boys, who were jerking around like crazy puppets. 'You certainly won't look as silly as *they* do.'

She took my hand and we got up to dance. She wasn't really an expert herself, tottering a little anxiously in her high heels, but she whirled me about, and once my feet caught the rhythm of the music, I started bouncing around, keeping to the beat, even improvising a few steps. I felt as if I could dance right across the ballroom, out of the window and up into the night, whirling round and round the clouds.

I was flushed and excited when I got back to our table, almost spilling my orange squash.

'Now, now, stop showing off,' said Biddy. 'Don't get above yourself, madam.'

But I *was* above myself, dancing and dancing with Diana, my new friend.

She had her very own single bedroom in the hotel, which impressed me enormously. John had to sleep on a put-you-up in her parents' room – and I still had to share with Biddy and Harry.

I tossed and turned that first night, too het up and excited to sleep properly. I was wide awake at six o'clock. I sat up stealthily in bed, reading *Wintle's Wonders* by Noel Streatfeild in the dawn light. I turned each page slowly and cautiously – but Harry suddenly started, turned over and opened his eyes.

I wriggled right down under the covers, hiding my book.

'Jac? What are you up to? Are you reading?'

I held my breath. For whatever crazy reason, I wasn't allowed to read if I woke up early. I was just supposed to lie there and try to get back to sleep. I was scared Harry would get cross with me. It would be terrible if he started a ranting fit right at the beginning of this beautiful Bournemouth holiday. But he leaned up on one elbow, actually smiling at me.

'It's OK. I can't sleep either. Shall we go for a walk before breakfast?'

'Oooh, yes!'

We took it in turns tiptoeing out of the bedroom to the lavatory and the bathroom. Hinton Firs was ultra posh to us but it didn't run to ensuite facilities. I pulled on my new blue jeans and checked shirt, hoping they might make me look like a real teenager, and hurried off with Harry.

We went along the quiet corridors, Harry shushing me, putting his finger to his lips. It was so strange thinking of all the sleeping guests the other side of each door, the men in their striped pyjamas, the women in artificial silk nighties, the children in white cotton patterned with teddies or tiny aeroplanes. We crept past Diana's small single room and I imagined her in a pink rosebud nightie, maybe a few curls pinned into place with kirby grips.

I wondered if she'd just been friendly at the dance because she had no one else to talk to, or whether she'd want to be my friend for the whole holiday. I imagined us walking along the sands, paddling in the sea, sharing secrets. Maybe she'd

let me try her pink lipstick, stagger in her high
sandals. I practised walking with precise steps,
swaying my hips as we went down the stairs.

'Why are you walking in that daft way?' Harry
whispered. It was all right, he wasn't cross, he
seemed amused.

I shrugged. 'How old do you think I look,
Daddy?' I asked.

'Oooh, twenty-two?'

'No, *really*.'

'Eleven.'

'Not maybe a bit older? I'll be twelve in
December, and then it's only a year and then I'll
be thirteen.'

'Your maths are improving,' Harry said dryly.

'I think I might almost look a teenager now,' I
said, glancing at Harry for confirmation, but he
only laughed at me.

Then we were outside the silent hotel in the
fresh early morning air, the sun already out, the
sky blue. There were tall pine trees and bright red
and yellow flowers in every green garden. The
hotels were white and pink and pale peach, one
with brilliant blue roof tiles. I felt like Dorothy
stepping into Oz.

'Oh glory, isn't it *lovely*!'

'Come on, let's see the sea,' said Harry, taking my
hand. 'We haven't even caught a glimpse of it yet.'

We walked towards the front of East Cliff, swinging our clasped hands. Then I broke free and ran. The sea sparkled below me, intensely blue, incredibly beautiful. The sands shone smooth and golden for miles. There was a zigzag path cut into the side of the cliff, going right and left, right and left, all the way down to the esplanade below. I forgot all about wanting to act like a teenager. I ran full tilt down the zigzag path, arms high in the air, going, 'Wheeeee!'

When I got to the bottom, I stood panting, waiting for Harry to catch me up, and then I declared, 'I think Bournemouth is the most beautiful place in the whole world!'

It was certainly a beautiful holiday. For once my real life lived up to my imaginary one. I was usually slightly out of synch, like a children's comic when the colour is misaligned and the yellows and reds and blues bleed past the black outlines. But now I was jolted into place, the real world as colourful as anything I could imagine.

Biddy was up and dressed in her best white top with the embroidered poppies when we got back to our bedroom. She smiled at us with matching poppy-red lips.

'Have you had a nice walk, you two? Come on, I want my bacon and eggs for breakfast!'

The Hilton family were sitting at a big table

with three free spaces. Diana waved to me.

'Come and sit here, Jacky!'

We spent the whole holiday with them. Biddy and Harry and Mr and Mrs Hilton sat in deckchairs on the beach, while Diana and I went off together, John leaping around us boisterously, cracking daft jokes that made us sigh. We spent every day on the beach, swimming in the freezing sea and then jumping around, pale blue and shivering, until the sun dried us.

We made friends with a newly engaged couple, Bob and Shirley. Bob was a dark, good-looking rugby player in his twenties, ultra fit. Harry and Mr Hilton held in their soft stomachs when they were all in their bathing costumes. Diana and I developed a crush on this Bob and followed him around like puppy dogs. Shirley indulged us fondly, making a fuss of both of us. She lay back on his towel and smoothed suncream all over, turning golden brown, while Bob splashed in the sea with Diana and me and hurled John around like a human rugby ball.

I loved Diana, I loved Bob, I loved Shirley – I was so happy I even loved John. I loved Biddy and Harry, who even seemed to love each other this one magical holiday. They didn't have a single row the entire fortnight.

I woke up early every morning. Once, when both

my parents were still sleeping soundly, I pulled on my favourite jeans and shirt and slipped out of the room all by myself. I crept out of the hotel, through the garden, out of the gate, down the road, all the way to the clifftop. I stood gazing out at the turquoise sea, trying to find the right words in my head to describe it.

I wondered if I'd ever be a real writer. I'd finished *Wintle's Wonders* and was now reading my Puffin paperback of E. Nesbit's *Five Children and It*. I wondered what I would wish for if I encountered the irritable Psammead hiding in Bournemouth's golden sands.

'I wish, I wish, I wish,' I whispered, not knowing what to wish for. It was no use wishing that Biddy and Harry would stay happy together. I knew them too well to wish for that. It was a waste wishing to be a teenager, because I *would* be one soon. I could wish for Diana and me to stay proper friends after the holiday – but we'd already exchanged addresses, promising to write to each other. So I wished my usual wish, the one I wished when I blew out my birthday candles, when I spotted the first star of the evening, when I hooked the Christmas turkey wishbone round my little finger.

'I wish I get to be a real writer and have a book published one day.'

I wonder what I'd have thought if I could have

gazed over that brilliant blue Bournemouth sea far into the future. I wouldn't have believed it possible that one day I'd have *ninety* books published, not just one. I'd laugh at the idea that one amazing day children would queue up outside a bookshop in Bournemouth for eight whole hours simply so I could sign their books. *My* books!

I stared at the sea, the early sun already warm on my face.

'Bournemouth,' I said, tasting the word as if it was a boiled sweet.

Then I started running all the way down the zigzag path for the sheer joy of it, still wondering if wishes ever came true.

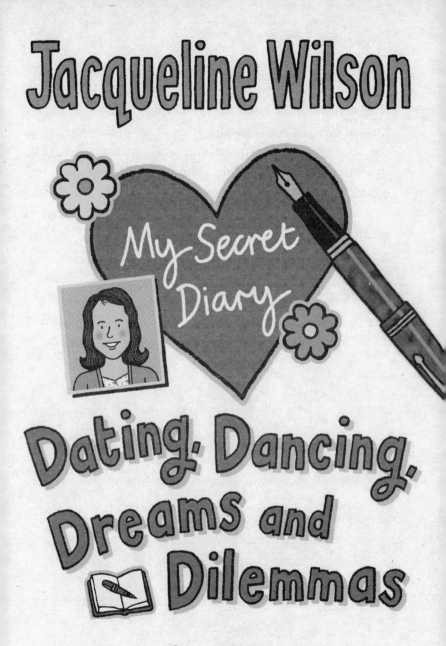

Jacqueline Wilson

My Secret Diary

Dating, Dancing, Dreams and Dilemmas

Illustrated by Nick Sharratt

For Chris

1
My Diary

I've kept a diary on and off all my life. When I was a little girl I had small Letts schoolgirl diaries. I kept them in my sock drawer, madly thinking this was an amazingly inventive hiding place. I didn't really record any riveting secrets in my blotchy biro: 'Mummy bought me a *Girl* comic. I think Joan of Arc is wonderful. Daddy and I went for a walk and I pretended to be a pony.'

I didn't write at length in a proper journal until I was in my teens. I read *The Diary of Anne Frank* and then re-read it so many times I could quote whole passages by heart. I especially loved the parts where Anne says she wants to be a writer when she grows up. I identified so strongly with that longing. I ached for Anne because she never had the chance to fulfil her huge potential. However, she also wrote that she wanted to be remembered after her death, and of course millions around the world read her wonderful diary. I knew this perfectly well but I still somehow felt she was writing her diary just for me, confiding all her secret fears and hopes and dreams. I slept with my pink Pan paperback copy of Anne's diary under my pillow and I kept a picture of her on my bedside table. I'd sometimes whisper to her at night.

I'd seen a photo of the actual red and white checked notebook that was Anne's first diary. I longed to own a similar notebook. Stationery was pretty dire back in the late fifties and early sixties. There was no such thing as Paperchase. I walked round and round the stationery counter in Woolworths and spent most of my pocket money on notebooks, but they weren't strong on variety. You could have shiny red sixpenny notebooks, lined inside, with strange maths details about rods and poles and perches on the back. (I never found out what they were!) Then you could have shiny *blue* sixpenny notebooks, etc. That was your lot.

I was enchanted to read in Dodie Smith's novel *I Capture the Castle* that the heroine, Cassandra, was writing her diary in a similar sixpenny notebook. She eventually progressed to a shilling notebook. My Woolworths rarely stocked such expensive luxuries. Then, two thirds of the way through the book, Cassandra is given a two-guinea red leather manuscript book. I lusted after that fictional notebook for years.

I told my mother, Biddy. She rolled her eyes. It could have cost two *hundred* guineas – both were way out of our league.

'Could I maybe have a special journal for my Christmas present?' I begged.

'Can't you use one of the notepads Harry brings home from work?' she asked.

My dad, Harry, was a civil servant. One of the few perks of his job was that he had an unlimited illegal supply of notepads watermarked SO – Stationery Office. I'd drawn on these pads for years, I'd scribbled stories, I'd written letters. They were serviceable but unexciting: thin cream paper unreliably bound at the top with glue. You couldn't write a journal in one of these notepads; it would fall apart in days.

'I need proper covers for my secret journal. I want it to be completely private,' I said.

Biddy scoffed at me. She didn't believe in privacy, especially where I was concerned. But she was always inventive with my Christmas presents even though we had very little money. She rose to the journal challenge.

On Christmas Day 1959, when I was just fourteen, she gave me a book, *The Devil and Mary Ann* by Catherine Cookson (I'd read the first two books about this tough little Tyneside girl and loved them); a *Filmgoers' Annual* with a special feature on Dirk Bogarde; a pair of American tan nylons and my first white lace suspender belt; a Yardley pressed powder compact in a gilt case – *and a proper journal*.

It wasn't quite a red-leather two-guinea job. It was grey plastic and it didn't cost a penny. Biddy worked as a book-keeper for Prince Machines. They supplied some of these machine tools to Thailand. Their customers sent them a diary as a seasonal token. The lettering was all Thai and therefore meaningless to me, but it was easy enough to work out which page was 1 January.

I was thrilled with my diary. It was the size of a book so I had quite a lot of room to write in. Here's that first entry:

Ever since I was little I have loved writing stories and poems. I would get an idea, buy a new exercise book, and start writing industriously, thinking myself the creator of a masterpiece. But by the end of the week I would think of another better idea and repeat the rigmarole. But now I have the better idea of writing a diary, as I hope I will never get sick of my own life. Besides, think of all the people who have been made famous by their diaries. Samuel Pepys, Fanny Burney, Marjorie Fleming, Anne Frank, etc., etc., so why shouldn't I? I'm only very ordinary, admittedly, but interesting things do sometimes happen to me. But perhaps the real reason for me starting this diary is because I find it 'irresistible, the pleasure of popping down my thoughts from time to time on paper'.

I was quoting Anne Frank of course. I said '*etc., etc.,*' one of my weird little writing tics, though I didn't know any other diarists, so I shouldn't have put even one etc., let alone two.

I wrote with a lovely old-fashioned mottled fountain pen. My handwriting was much neater then than it is nowadays. My spelling wasn't always too hot. It still isn't. Thank goodness for the spellcheck on my computer!

I had a list of new year's resolutions too. They didn't vary from year to year. Two out of three of them are pretty embarrassing.

Number one: Grow my hair.

When I was a baby I'd had fine, dark, straight hair. Biddy wound the top wisp round her finger so it stuck up in a fetching little wave. Sadly, my hair stayed thin and straight and wispy. Biddy continued to wave the top, forcing me to sleep with wicked curling grips seemingly stuck directly into my scalp. She had the rest cut very short to try to keep it tidy. I hated my hairstyle, though I liked going to Bentalls children's hairdresser's because you got to crouch on a special seat with a horse's head sticking out between your knees. You could stroke the horse's mane and tickle his ears while having your hair clipped. If you were very good and didn't make a fuss, the hairdresser (Pam or Maureen or Marilyn) would spin you round and round when she'd finished snipping.

Biddy was still dissatisfied with my wispy waif appearance. She wished I had Shirley Temple ringlets so she dragged me to her own hairdresser's and had them perm my hair. I had one perm after another throughout my childhood. I hated hated hated perms. I looked as if I'd been plugged into a light socket. I still had violent perms the first couple of years of secondary school and got royally teased about my frizzy hair. Girls on the bus would snigger at my precariously balanced school beret.

'Does your mother have to put your beret on with a battering ram?'

Oh, very funny. As I got older I argued more and utterly refused to have any more perms.

'I'm going to grow my hair long,' I said firmly.

'But it won't suit you, Jac. And it's too fine. It'll go all straggly.'

'I don't care,' I said.

It *did* go straggly in that awful in-between stage. It took such a long time to grow. I'd take hold of it a lock at a time and pull it sharply, or I'd sit hunched up with my neck tucked in just so that I could kid myself my hair was nearly shoulder-length.

It started to get horribly greasy too, much to my horror. In those long-ago days you only washed your hair once a week with Drene shampoo. *Anyone's* hair would look greasy. I'd attack my head with dry shampoo, a ghastly white powdery substance like chalk. It *looked* as if I'd been rubbing chalk through my hair after I'd applied it. I can't understand why I didn't wash my hair properly each day. There was some mumbo-jumbo that it made you lose your strength!

I'd wince every time I looked in the mirror and suddenly weaken. I'd have my hair cut and permed, instantly hate my new middle-aged hairstyle and vow to grow my hair all over again.

I didn't just want long hair. I wanted *fair* hair too, though I didn't dare contemplate peroxide. Biddy said Peroxide Blondes were as Common as Muck. I longed ludicrously for natural long blonde hair. There was a girl called Susan Wooldridge in my year at school. She had shiny straight fair hair, neatly plaited in two long braids tied with green satin ribbon to match our green and grey school uniform. I'd stand behind Susan in assembly and stare enviously at her beautiful hair. Susan was a pretty pink-and-white complexioned girl with a perky personality. I didn't know her very well because we weren't in the same class but I longed to *be* her.

When I woke up in the morning I'd keep my eyes shut, clench my fists and *will* myself to change places with Susan. Sometimes I'd kid myself it was actually working. I'd feel as if I was wafting way above the clouds, diving down over the rooftops of New Malden and slipping into Susan's open window. But when I dared open my eyes I always found myself under my own ugly brown eiderdown, and the mirror in my bedroom reflected my own artificial curls.

My second resolution was equally embarrassing: Get a boyfriend.

I'd had boyfriends at my primary school – David and then Alan – but of course they weren't *real* boyfriends, though we held hands and occasionally gave each other film-star kisses. We didn't keep in touch when we all went on to secondary school. I went to Coombe, an all-girls school, so I obviously wasn't going to find a new boyfriend there.

I didn't truthfully *want* a boyfriend, but it was such a status symbol, especially at school. When we all gathered together in the first year (Year

Seven) it was the first question everyone asked. *Have you got a boyfriend?*

Very few of us had boyfriends the first and second years so we could relax and not bother about it too much, but by the third year (Year Nine) it was starting to become imperative.

I still didn't know *how* to get a boyfriend. There were lots of boys who lived in our flats – in fact I lived right next door to two teenage boys, Jeremy and Anthony, but I didn't *know* them. I just mumbled hello if I bumped into them on the balcony.

I was painfully aware that Biddy thought me very backward when it came to boys. I knew she'd had heaps of boyfriends when she was fourteen.

'Don't worry, you'll get a boyfriend soon, Jac,' she'd say. 'Just smile at the first boy you fancy and start chatting to him.'

'What should I *say*?'

'*I* don't know. The first thing that comes into your head.'

I had a head full of daydreams. I couldn't imagine telling any boy about my private imaginary games, all my made-up characters and stories-in-progress. I didn't even talk about them to my best friends, Chris and Carol. I certainly didn't talk about them to Biddy, who thought me weird enough already.

'I don't know how to talk to boys,' I said despairingly.

'If only you weren't so *shy*,' said Biddy. 'Still, you can't help that, you take after your father.'

I didn't ask Harry how to talk to boys. I didn't know how to talk to *him*. We could spend a whole day together in the flat without saying a word to each other. It was hard remembering that Harry had once been Biddy's boyfriend. They weren't boy and girl now – and they certainly weren't friends either.

My third and final new year resolution was more heartfelt and personal:

Write a book!

I'd *written* so-called books, heaps of them, but they were twenty-page hand-written efforts in my Woolworths notebooks. Most petered out halfway through. Some only progressed for a page or two. I didn't restrict myself to novels. I wrote a fifteen-page biography of the child actress Mandy Miller, embellished with photos and drawings. It was pretty similar to all the Jacqueline Wilson projects children show me nowadays.

I wrote the odd play too – odd being the operative word. I once wrote about the story of Moses from his sister Miriam's point of view. I tried poetry too, most of it abysmal. I tried to be versatile as a writer but at heart I've always been a novelist. I tried so hard with my stories but I knew that none of them were good enough to get published. I just hoped that *one* day I'd write something worth while.

I kept that 1960 diary all the way through to the summer, writing very detailed entries day after day. I'll be quoting from almost every page – and blushing frequently!

Jacqueline with her grandparents

2
My Family

We were a small family, just Biddy, Harry and me, cooped up in our claustrophobic council flat in Kingston. There were a lot of arguments. Biddy and me, Harry and me, Biddy and Harry against me – and, most frequently of all, Biddy and Harry arguing between themselves.

I rarely go into details of these arguments in my 1960 diary. I just write at the bottom of many pages: 'Mummy and Daddy had a row.' These rows could blow up over the silliest things. Harry might moan about the way Biddy tucked his socks into a tight ball, or Biddy might raise her eyebrows and sniff in a snobbish way if Harry said, *'Pardon?'*. These tiny irritations would be like a starter's gun. Suddenly they were *off* – and the row would escalate until they were both shouting at the tops of their voices.

'For God's sake, what will the neighbours think?' Biddy would hiss when Harry was in mid rant. Harry would bellow that he couldn't care less about the neighbours – or words to that effect.

The Grovers at number eleven and the Hines at

number thirteen must have sighed and turned up their televisions, muttering 'Those dreadful Aitkens' again.

Yet it wasn't *all* rows and ranting. Biddy and Harry couldn't stand each other, and like all teenagers I sometimes felt I couldn't stand them – but we could still have fun together. On Sunday mornings, if Harry was in a good mood, he'd get up and make us breakfast. We weren't healthy eaters then. My absolute favourite Sunday-treat breakfast was fried potatoes on buttered toast, followed by another piece of toast spread with thick white sugary condensed milk. My mouth is puckering as I write this. Nowadays I couldn't swallow so much as a teaspoon of ultra-sweet condensed milk to save my life, but when I was fourteen I could have slurped up a whole tin at a time.

We ate a large Sunday roast together too while listening to *The Billy Cotton Band Show* and *Family Favourites* on the radio. We particularly enjoyed listening to *Hancock's Half Hour* as a family, all three of us convulsing with laughter. We watched television together in the evenings. For a long time we only had one television channel so there weren't any arguments about which programme to pick.

There must have been many ordinary cosy evenings like this:

Thursday 3 March
I'm sitting at the table. The time is twenty to eight.
'Life of Bliss' is on the T.V. Daddy has just got in
from work. I ask Mummy what happened at her
office. Mr Lacy was in a good mood, she replies,
and goes back to her newspaper. What are you
looking for? Mummy asks Dad. My black pen, he
replies, have I got time for a bath before supper?
Only an in and out says Mummy. Daddy has his
bath. We sit down to our supper of macaroni cheese
(one of my favourites). After supper I do my maths
homework. Daddy helps, bless him. Then I watch
T.V. It is a Somerset Maugham play, and very good.
P.S. Mum bought me some sweet white nylon
knickers.

I was still very close to Biddy and struggled hard
to please her. I took immense pains to find an
original Mother's Day present for her. I went
shopping in Kingston with my friends Carol and
Cherry, all of us after Mother's Day presents –
though we got a little distracted first.

We first went to Maxwells the record shop, and I
bought the record 'A Theme from a Summer Place'.
It was lovely. Then we went to Bentalls. First we

went to the Yardley make-up, and a very helpful woman sold me my liquefying cleansing cream and Cherry a new lipstick. Then we bought our mothers some cards, and Cherry bought her mother some flowers, and Carol bought her mother some chocs. But I knew what I wanted for my adorable, queer, funny, contemporary mother. A pair of roll-on black panties, a pair of nylons and a good (expensive) black suspender belt.

I record happily on Sunday: '*Mum was very pleased with her panties, belt and nylons.*'

I tried to please Harry too. I didn't buy him a vest and Y-fronts for Father's Day, thank goodness – but I did make an effort.

Saturday 4 June
I bought a card for Father's Day, and some men's talcum and three men's hankies as well.

Biddy and Harry bought me presents too, sometimes vying with each other, to my advantage: '*Biddy gave me a pound to spend for when I'm going round Kingston with Carol – and then Harry gave me <u>five</u> pounds. For nothing!!!*'

They could be imaginative with gifts. Biddy not

only bought me all my clothes, she bought me books and ornaments and make-up. Harry tried hard too. He was away up in Edinburgh for a week on business (I wrote, 'It feels so strange in the flat without Daddy'), but when he came back he had bought lavish presents for both of us:

Saturday 21 May
Daddy came back from Scotland today. He gave me a little Scotch doll, a typewriter rubber, a coin bracelet, an expensive bambi brooch, and a little book about Mary, Queen of Scots. He gave Mummy a £5 note.

Harry could be generous with his time too. That summer of 1960 I had to do a Shakespeare project so he took a day off work and we went to Stratford. It was a *good* day too. We went round Shakespeare's birthplace and Anne Hathaway's cottage and collected various postcards and leaflets. My project was the most gorgeously illustrated of anyone's. But he mostly kept to himself, out at work on weekdays, still playing tennis at the weekends, and when he was at home he hunched in his armchair, surrounded by piles of *Racing Posts* and form books. If he wasn't going out he rarely bothered to get dressed, comfortable in our centrally heated flat in pyjamas and dressing gown and bare feet.

Biddy frequently changed into her dressing gown too and sat watching television, tiny feet tucked up, her Du Maurier cigarettes on one arm of the chair and a bag of her favourite pear drops on the other. As the evening progressed, one or other of them would start nodding and soon they would both be softly snoring. I'd huddle up with my book, happy to be left in peace way past my bed time.

They never went out in the week but they started going out on Saturday nights with Biddy's friend Ron. They must have been strange evenings, especially as my parents were practically teetotal. Biddy stuck with her bitter lemons. Harry tried a pint of beer occasionally but hated it. One Saturday night he pushed the boat out and had two or three and came home feeling so ill he lay on the kitchen floor, moaning.

'Well, it's all your own fault, you fool. You were the one who poured the drink down your throat,' said Biddy, poking him with her foot.

Harry swore at her, still horizontal.

'Don't you start calling me names! Now get up, you look ridiculous. What if someone walks along the balcony and peers in the kitchen window? They'll think you're dead.'

'I wish I was,' said Harry, and shut his eyes.

I don't think he enjoyed those Saturday nights one iota – and yet he agreed to go on a summer holiday that year with Ron and his wife, Grace. I don't know if Harry had any particular secret lady friends at that time – he certainly did later on in his life. I think Biddy and Harry came very close to splitting up when I was fourteen or so. I know Ron had plans to go to Africa and wanted Biddy to go with him. But I was the fly in the ointment, flapping my wings stickily. Biddy wouldn't leave me, so *she* was stuck too.

We went out very occasionally on a Sunday afternoon, when we caught the bus to the other end of Kingston and went to tea with my grandparents, Ga and Gongon. The adults played solo and bridge and bickered listlessly and ate Cadbury's Dairy Milk chocolates. I ate chocolates too and curled up with my book. If I finished my own book I read one of Ga and Gongon's Sunday school prize books or flipped through their ten volumes of Arthur Mee's *Children's Encyclopedia*.

I preferred visiting Ga by myself. I'd go on Wednesday afternoons after school. She'd always have a special tea waiting for me: thinly sliced bread and butter and home-made loganberry jam, tinned peaches and Nestlé's tinned cream, and then a cake – a Peggy Brown lemon meringue tart if Ga had shopped in Surbiton, or a Hemming's Delight (meringue and artificial cream with a glacé cherry) if she had been to Kingston marketplace.

Ga would chat to me at tea, asking me all about school, taking me ultra seriously. I should have been the one making *her* tea as her arthritis was really bad now. She had to wear arm splints and wrist supports, and for a week or so before her monthly cortizone injection she could only walk slowly, clearly in great pain. It's so strange realizing that Ga then was younger than me now. She looked like an old lady in her shapeless jersey suits and black buttoned shoes.

One Wednesday it was pouring with rain and I was sodden by the time I'd walked to Ga's, my hair in rats' tails, my school uniform dripping. Ga gave me a towel for my hair and one of her peachy-pink rayon petticoats to wear while my clothes dried. But when it was time for me to go home they were still soaking wet. I didn't particularly mind but Ga wouldn't hear of me walking the three quarters of an hour home up Kingston Hill in sopping wet clothes. She was sure I'd catch a chill. She insisted I borrow one of her suits. She meant so well I couldn't refuse, though I absolutely died at the thought of walking home in old-lady beige with her long sagging skirt flapping round my ankle socks.

Ga could no longer make her own clothes because her hands had turned into painful little

370

claws due to her arthritis – but she would press her lips together firmly and *make* herself sew if it was for me.

Wednesday 27 January
After school went up to Ga's. She has made my Chinese costume for the play, and also gave me a lovely broderie anglaise petticoat. Isn't she kind?

Yes, she was *very* kind, in little sweet ways. On 14 February I always received a Valentine. That year it was two little blue birds kissing beaks, perching on two red hearts outlined with glitter. There were forget-me-nots and roses sprinkled across the card, and inside a little printed verse and an inked question mark. I knew it wasn't from a boy, although I was supposed to assume it came from a secret admirer. I was pretty certain it was Ga wanting to give me a surprise, sending me a Valentine so I could show it off at school.

She was always so reassuring and comforting.

Wednesday 24 February
Back to school, worst luck. Going to school all Wolverton Avenue was dug up and there were many

workmen standing around and digging under the pavement. Sue at once crossed the road, but I stayed on the left side where they were working and each time they smiled and said hello and how are you, etc. in the friendly way workmen do, I smiled back and said hello, and I feel fine. Afterwards Sue was ever so crabby and said in what I call her 'old maid' voice, 'I saw you smile at all those <u>work</u> men.' Talk about a bloody snob! She makes me MAD at times. I told Ga when I went up there this afternoon after school and she (the darling) said I had a nice little face and naturally they would smile and talk to me, and that it was only polite that I should do the same back.

Ga was so gentle with me, letting me rant on in a half-baked manner about becoming a pacifist and banning the bomb and being anti-apartheid, while she nodded and smiled. I got tremendously steamed up at the end of term because we were having a party for all the girls at school, with music and non-alcoholic punch.

'It's not *fair*!' I said.

'You can't have real punch at a school party,' she said reasonably.

'Oh no, I don't mind the non-alcoholic punch part. I don't *like* proper drink,' I said.

She looked relieved. 'So *what* isn't fair?' she asked.

'We can't have boys! Can you imagine it, just us girls dancing together all evening. That's not a proper party, it's just like dancing school. We're all furious, wanting to take our boyfriends.'

Ga blinked. 'So, have you got a boyfriend, Jac?'

'Well . . . no, I haven't, not at the moment. But that's not the point, it's the *principle* that matters,' I said, determined not to lose face.

Ga was kind enough not to laugh at me.

3

Clothes

Saturday 2 January
I went to Bentalls' sale with Mum. We got some
smashing bargains so I'm jolly glad I went. First
a very full pink and mauve mohair skirt, and to go
with it a lovely pink thick-knit Austrian cardigan.
We got it for 45 bob, but previously it had been
£9.9s!! I also got a good book and a new lipstick. I
tried it out this afternoon and wore my new outfit,
and I think I looked quite nice. I looked warm, cosy
and fashionable, nice and teenager-y, but not
looking too grown up.

I can't believe I once used words like *jolly* and
smashing! I sound like someone out of Enid
Blyton's Famous Five books. That pink and mauve
mohair skirt and Austrian cardigan sound
absolutely hideous too, though I obviously liked
them at the time. I didn't actually *want* to look
'nice and teenager-y'.

If you wanted to look truly cool in 1960 you
dressed like a Beatnik. You had long straight hair

(sigh!). You wore black: black polo-neck jumper, black skirt, black stockings, black pointy boots, with a black duffel coat over the top. You were probably roasting to death in all these woolly layers but you *looked* cool. I'd have given anything to be a Beatnik but it would have looked like fancy dress on a schoolgirl living on a suburban council estate. Beatniks were exotic adults who lived in London and haunted smoky jazz cellars.

The cool look at school was totally different. Girls backcombed their hair into bouffant styles and then sprayed it until it hardened into a helmet. They cinched in their waists with elasticated belts and stuck out their skirts with nylon petticoats. You could get wonderfully coloured petticoats at Kingston Monday market – pink, blue, even bright yellow, edged with lace. You washed these petticoats in sugar water, which made them stiff. Your skirts bounced as you walked, showing your layers of petticoat. You wobbled when you walked too, in stiletto heels.

I say 'you'. *I* didn't have bouffant hair, elasticated belts, flouncy petticoats or stiletto heels.

'You're not going out looking as Common as Muck,' said Biddy.

I rather wanted to look as Common as Muck, but I couldn't manage it, even behind Biddy's back. I didn't know *how* to tease my hair into that amazing bouffant shape. It was either too frizzy or too limp, depending on whether I'd just had another dreaded perm or not.

I didn't have enough of a waist to cinch, and my petticoats were limp white garments that clung to my legs. I didn't have proper stilettos. My first pair of heels were barely an inch high. They were called Louis heels, squat, stumpy little heels on a slip-on shoe. I was used to straps or laces and I had to walk with my feet stuck out like a ballet dancer to keep them on. They were pale green. 'Eau de nil,' said Biddy. She bought me a silly little clutch purse too, also in eau de nil. I had Biddy's pass-me-down cream swagger coat that year. It draped in an odd way and had weird wide sleeves. I didn't swagger in my coat, I slouched, walking with kipper feet in my silly shoes, clutching the purse.

'You look so ladylike in that outfit,' said Biddy, smiling approvingly.

Biddy wasn't alone in wanting her daughter to look ladylike. At school that spring of 1960 we had a visit from the Simplicity paper-pattern people. I'd never sewn a garment in my life apart from a school apron I'd laboured over in needlework, but I certainly knew my way around the Simplicity fashion books. I'd been buying them for years so that I could cut out all the most interesting models and play pretend games with

377

them. It was strange seeing familiar dresses made up, worn by real girls.

Thursday 17 March
We missed Latin today! The fashion people, Simplicity, had made up some of their teenage patterns and our girls dressed up in them, and we had a fashion parade. It was quite good, and our girls looked quite different, being all posh, and wearing white gloves, and walking like proper models. (Only they looked a bit daft.) I didn't mind the dresses, but I didn't see one I really liked. Afterwards the lady told us that we should wear bras to define and shape our figures (we already do wear them of course), that we should use deodorants (which I at any rate do), that we should pay attention to our deportment (which I try to do), that we should think carefully whether our lipsticks go with our dresses (which I do) etc., etc.

Heavens! I might go in for a spot of lipstick coordination but I certainly didn't want to wear ladylike *white gloves*. The very last thing in the world I wanted to look was *ladylike*. At least the pink of the mohair skirt wasn't pastel, and the skirt was full enough to bunch out as much as possible.

I could hide my lack of waist under the chunky cardigan. I expect the lipstick was pink too. Later on in the sixties make-up changed radically and I'd wear *white* lipstick and heavy black eye make-up, but in 1960, when I was fourteen, the 'natural' look was still in vogue.

I wasn't great at putting on make-up. I rubbed powder on my face, smeared lipstick on my lips, brushed black mascara on my lashes and hoped for the best. It didn't help that I wore glasses. I had to take them off when I applied my make-up and consequently couldn't quite see what I was doing.

I've looked through the photo album covering my teenage years and I can't find a single picture of me wearing my glasses. I hated wearing them. I'm not sure contact lenses were widely available in those days. I'd certainly never heard of them. I was stuck wearing my glasses in school. I couldn't read the blackboard without them. I could barely see the board itself. But *out* of school I kept them in the clutch bag.

I had to whip them on quick while waiting at a bus stop so I could stick my hand out for the right number bus, but the moment I was *on* the bus I'd shove the glasses back in the bag. I spent most of my teenage years walking round in a complete haze, unable to recognize anyone until they were nose to nose with me. I was clearly taking my life in my hands whenever I crossed the road. I was an accident waiting to happen, especially as I made up stories in my head as I walked along and didn't even try to concentrate on where I was going.

I was in the middle of an imaginary television interview one day going home from school.

'Do tell us what inspired you to write this wonderful novel, Miss Aitken,' the interviewer asked as I jumped off the bus.

He never got an answer. I stepped out into the road and walked straight into a car. I was knocked flying, landing with a smack on the tarmac. The interviewer vanished. *I* vanished too, losing consciousness. I opened my eyes a minute or two later to find a white-faced man down on his knees beside me, clutching my hand.

'Oh, thank God you're not dead!' he said, nearly in tears.

I blinked at him. It was almost like one of my own fantasies. When Biddy or Harry were especially impatient with me I'd frequently imagine myself at my last gasp on my deathbed, with them weeping over me, begging my forgiveness.

'I'm so sorry!' he said. 'It wasn't my *fault*, you just walked straight in front of me. I braked but I couldn't possibly avoid you. Where do you hurt?'

'I don't think I actually hurt anywhere,' I said, trying to sit up.

'No, you shouldn't move! I'd better find a phone box to call an ambulance.'

'Oh no, I'm fine, really,' I said, getting very worried now.

I *did* feel fine, though in a slightly dream-like, unreal way. I staggered to my feet and he rushed to help me.

'You really shouldn't stand!' he said, though I was upright now. 'Are your legs all right? And your arms?'

I shook all four of my limbs gingerly. One of my arms was throbbing now, *and* one of my legs, but I didn't want to upset him further by admitting this.

'Yes, they're perfectly OK,' I said. 'Well, thank you very much for looking after me. Goodbye.' I started to walk away but he looked appalled.

'I can't let you just walk off! The very least I can do is take you home to your mother. I want to explain to her what happened.'

'Oh no, really!'

'I insist!'

I dithered, nibbling my lip. I couldn't think clearly. Alarm bells were ringing in my head. Biddy had drummed it into me enough times: *Never get into a car with a strange man!* But he seemed such a nice kind strange man, and I was worried about hurting his feelings.

I tried to wriggle out of his suggestion tactfully.

'My mum isn't *at* home,' I said. 'So you won't be able to explain to her. *I'll* tell her when she gets home from work. I promise I'll explain it was all my fault.'

I went to pick up my satchel. I used the aching arm and nearly dropped it. I tried to hurry away, but the aching leg made me limp.

'You *are* hurt, I'm sure you are,' he said. 'Where does your mother work? I'm driving you there straight away, and then I'll drive you both to the hospital.'

I didn't have the strength for any more arguing. I let him help me into his car. Biddy's workplace, Prince Machines, was only five minutes' drive away. If he drove fast in the wrong direction, intent on abducting me, then I'd simply have to fling open the car door and hurl myself out. I'd survived one car accident, so hopefully I'd survive a second.

Yes, I know. I was mad. Don't anyone ever get in a car with a stranger under any circumstances whatsoever.

However, my stranger proved to be a perfect gentleman, parking the car in the driveway of Prince Machines, supporting me under the arm, carrying my satchel on his own back. Biddy looked out of the office window and saw us approaching.

She shot out of the office and came charging up

382

to us. 'Jac? What's happened? Who's this? Are you all right?'

'This is my mum,' I said unnecessarily.

The stranger explained, anxiously asserting again that it really wasn't his fault.

Biddy didn't doubt him. 'You're so *hopeless*, Jac! Haven't I told you to look where you're going? You were daydreaming, weren't you? When will you *learn*?'

I hung my head while Biddy ranted.

'Still, thank goodness you're all right,' she said finally, giving me a quick hug.

'Well, I'm not quite sure she *is* all right,' said my rescuer. 'I think she was unconscious for a minute or two. She seems pretty shaken up. I'm very happy to drive you to hospital.'

'Oh, for goodness' sake, she's fine. There's no need whatsoever,' said Biddy. 'Who wants to hang around the hospital for hours?'

Biddy had once worked there delivering newspapers to patients and had a healthy contempt for the place. She always swore she'd never set foot in the hospital even if she was dying.

She had more authority than me and sent the stranger on his way. He was kind enough to pop back the following day with the biggest box of chocolates I'd ever seen in my life. I'd never been given so much as a half-pound of Cadbury's Milk

Tray before. I lolled on my bed in my baby-doll pyjamas all weekend with my giant box beside me. I'd seen pictures of big-busted film starlets lounging on satin sheets eating chocolates. I pretended I was a film star too. I can't have looked very beguiling: I had one arm in a sling and one leg was black with bruises from my thigh down to my toes.

Biddy had had to drag me up to the dreaded hospital after all. My aching arm became so painful I couldn't pick anything up and my bad leg darkened dramatically. We spent endless hours waiting for someone to tell us that I'd sprained my arm badly and bruised my leg.

'As if that wasn't blooming obvious,' Biddy muttered.

At least it got me out of PE at school for the next couple of weeks, so I didn't have to change into the ghastly aertex shirt and green divided shorts.

I cared passionately about clothes, but most of the time I was stuck wearing my school uniform. The winter uniform wasn't too terrible: white shirts, green and yellow ties, plain grey skirts and grey V-necked sweaters. We had to wear hideous grey gabardine raincoats, and berets or bowler-type hats with green and yellow ribbon round the brim. Earnest girls wore the hats, cool girls wore berets.

We had to wear white or grey socks or pale stockings kept up with a suspender belt or a 'roll-on'. Oh dear, underwear was so not sexy in 1960! Those roll-ons were hilarious. They weren't as armour-plated as the pink corsets our grannies wore, but they were still pretty fearsome garments. You stepped into them and then yanked them up over your hips as best you could, wiggling and tugging and cursing. It was even more of a performance getting out of them at the end of the day. I'm sure that's why so many girls never went further than chastely kissing their boyfriends. You'd die rather than struggle out of your roll-on in front of anyone. They had two suspenders on either side to keep up your stockings. Nylons took a sizeable chunk of pocket money so we mostly wore old laddered ones to school. We stopped the ladders running with dabs of pink nail varnish, so everyone looked as if they had measles on their legs.

We had to wear clunky brown Clarks shoes – an outdoor and an indoor pair – though some of the older girls wore heels on the way home if they were meeting up with their boyfriends. They customized their uniforms too, hitching up their skirts and pulling them in at the waist with those ubiquitous elasticated belts. They unbuttoned the tops of their blouses and loosened their ties and folded their berets in half and attached them with kirby grips to the back of their bouffant hair. We were younger and meeker and nerdier in my year and mostly wore our uniform as the head teacher intended.

Everyone cordially hated the summer uniform: canary-yellow dresses in an unpleasant synthetic material. There is not a girl in existence who looks good in canary yellow. It makes pale girls look sallow and ill, and rosy-cheeked girls alarmingly scarlet. The dresses had ugly cap sleeves, like silly wings, unflattering to any kind of arm and embarrassing when you put up your hand in class.

Very few people had washing machines in those days. You did your main wash once a week, so by Friday our canaries were stained and dingy. We had to wear straw boaters going to and from school even if there was a heatwave. These were hard, uncomfortable hats that made your head itch. They could only be kept in place with elastic. Nasty boys would run past and tip our boaters so that the elastic snapped under our chins. *Particularly* nasty boys would snatch at our backs to twang our bra elastic too. I often wonder *why* I wanted a boyfriend!

I looked younger than my age in my school uniform, but I did my best to dress older outside school – sometimes for particular reasons!

Thursday 4 February
After school I went to the pictures with Sue and Cherry. I wore my red beret, black and white coat and black patent shoes and managed to get in for 16 as the picture was an 'A'.

I sound too twee for words. A beret? But at least it was a change from eau de nil. Green still figured prominently in my wardrobe though.

Saturday 12 March
In the afternoon I went shopping with Mummy and we bought me a pale green checked woolly shirtwaister for the Spring to go with my green shoes and handbag.

Just call this the lettuce look. However, I seemed to like it then. In May I wrote:

After dinner I got dressed in my new green shirtwaister, that I think suits me very well. Then, loaded down with records, I called for Sue and we went to Cherry's party. Everyone had brought lots of records, and did my feet ache after all that jiving!

Carol wore her new black and white dress which looked nice.

My writing was certainly as limp as a lettuce in those days. *Nice!*

So I liked my green dress, but my favourite outfit was 'a cotton skirt patterned with violets and nice and full'. It's about the only one of those long-ago garments I wouldn't mind wearing now on a summer day.

Biddy was generous to me, buying me clothes out of her small wage packet.

Saturday 4 June
In the afternoon Mummy and I went to Richmond and after a long hunt we bought me a pair of cream flatties, very soft and comfortable. Then, back in Kingston, we went into C & A's and found a dress in the children's department that we both liked very much. The only trouble with it was that it had a button missing at the waist. Mummy made a fuss about it, but they didn't have another dress in stock or another button, so we bought it minus the button as we liked it very much indeed. It is a lovely powder blue colour with a straight skirt and Mummy

has transferred the bottom button to the waist so that it doesn't notice so much.

I sound like little Goody-Two-Shoes, trotting round with Mummy, being ever so grateful for my girly frock. It's reassuring to see that I revert to surly teenager the very next day.

Sunday 5 June
I AM A PIG. I was rude and irritable today and I just didn't care, and I spoilt Mummy's day at the coast. (Daddy wasn't very well-behaved either though!) I won't write any more about a very unfortunate day.

I wish I had. It would have been a lot more interesting than painstaking accounts of buttons missing on powder-blue dresses!

4
Chris

Chris and Carol are my best friends, and there is also Sue who lives next door, and Cherry down the road. They all go to Coombe, my school.

I met my very special friend, Chris, on my first day at Coombe County Secondary School for Girls. I'd had *another* Christine as my special friend when I was at primary school but we'd sadly lost touch when we both left Latchmere. I think she moved away after her mum died.

I'd never set eyes on my new friend Chris before that first day at secondary school. I didn't know anyone at all. It's always a bit scary going to a brand-new school. Coombe was in New Malden, two or three miles from our flats in Kingston. I hadn't made it through my eleven plus to Tiffin Girls' School, but I'd been given a 'second chance' and managed to pass this time. I could now go to a new comprehensive school instead of a secondary modern.

Coombe was one of the first comprehensives, though it was divided firmly into two teaching streams – grammar and secondary modern. In an effort to make us girls mix in together, we were in forms for non-academic lessons like singing and PE, and in groups graded from one all the way to nine for lessons like maths and English. This system didn't make allowances for girls like me. I'd been put in group one, where I held my own in English and most of the arts subjects – but I definitely belonged in group nine for maths! Still, compiling that timetable must have been nightmare enough without trying to accommodate weird girls like me – very good in some subjects and an utter dunce in others.

I couldn't even get my head around the densely printed timetable, and the entire geography of the school was confusing. We weren't shown around beforehand or even given a map when we arrived the first day. We were somehow expected to *sense* our way around.

I managed to fetch up in the right form room, 1A. We stood around shyly, eyeing each other up and down. We were a totally mixed bunch. A few of the girls were very posh, from arty left-wing families who were determined to give their daughters a state education. Some of the girls were very tough, from families who didn't give their daughters' education a second thought. Most of us were somewhere in the middle, ordinary suburban girls fidgeting anxiously in our stiff new uniforms, wondering if we'd ever make friends.

'Good morning, Form One A! I'm Miss Crowford, your form teacher.'

'Good-morning-Miss-Crowford,' we mumbled.

She was small and dark and quite pretty, so we could have done a lot worse. I hoped she might teach English, but it turned out she was the gym teacher. I started to go off her immediately, though she was actually very kind and did her best to encourage me when I couldn't climb the ropes and thumped straight *into* rather than over the wooden horse.

Miss Crowford let us choose our own desks. I sat behind a smallish girl with long light-brown hair neatly tied in two plaits. We all had to say our names, going round the class. The girl with plaits said she was called Christine. I was predisposed to *like* girls called Christine so I started to take proper notice of her.

Miss Crowford was busy doing the Jolly-Teacher Talk about us being big girls now in this lovely new secondary school. She told us all about the school badge and the school motto and the school hymn while I inked a line of small girls in school uniform all round the border of my new and incomprehensible timetable.

Then a loud electronic bell rang, startling us. We were all used to the ordinary hand-bells rung at our primary schools.

'Right, girls, join your groups and go off to your next lesson,' said Miss Crowford. 'Don't dawdle! We only give you five minutes to get to the next classroom.'

I peered at my timetable in panic. It seemed to indicate that group one had art. I didn't have a clue where this would be. All the other girls were getting up purposefully and filing out of the room. In desperation I tapped Christine on the back.

'Excuse me, do you know the way to the art room?' I asked timidly.

Chris smiled at me. 'No, but I've got to go there too,' she said.

'Let's go and find it together,' I said.

It took us much longer than five minutes. It turned out that the art room wasn't even in the main school building, it was right at the end of the playground. By the time we got there I'd made a brand-new best friend.

Coombe had only been open for two years, so there weren't that many girls attending, just us new first years, then the second and third years. We barely filled half the hall when we filed into

394

assembly. It was a beautiful hall, with a polished parquet floor. No girl was allowed to set foot on it in her outdoor shoes. We had to have hideous rubber-soled sandals so that we wouldn't scratch the shiny floorboards. We also had to have black plimsolls for PE. Some of the poorer girls tried to make do with plimsolls for their indoor shoes. Miss Haslett, the head teacher, immediately protested, calling the offending girls out to the front of the hall.

'They are *plimsolls*,' she said. 'You will wear proper indoor shoes tomorrow!'

I couldn't see what possible harm it would do letting these girls wear their plimsolls. Why were they being publicly humiliated in front of everyone? It wasn't their fault they didn't possess childish Clarks sandals. None of us earned any money. We couldn't buy our own footwear. It was a big struggle for a lot of families to find three pairs of shoes for each daughter – *four* pairs, because most girls wouldn't be seen dead in Clarks clodhoppers outside school.

However, the next day all the girls were wearing regulation sandals apart from one girl, Doreen, in my form. She was a tiny white-faced girl with bright red hair. She might have been small but she was so fierce we were all frightened of her. Doreen herself didn't seem frightened of anyone, not even Miss Haslett.

Doreen danced into school the next day, eyes bright, chin up. She didn't flinch when Miss Haslett called her up on the stage in front of everyone. None of Doreen's uniform technically passed muster. Her scrappy grey skirt was home-made and her V-neck jumper hand-knitted. She wore droopy white socks – and her black plimsolls.

Miss Haslett pointed at them in disgust, as if they were covered in dog's muck. 'You are still wearing plimsolls, Doreen! Tomorrow you will come to school wearing *indoor shoes*, do you hear me?'

Doreen couldn't help hearing her, she was bellowing in her face. But she didn't flinch.

We all wondered what would happen tomorrow. We knew Doreen didn't *have* any indoor shoes, and she didn't come from the sort of family where her mum could brandish a full purse and say, 'No problem, sweetheart, we'll trot down to Clarks shoeshop and buy you a pair.'

Doreen walked into school assembly the next morning in grubby blue bedroom slippers with holes in the toes. I'm certain this was all she had. She didn't look as if she was being deliberately defiant. There was a flush of pink across her pale face. She didn't want to show off the state of her slippers to all of us. Miss Haslett didn't understand. She flushed too.

'How *dare* you be so insolent as to wear your slippers in school!' she shrieked. 'Go and stand outside my study in disgrace.'

Doreen stood there all day long, shuffling from one slippered foot to the other. She didn't come into school the next day. The following Monday she wore regulation rubber-soled school sandals. They were old and scuffed and had obviously belonged to somebody else. Maybe someone gave them to her, or maybe her mum bought them for sixpence at a jumble sale.

'At last you've seen sense, Doreen,' said Miss Haslett in assembly. 'I hope this has taught you all a lesson, girls.'

I hadn't seen sense. I'd seen crass stupidity and insensitivity on Miss Haslett's part. It taught me the lesson that some teachers were appallingly unfair, so caught up in petty rules and regulations that they lost all compassion and common sense.

A couple of years later *I* ended up standing in disgrace outside Miss Haslett's study door. She'd seen me walking to the bus stop without my school beret and – shock horror! – I was sucking a Sherbet Fountain. I'd committed not one but two criminal offences in her eyes: eating in school uniform and not wearing my silly hat.

Miss Haslett sent for me and started telling me

off. 'Why were you eating that childish rubbish, Jacqueline?' she asked.

The obvious answer was that I was hungry, and I needed something to keep me going for the long walk home. (I'd stopped taking the bus after the dramatic accident.) However, I sensed Miss Haslett would consider an honest answer insolent, so I kept quiet.

'And *why* weren't you wearing your school beret?' she continued.

This was easier. 'I've lost it, Miss Haslett,' I said truthfully.

It had been there on my coat hook that morning. Someone had obviously snatched it for themselves when their own beret had gone missing.

'That's just like you, Jacqueline Aitken,' said Miss Haslett. 'Stand outside!'

I stood there. My legs started aching after a while so I leaned against the wall. I didn't feel cast down. I was utterly jubilant because I was missing a maths lesson. I gazed into space and started imagining inside my head, continuing a serial – a magic island story. Pupils squeaked past in their sandals every now and then, good girls trusted to take important messages to Miss Haslett. The odd teacher strode past too, several frowning at me to emphasize my disgrace. But then dear Mr Jeziewski, one of the art teachers, came sloping along in his suede shoes. He raised his eyebrows at me in mock horror, felt in his pocket, put two squares of chocolate on the window ledge beside me and winked before he went on his way.

I smiled at Mr Jeziewski and savoured my chocolate. I couldn't resist writing a similar scene in my book *Love Lessons*, in which my main girl, Prue, falls passionately in love with her art teacher, Mr Raxbury. I promise I *didn't* fall for Mr Jeziewski, who was very much a family man and rather plain, with straight floppy hair and baggy cords – but he was certainly my favourite teacher when I was at Coombe.

Having Chris for a friend was an enormous help in settling into secondary school life. She wasn't quite as hopeless as me at PE, but pretty nearly, so we puffed along the sports track together and lurked at the very edge of the playing field, pretending to be deep fielders.

We managed to sit next to each other in maths lessons so they were almost enjoyable. We didn't *learn* anything, though our teacher, Miss Rashbrook, was very sweet and gentle and did her best to explain – over and over again. I could have put poor Miss Rashbrook on a loop and played her explanation twenty-four hours a day, it would have made no difference whatsoever.

Chris and I pushed our desks close and tried to do our working out together – but mostly we chatted. We daydreamed about the future. We decided we'd stay friends for ever. We even wanted to live next door to each other after we got married. We could see the row of neat suburban houses outside the window and picked out two that were ours. (I had private dreams of a more Bohemian adult life, living romantically in a London garret with an artist – but wondered if I could do that at the weekends and settle down in suburbia Monday to Friday.)

We don't live next door to each other now but we *did* stay great friends all through school and went on to technical college together. We used to go dancing and I was there the evening Chris met her future husband, Bruce. I was there at Chris's wedding; I was there – in floods of tears – at Bruce's funeral. We've always written and phoned and remembered each other's birthdays. We've been on several hilarious holidays, giggling together as if we were still schoolgirls.

Chris lived in New Malden so she went home for dinner, and at the end of school she walked one way, I walked the other, but the rest of the time we were inseparable. Chris soon asked me home to tea and this became a regular habit.

I *loved* going to Chris's house. She had a

storybook family. Her dad, Fred Keeping, was a plumber, a jolly little man who called me Buttercup. He had a budgie that perched on his shoulder and got fed titbits at meal times. Chris's mum, Hetty, was a good cook: she made Victoria sponges and jam tarts and old-fashioned latticed apple pies. We always had a healthy first course of salad, with home-grown tomatoes and cucumber and a little bit of cheese and crisps. I had to fight not to be greedy at the Keepings. I could have gone on helping myself to extra treats for hours. Chris's sister, Jan, was several years older and very clever but she chatted to me as if she was my friend too. We were all passionate about colouring. Chris and Jan shared a magnificent sharpened set of Derwent coloured pencils in seventy-two shades.

After Mrs Keeping had cleared the tea things and taken the embroidered tablecloth off the green chenille day cloth, we three girls sat up at the table and coloured contentedly. We all had historical-costume colouring books. Jan had the Elizabethans and coloured in every jewel and gem on Queen Elizabeth's attire exquisitely. Then she settled down to all her schoolwork while Chris and I went up stairs. We were supposed to be doing *our* homework up in Chris's bedroom, but we muddled through it as quickly as possible.

We did some mad projects together. For the first

two years at Coombe we did a combined history and geography lesson called 'social studies'. We learned all about prehistoric times, and made a plasticine and lolly-stick model of an early stilt village. We also started to write a long poem about a caveman family. We thought up our first line – *Many millions of years ago* – but then got stuck. We couldn't think of a rhyme for *ago*, so Chris looked up the word in Jan's rhyming dictionary. We ended up with:

> *Many millions of years ago*
> *Lived a woman who was a virago.*

perhaps the worst rhyme in many millions of years.

Mostly we simply played games like Chinese Chequers, Can You Go?, and Beetle, and made useless items with Scoubidou.

I loved Chris's bedroom, though it was very small and she didn't have anywhere near as many books as me. She had a little stable of china horse ornaments, big and small, because she longed passionately to go horse-riding, and saved up all her pocket money and birthday money for lessons. Her only other ornaments were plaster-cast Disney replicas of Snow White and the Seven Dwarfs. A few childhood teddies drooped limply on a chair, balding and button-eyed. Her clothes were mostly more childish than mine, though I hankered after her kingfisher-blue coat, a colour Biddy labelled vulgar – goodness knows why.

Chris's bedroom felt *safe*. You could curl up under her pink candlewick bedspread, read an old Blyton mystery book, and feel at peace. You wouldn't fall asleep and dream of mad men walking out of your wardrobe or monsters wriggling up from under your bed. You wouldn't wake to the sound of angry voices, shouts and sobbing. You would sleep until the old Noddy alarm clock rang and you could totter along to the bathroom in your winceyette pyjamas, the cat rubbing itself against your legs.

I'd slept at Chris's house several times, I'd been to lunch with her, I'd been to tea, I'd been on outings in their family car to Eastbourne, I'd been to Chris's birthday party, a cosy all-girls affair where we played old-fashioned games like Squeak Piggy Squeak and Murder in the Dark.

It was way past time to invite Chris back to my flat at Cumberland House. So Chris came one day after school and met Biddy and Harry. My home was so different from hers. Chris was very kind and a naturally polite girl. She said 'Thank you for having me' with seeming enthusiasm when she went home. I wonder what she *really* thought.

403

Maybe she liked it that there was no one in our flat to welcome us after school. It was fun having the freedom of the whole place, great to snack on as many chocolate biscuits as we wanted. When Biddy came home from work she cooked our tea: bacon and sausage and lots of chips, and served a whole plate of cakes for our pudding – sugary jam doughnuts, cream éclairs, meringues. Biddy considered this special-treat food and Chris nibbled her cakes appreciatively – but all that fatty food was much too rich for her sensitive stomach. She had to dash to the lavatory afterwards and was sick as discreetly as possible, so as not to offend Biddy. When Harry came home from work he was in a mood. He didn't call Chris Buttercup, he didn't say anything at all to her, just hid himself behind the *Sporting Life*.

Chris came on a sleepover once, and thank goodness everything went well. It was just like having a sister: getting ready for bed together and then whispering and giggling long into the night. We weren't woken by any rows, we slept peacefully cuddled up until the morning.'

However, Biddy and Harry couldn't always put on an amicable act. I remember when we got our first car, a second-hand white Ford Anglia. Biddy learned to drive and, surprisingly, passed her test before Harry. We decided to go on a trip to Brighton in our new car, and as a very special treat Chris was invited along too.

We sat in the back. I was dosed up with Quells, strong travel pills, so that I wouldn't be sick. They made me feel very dozy, but there was no danger of nodding off on *this* journey. Biddy and Harry were both tense about the outing and sniped at each other right from the start.

'Watch that lorry! For Christ's sake, do you want to get us all killed?' Harry hissed.

'Don't you use that tone of voice to me! And it was *his* fault, he was in the wrong ruddy lane,' said Biddy, her knuckles white on the steering wheel.

'*You're* in the wrong lane, you silly cow, if we're going to turn off at the Drift Bridge.'

'Who's driving this car, you or me? Ah, *I'm* driving because I'm the one who's passed the test!'

They chuntered on while I sat in the back with Chris, my tummy churning. I talked frantically, nattering about school and homework to try to distract her from my angry parents. I madly hoped she wouldn't even hear what they were saying. She talked back to me, valiantly keeping up the pretence, though she was very pale under her freckles.

Biddy and Harry had gone past the stage of being aware of us. We were stuck in a traffic jam going up Reigate Hill. The car started to overheat, as if reacting to its passengers. Biddy had to pull over and open the bonnet so the engine could cool down.

'It's your fault, you're driving like a maniac. You do realize you're ruining the car!' Harry said.

'If you don't like the way I drive, then *you* blooming well have a go,' said Biddy, bursting into tears.

'Oh yes, turn on the waterworks,' said Harry.

'Just shut up, will you? I'm sick of this,' Biddy sobbed. She opened her door and stumbled into the road. She ran off while we stared.

'That's so typical! Well, *I* can't ruddy well drive, as she's all too well aware,' said Harry – and *he* got out of the car, slammed the door with all his strength, and marched off in the opposite direction.

Chris and I sat petrified in the back of the car, our mouths open. Cars kept hooting as they swerved around us. I reached out for Chris's hand and she squeezed mine tight.

'You won't tell anyone at school?' I whispered.

'No, I promise,' she said. She paused. 'Jac, what if . . . what if they don't come back?'

I was wondering that myself. I couldn't drive, Chris couldn't drive. How would we ever get home? I thought about jumping out and flagging down a passing car to give us a lift. But they'd all be total strangers, it was far too dangerous. It was also obviously dangerous to be sitting in the back of a car parked at a precarious angle halfway up a hill heaving with traffic.

'They *will* come back,' I said firmly, trying to make myself believe it as well as Chris. I made my voice sound worldly wise and reassuring. 'They just need a few minutes to calm down.'

I was wondrously right. As I spoke I saw Biddy tottering back up the hill – and Harry appeared on the horizon too, strolling down towards us with his hands in his pockets. They both got back into the car as casually as if they'd just nipped out to spend a penny in the public toilets.

Biddy started up the car and we went up and over the hill, off to Brighton. Biddy and Harry barely spoke for the rest of the journey.

We had chicken and bread sauce for our lunch in a café near the beach, and then Chris and I were allowed to go off together. Biddy and Harry both gave us money. We scrunched up and down the pebbly beach, walked to the end of the pier and back, went all round the ornate pavilion, and treated ourselves to Mars bars and Spangles, two Wall's vanilla ice creams, and two portions of chips with salt and vinegar.

Heaven help us if Biddy and Harry had had another big row on the journey back. We'd have both been violently sick.

Jacqueline and Carol,
14-year-old schoolgirls

Jacqueline and Carol,
14-year-old young ladies

5
Carol

Girls' friendships are often complex. Chris was my best friend – but Carol was too. She lived in Kingston so we went home from school together, and we spent a lot of time in the holidays with each other. Both our mothers worked full-time so Carol and I spent day after day together.

I can't clearly remember going to Carol's house. I hardly knew her family. I met her mother but I can't remember her father. Carol had an older sister, Margaret, but she wasn't chatty and cosy like Jan, Chris's sister. I don't think she ever even spoke to me. Margaret looked years older than her age. She wore lots of make-up and high stiletto heels and had many boyfriends.

Carol seemed to be heading that way too. She was a dark, curvy girl with very white skin and full lips. By the time we were fourteen she could easily pass for seventeen or eighteen. She effortlessly managed all those teenage female things that I found a bit of a struggle: she plucked her eyebrows into an ironic arch, she shaved her legs smooth, she styled her hair and tied a silk scarf round it just like a film star. She was as expert as her sister with make-up, outlining her eyes and exaggerating her mouth into a moody coral pout.

Carol could be moody, full stop. I went round with her for several years but I never felt entirely at ease with her. We'd share all sorts of secrets but I always felt she was privately laughing at me, thinking me too earnest, too intense, and much too childish. Carol had two other friends, Linda and Margaret, sophisticated girls who flicked through the beauty pages of women's magazines in the lunch hour and yawned languidly because they'd been out late the night before with their boyfriends. I'd sit with the three of them each lunch time and feel utterly out of things. I'd risk a comment every now and then and catch Carol raising her immaculate eyebrows at Linda and Margaret.

She never openly criticized me, but sometimes it was the things she *didn't* say that hurt the most. I remember one time in the holidays I'd been maddened by my wispy hair straggling out of its annual perm. I'd taken myself off to a hairdresser's and asked for it to be cut really short. A few avant-garde girls were sporting urchin cuts that year and I thought they looked beautiful.

The trouble was, *I* wasn't beautiful. I was

appalled when I saw my terrible new haircut. It cruelly emphasized my glasses and my sticky-out ears. I went home and howled.

I was meeting Carol that afternoon. I felt so awful walking up to her and seeing her expression. I badly wanted her to say, 'Oh, Jacky, I love your new haircut, it really suits you.' We'd both know she was lying but it would be so comforting all the same.

Carol didn't say a word about my hair – but every now and then I caught her staring at me and shaking her head pityingly.

However, we did sometimes have great fun together. We both loved to go shopping, though neither of us had much pocket money. Kingston has always been a good town for shopping, though in 1960 Bentalls was just a big department store, not a vast shopping centre. We wandered round the make-up and clothes but we never actually bought anything there.

We had two favourite haunts, Woolworths and Maxwells. When I was fourteen, Woolworths was considered cool, a place where teenagers hung out. There was no New Look or Claire's Accessories or Paperchase or Primark or TopShop. I spent my pocket money in Woolworths. I walked straight past the toy counter now (though when Carol wasn't watching I glanced back wistfully at the little pink penny dolls) but I circled the stationery counter for hours.

It was there that I bought the red and blue sixpenny exercise books, or big fat shilling books if I was really serious about a story idea. I was forever buying pens too – red biro, blue biro, black biro, occasionally green – that was as varied as it got. There were no rollerballs, no gel pens, no felt tips. There were fountain pens but they didn't have cartridges then, so you needed a bottle of royal-blue Quink, and I always ended up with ink all over my fingers. I used to think that if I could only find the perfect notebook, the most stylish pen, my words would flow magically.

There's a little childish bit of me that still thinks that. I've got more ambitious in my taste. I thumb through beautiful Italian marbled notebooks now, trying to choose between subtle swirling blues and purples, pretty pale pinks and blues, bold scarlet with crimson leather spines and corners, wondering which is the luckiest, the one that will help me write a truly special story. I've bought a handful of expensive fountain pens, but I *still* end up with ink all over me so I generally stick to black miniballs.

I liked Woolworths jewellery too, big green or red or blue glass rings, 'emeralds' and 'rubies' and 'sapphires', for sixpence, and I loved the Indian glass bangles, treating myself to three at a time: pink and purple and blue. Biddy said it was common wearing so much jewellery at once. We'd both have been astonished to see me now, huge silver rings on every finger and bangles up to my elbows!

Monday 4 January
Met Carol in Kingston this morning. (We are still on holiday, go back to school next Wed. worst luck.) I bought a new pen from good old Woolworths, a pair of red mules, and some tomatoes for my lunch.

Woolworths sold old-lady slippers, cosy tartan with pompoms on the top, but of course I didn't want a pair of these. They were definitely grandma territory, and much as I loved Ga, I didn't want to look like her. No, these were special Chinese scarlet satin embroidered mules, incredibly exotic for those days. I was particularly keen on anything Chinese since reading a highly unsuitable adult book called *The World of Suzie Wong* by Richard Mason. Biddy might fuss excessively about the way I looked but she didn't always manage to monitor my reading matter.

Suzie Wong was a Chinese prostitute living in a

house of ill repute in Hong Kong. I thought her incredibly glamorous. I didn't necessarily want to copy her career choice, but I wished I *looked* like Suzie Wong: long straight glossy hair, and wearing a silk embroidered cheongsam split to the thighs. Both were way beyond my reach, but I *could* sport Chinese slippers from Woolworths. Well, I *couldn't* wear them actually. They were flat mules and I had the greatest difficulty keeping them on my feet. I walked straight-legged, toes clenched, but could only manage a couple of steps before walking straight out of them. I didn't care. I could simply sit with my legs stuck out and *admire* them.

We never went shopping in Kingston without going into Maxwells. It sold records. There weren't any HMV shops selling CDs in those days, let alone songs to buy on iTunes. Singles came on little '45' records in paper sleeves. They were actually doubles rather than singles, because each record had an A side (the potential chart topper), and then you flipped it over to the B side. You listened to the top twenty records in the hit parade on your little portable radio – only I didn't have one till I was fifteen, and I couldn't tune our big old-fashioned Home Service wireless to trendy Radio Luxembourg. I simply had to go to Maxwells with Carol and listen there. You told the spotty guy behind the desk that you wanted

414

to listen to several records – Carol would reel off three or four likely titles – and then he would give them to you to take into the special listening booth.

We'd squash in together and then, when we started playing the records, we'd bob up and down in an approximation of dancing and click our fingers in time to the music. We considered ourselves very hip.

Sometimes there were other girls in the next listening booth. Sometimes there were boys, and then we'd bob and click a little more and toss our heads about. Sometimes there were older men, often comic stereotype leery old men in dirty raincoats. They'd peer through the window at us, their breath blurring the glass. We'd raise our eyebrows and turn our backs, not too worried because we were together.

We rarely *bought* a record. We played them several times and then slipped them back into their sleeves and returned them to the spotty boy.

'Sorry, we can't quite make up our minds,' we'd chorus, and saunter out.

Up until January 1960 I didn't even have a record player so it would have been a pointless purchase anyway. We had my grandparents' gramophone, one of those old-fashioned wind-up machines with a horn, but it wouldn't play modern

45 records. We had a pile of fragile 78s, that shattered if you dropped them, and I had my childhood Mandy Miller records, 'The Teddy Bears' Picnic', 'Doing the Lambeth Walk', and some Victor Silvester dance music. They weren't really worth the effort of strenuous handle-winding. But on 9 January everything changed.

I did the shopping with Dad and you'll never guess what we bought! A RECORD PLAYER! It had previously been £28 but had been marked down to £16. It is an automatic kind and plays beautifully. We bought 'Travelling Light' by Cliff Richard and Dad chose a Mantovani long player. It sounds very square but actually it is quite good with some nice tunes like 'Tammy', 'Que Sera Sera', 'Around the World in 80 Days'. I've been playing them, and all our old 78 records, all the afternoon.

I know, I know – Cliff Richard! But this wasn't the elderly Christian Cliff, this was when he was young and wild, with sideburns and tousled hair, wearing white teddy-boy jackets and tight black drainpipe trousers, very much an English Elvis, though he was never really as raunchy as Presley. I remember Celia, a lovely gentle girl in my class who was very into pop music. Her mother was too, surprisingly.

'My mum says she'd like to put Cliff to bed and tuck him up tight and give him a goodnight kiss – and she'd like to put Elvis to bed and get in beside him!' said Celia, chuckling.

Celia knew the words to every single pop song and would sometimes obligingly write them out for me in her beautiful neat handwriting. I would solemnly learn every single *bam-a-wham-bam* and *doobie-doobie-do* and also try hard to copy Celia's stylish script. There are passages in my diary where I'm trying out different styles, and it's clear when I'm doing my best to copy Celia.

I saved up my pocket money to buy another record the very next week: Michael Holliday's 'Starry Eyed'. It was currently Carol's favourite song and so we could do a duet together, though neither of us could sing to save our lives.

I didn't buy another record until March, when I decided on the theme tune from *A Summer Place,* a very sugary recording, all swirly violins, but I declared it 'lovely'. I had no musical taste whatsoever at fourteen. I'm astonished to see I next bought a Max Bygraves record, 'Fings Ain't Wot They Used t'Be'. I can hardly bear to write those words on the page!

By August I was staying up late on Saturday nights listening to David Jacobs's *Pick of the Pops*, and hearing 'Tell Laura I Love Her' by Ricky Valance for the first time. I *adored* 'Tell Laura'. It was like a modern ballad poem, a tragic sentimental song about a boy called Tommy trying to win a stockcar race in order to buy his girl a diamond ring. Each verse had a chorus of *'Tell Laura I love her'* – and of course Tommy's dying words from his wrecked car were *'Tell Laura I love her'*. I didn't take the song *seriously* but loved singing it over and over again in a lugubrious voice until Biddy screamed at me to stop that stupid row *now*.

Thank goodness my taste developed a little over the next year – in the summer of 1961 I discovered traditional jazz. I fell in love with all the members of the Temperance Seven, a stylish crowd of ex-art students who dressed in Edwardian costume. 'Whispering' Paul McDowell sang through a horn to make an authentic tinny sound. It was the sort of music my grandparents must once have played on their wind-up gramophone, but it seemed mint-new and marvellous to me: 'I bought Pasadena, it's an absolutely fab record and I've now played it at least 50 times.'

I went to see the Temperance Seven at Surbiton Assembly Rooms, and when I was sixteen I used to go up to London to various jazz cafés in Soho with a boyfriend. That was way in the future though. I might manage to just about *pass* for sixteen when I wanted to get into an A film at the cinema – but I certainly didn't act it.

Jacqueline with film star Jack Hawkins

TROY DONAHUE

AUDREY HEPBURN

CLIFF RICHARD

SANDRA DEE

NORMAN WISDOM

6
Films

I went to so many films – most of them pretty dire too! There were lots of cinemas in Kingston then, but each only had one screen. The Granada and the Regal and the Empire were all perfectly respectable, but Kingston Kinema was a total fleapit. It showed arty, less mainstream films, and we sometimes went there too, though we weren't supposed to.

The Kinema attracted Dirty Old Men – far dirtier than the ones who hung around Maxwells music shop. The pitch-black of the Kinema made them bold. They'd shuffle along the empty rows and sit right next to you. You'd strain as far away from them as possible, staring up at the screen, heart thumping. You'd keep telling yourself it was going to be fine, he wouldn't *do* anything, but then a clammy hand, repulsive as a jellyfish, would slither onto your knee. You'd jerk your knee away from it, trembling, but you knew that hand would come back. Sometimes it changed into a crab and tried to scuttle underneath your skirt. Then at long long last this would galvanize you into action and you'd grab your friend and sidle down the row away from him.

Why on earth did we put up with this? Why didn't we complain loudly and go and find an usherette? We were all as hopeless as each other – Carol, Chris, all my other friends: we sat paralysed with shame and fear while these hateful men dabbed at us disgustingly. It was as if *we'd* done something bad and embarrassing. We might joke about it afterwards, even getting fits of the giggles, but at the time it was terrifying.

So why did we *go* to the Kinema? Well, we wanted to see those arty movies, a lot of them X-rated. They would probably be considered very bland kids' stuff nowadays. We were so totally innocent, even a Cliff Richard film could shock us. We all wanted to see his new film, *Expresso Bongo*, because it was set in Soho where all the strip joints were.

Friday 22 January
In the evening I went to see 'Expresso Bongo' with Carol at the Regal. We saw tons of girls from school there, all dressed up pretending to be sixteen. Jill, Susan and Joyce were there in the 'ninepennies' and Jill told me afterwards that she had seen Peter there and he had smiled at her. She also said that Joyce had asked Susan and her to club together and

buy some cigarettes. They reluctantly agreed, but
Susan wouldn't smoke any. Jill had three and
wasn't very impressed, but Joyce finished the lot
off! I think she's only 13!
P.S. 'Expresso Bongo' was very good.

I was too shy to write in my diary about the
astonishing scene set in a Soho club where you saw
topless showgirls. There was an audible gasp from
the cinema audience as this line of girls jiggled
across the screen. They weren't even entirely
topless: they had little stars in pertinent places,
presumably stuck on. It must have been pretty
painful removing them each night.

You didn't get topless models in newspapers
in 1960, not the papers we had at home anyway.
You didn't get girly magazines openly displayed on
newsagents' shelves either. The only bare breasts
I'd ever seen were on African women in the *National
Geographic* magazine. Those *Expresso Bongo* girls
made a big impression on all of us. We talked about
them excitedly at school the next morning.

Mostly our film-going was a lot less adventurous.
I seemed very easy to please. On Monday 4 January
I went to see Tommy Steele in *Tommy the Toreador*
and pronounced this film 'very good.' The next day
I saw Norman Wisdom in *Follow a Star*, which I

said was 'very funny'. You would have to tie me to my seat to get me to watch either film now.

Carol and I went to the pictures two or three times a week in the holidays. We went after school too, sometimes with Sue and Cherry. They lived in Kingston too. Sue literally lived next door to me, at number eleven Cumberland House, where we'd both lived since we were six.

This was 'a better class of council estate', according to my mother – and she did her level best to bring me up a better class of child. Sue's mother, Nancy, was equally ambitious for her daughter. No other children in Cumberland House had such white socks and blouses, such polished brown sandals, such expensive school satchels.

Sue and Nancy had heated arguments nowadays. Nancy wouldn't let Sue use make-up and still liked her to wear smocked Viyella dresses with long blue socks and flat shoes, whereas we were all allowed lipstick and eyeshadow, nylons and little heels. Sue secretly used her birthday money on her own lipstick and nylons and spent two minutes in the ladies' toilets each time she went out, turning herself into a teenager.

Cherry lived in a flat too, but it was part of a very large house further down the road. When she was a little girl she'd had a pageboy haircut, but now she had a blonde ponytail that bounced as she walked. Cherry was part of a different teenage world altogether. She went riding, she joined a tennis club, she sang in amateur Gilbert and Sullivan productions. (Biddy perversely sneered at these harmless middle-class hobbies.)

I'd been friends with Sue and Cherry when we were children but they'd gone to different secondary schools. However, now we were in the third year (Year Nine), Coombe had expanded and Sue and Cherry started going there too.

Thursday 4 February
After school I went to the pictures with Sue and Cherry. Carol still has a chill. It was 'Please Turn Over', and all three of us enjoyed it very much. Julia Lockwood was in it who I quite like. In the film she wrote a book called 'Naked Revolt' about her suburban family, with some shocking results. It showed you excerpts from the book, and I would have given anything to have been able to read it. The other film was good too; it was called 'The Desperate Man'. Conrad Phillips (William Tell) was in it, and also a very attractive girl called Jill Ireland.

You got good value for money going to the

pictures in 1960. There were always two films, the main feature film and then a shorter film, usually a thriller. In between you got Pathé News, introduced by a noisy cockerel, and a ten-minute documentary called *Look at Life*. If you had nothing else to do, you could sit there in your red plush seat watching the entire programme all over again. You'd only have to get up when they played the National Anthem. It sounds so strange now, but they truly did play 'God Save the Queen' after every cinema performance, and everyone stood to attention, looking solemn.

Thursday 11 February
After school I dashed home and changed, slapped some powder and lipstick on my face, called for Sue, and then we went to the flicks. We met Carol there and saw 'A Summer Place' with Sandra Dee and Troy Donahue. It was quite good, but a little too dramatic. Everyone seemed to have a love affair with someone else, and crept hand in hand to the boat house, beach or park respectively. It was rather like a women's magazine story, taking you to the bedroom door and no further.

I don't think I knew much about what happened

behind the bedroom door at fourteen, but I wanted to sound sophisticated.

I nearly always went to the pictures with my friends. Harry had taken me when I was a little girl but we didn't go anywhere together now. I *did* occasionally go with Biddy:

Saturday 13 February
Mum said she wanted to see the film 'The Reluctant Debutante' so we went together. On the way we went into the Bentalls' record department. I saw P. Wilson and Y. McCarthy in turquoise duffel coats, extremely tight jeans and cha-cha shoes being cuddled by a group of horrible spotty teddy boys. 'The Reluctant Debutante' was very good, and Mum and I also enjoyed the other film 'Watusi' very much.

Oh dear, it would have been *so* much cooler to be wearing a duffel coat and tight jeans and cuddling a teddy boy rather than going to the cinema with my mum.

The following Saturday I 'went to see "Pillow Talk" with Carol and Sue'. *Pillow Talk sounds* sophisticated, but it was a frothy comedy. I vastly preferred the next film I saw, *The Nun's Story*, with Audrey Hepburn. Audrey made thousands of

427

girls decide they wanted to be nuns, although sadly no *real* nun ever looked so ethereally exquisite in her veil and wimple. I fell in love with Audrey like everyone else, but the nun's vow of obedience appalled me.

Monday 22 February
In the evening I met Carol and we went to see 'The Nun's Story'. It was a really wonderful film, one of the best I've seen. It showed you what a nun's life is really like. I know one thing, and that is that I would never make a good nun, not even a makeshift one. Never, never could I have such sheer obedience; if I think I am right I cannot obey humbly but I must argue my point. But humility is the quality I lack most. If anyone says anything humiliating to me, something inside me is hurt and angry and tells me to hit back at that person with cutting remarks. Besides, I could not bear a life minus men and children.

I saw delicious melodramas like *Conspiracy of Hearts* with Carol – but occasionally I went to a comedy with Chris. We saw *Please Don't Eat the Daisies* – and sang '*Please, please,* don't *eat the daisies*' up and down Coombe's corridors for weeks afterwards. We had a lovely cosy day when we went to see *School for Scoundrels*.

Thursday 19 May
I went home with Chris at dinner time. It was raining, and we had to wait for 4 buses. When we eventually got to the Keepings' we were absolutely <u>drenched</u>. For dinner we had liver, baked beans, cauliflower and new potatoes; then rhubarb and evaporated milk! <u>Very nice</u>! Then we did our maths together, and then caught the train to Kingston, and saw 'School for Scoundrels'. It was very funny, but Chris and I laughed far more at the other film which was meant to be VERY SERIOUS. The main character was called Julian Caesar, his best friend Marc Antony, another friend Brutus, his girlfriend Portia, and his enemy Cassius. <u>How daft</u>.

It could well have been a brilliant contemporary reworking of Shakespeare but clearly it didn't work for us! We must have infuriated everyone sitting near us, going giggle giggle giggle, but only half the audience seemed interested in watching the film:

Sitting in front of us were these girls and teds snogging (if you'll pardon the vulgar expression)

79

*and Chris and I are positive that one of them (the
one on the end without a boy) was Jennifer D!*

Oh dear, how awful to be the one on the end
without a boy!

I wasn't a particularly religious girl, but I adored
the film *The Ten Commandments*. In an age long
before videos and DVDs it was a rare treat to find
a film repeated after its original release. I saw *The
Ten Commandments* was on again at the cinema
and begged Carol to go with me.

It was extremely long, but we watched
enraptured. It was filmed very solemnly, with
the actors frequently standing still as if in a
tableau, gesturing bizarrely, but we soon got used
to that. It was very stirring when they were
building the pyramids and Moses saved the old
woman – she's actually his real mother but he
didn't know this.

The colours of *The Ten Commandments* were so
rich and beautiful and the miracles themselves
seemed wondrous. In our age of computer-
generated trickery the parting of the Red Sea would
probably seem pretty pathetic – but I held my
breath when Charlton Heston made his way
through those waves. The whole cinema whispered,
'*How did they* do *that?*'

The film was about the very good and the very

bad – and I'm afraid I was mostly on the bad guy's side. I thought irreverently that the film's Voice of God was a little like the voice of the Wizard of Oz. I quite liked Charlton Heston as Moses but I vastly preferred his enemy, Yul Brynner, playing bald, sexy Rameses, who was unhappily married to dark, scheming Nefertiri. She was one hundred per cent a baddie, a callous murderer, but Anne Baxter, who played her, was so beautiful that I thought her wonderful. I didn't want to be blonde Susan Wooldridge any more. I wanted to be dark and sultry with long shiny black hair and crimson lips.

I went to some classic adaptations with the wrong attitude entirely. Carol and I hadn't read D. H. Lawrence's *Sons and Lovers* (and *Lady Chatterley's Lover* hadn't even been published yet) but we thought it would be pretty sexy. We watched the film restlessly and grew impatient at the end.

'What a swizzle. It wasn't a *bit* sexy,' I said. 'I don't think much of D. H. Lawrence.'

But sometimes these adaptations worked wonders.

Saturday 23 July
In the afternoon I went to the flicks again, this time with Sue, and saw 'Wuthering Heights', on at the

Kinema. It was very good, and at the end I could hear Sue sniffling away as if her heart was broken. I think I will read the book, as it is one of the classics Miss Pierce told us to read.

I read it that summer, waking up early every morning and reading for hours until I reached that beautiful last paragraph.

7

Books

I read voraciously right through my teens. I didn't read teenage books: there were no such things in those days. Well, there *was* a small shelf in the library labelled TEENAGE BOOKS, but they were dull-as-ditchwater career books with ridiculous titles like *Donald is a Dentist* and *Vera is a Vet*. Donald and Vera were barely characterized and there was no plot whatsoever. Each book was a dreary account of how to pursue the relevant career. I didn't want to give people fillings or spay cats so I left them gathering dust on the shelf. (I *might* have been tempted by *Jacky is a Journalist*.)

I read children's books up to the age of eleven or so and then I switched to adult books. I didn't just read classics like *Wuthering Heights,* of course. I read all sorts of books – some trashy, some tremendous, some wildly unsuitable.

I spent most of my pocket money on paperbacks and borrowed three books from the library every week, sometimes twice a week. If I was particularly interested or irritated by a book I wrote about it in my diary, but sadly I didn't record every book I read. That would have been like writing 'Today I brushed my teeth with Colgate toothpaste', something I simply took for granted as part of my daily life.

I had various favourite books and I read these again and again. I kept my bright pink Pan paperback of *The Diary of Anne Frank* on my bedside table, with a carefully cut-out photograph of Anne pinned above my bed. The Holocaust had happened less than twenty years before. I could barely take it in. It seemed so unbelievably terrible that Anne and six million others had lost their lives because they were Jews.

I thought of her as a martyr but she was certainly no saint. I loved reading the passages in her diary when she complained bitterly about her mother and longed for a proper boyfriend. But as I said in the first chapter, it was her diary entries about writing that meant the most to me and I learned them by heart. I mentioned my other all-time favourite book in the first chapter too: *I Capture the Castle* by Dodie Smith.

It's the story of Cassandra and her sister Rose, living in poverty in a dilapidated castle with their writer father and eccentric stepmother, Topaz; then two rich American brothers come to live nearby . . .

It sounds absolute toffee, a ridiculous romantic fairytale, but trust me, it's a wonderful book and Cassandra is such an endearing and compelling narrator that you are swept into the story and believe every single word of it.

I didn't just envy Cassandra her two-guinea red-leather notebook. I wanted to dab myself with her bluebell scent and drink green crème de menthe and swim in a moat at midnight.

I loved reading *sad* stories. I found *The Wind Cannot Read* wondrously moving:

Tuesday 2 February
Morris and Iris [friends of Biddy's] *have lent me 'The Wind Cannot Read', by Richard Mason, author of my favourite 'The World of Suzie Wong'. I'm enjoying it very much at the moment.*

Wednesday 3 February
I finished reading 'The Wind Cannot Read'. It is a lovely book, but very sad at the end. I almost cried, and I'm definitely not the sentimental type.

I'm sure I'd remain dry-eyed if I ever tried to plough through it now, but one book that would still make me cry is *The Story of Gabrielle*.

Tuesday 23 February
I went to the library and got 3 books. I have finished
one already called 'The Story of Gabrielle'. It is a
wonderful story of a truly amazing child who dies
of cancer. It is very moving, and I really love and
admire Gabby.

The Story of Gabrielle was beautifully and
movingly written by Gabrielle's mother. I own it
now but can't even bring myself to look at it
because I find it unbearable to read about the death
of a child, maybe because I've known so many
special children who have died of cancer. Over the
years I've made many visits to sick children who
have written to me. They are always very brave so
I try hard to be brave too, though when I get home
I often cry.

I know *I* sometimes write sad books now. I wept
when I wrote *Kiss* – and I cried and cried when I
wrote the last chapter of *My Sister Jodie*. I tried
hard not to let *Vicky Angel* be too upsetting, even
though it was very sad. I cut out one of the early
chapters, with detailed descriptions of Vicky
in hospital.

I was certainly wary of hospital scenes in fiction
back in 1960:

Wednesday 3 February
I carried on reading [after finishing *The Wind Cannot Read*] *'Not As a Stranger', but I'm not going to read it any more. First it told you about digging a boil out of a neck and the pus etc. etc., and it made me feel sick, and then a little boy cuts off his w— with a razor blade. Ugh! I very nearly was sick then, and I'm not going near the horrible book again.*

I read historical fiction too. I had a thing about Queen Elizabeth I in my early teens and read anything I could find about her and the times she lived in.

Wednesday 20 January
I got a good book out of the library called 'Young Bess' by Margaret Irwin. It is all about Elizabeth 1st when she was about 12–15. She wasn't half advanced for her age! There is a portrait of her in the book painted when she was 13. She looked at least 18! Also Tom Seymour, a man of over thirty, was in love with her! I can't imagine a man loving me like that at this age.

Thursday 21 January
I'm enjoying 'Young Bess' very much. It makes you

think of Elizabeth as if she was still living. The book is very witty, but you have to use your brains to understand the jokes.

Tuesday 17 May
After school I went to the library. I got a very interesting book about Elizabethans. I specially enjoyed the chapters about cosmetics and ailments. It's amazing that the Elizabethans managed to live at all! They used to put cerise (white lead) on face, neck and chest, which slowly turned the skin withered, and gave the women gastro-intestinal diseases and palsy. They put rouge on cheeks and lips that simply ate into the flesh after a time. Also, if they had scars, spots or freckles they put on this ointment that destroyed all skin tissue, which, naturally, left horrible scars. So the Elizabethans put on more and more ointment to get rid of the scars until they had hardly any skin left at all.

I wished we studied the Elizabethans in history. I sat next to a funny, lively, dark-haired girl called Jill in history lessons and we bonded terrifically when she said she hero-worshipped Elizabeth too.

Tuesday 1 March
Had double History. Mr Stokes looked at Jill's library
book and roared with laughter when he saw it was
entitled 'Lovers of my Lord Admiral'. Jill explained
that she was an Elizabeth fan, and when Mr S. looked
at my book and saw it was 'The Bright Pavilions'
(an Eliz. Book) he realised I was too.

Jill was more flexible than me when it came to
periods of history.

Friday 12 February
Jill lent me a book 'Our Dearest Emma' by Lozania
Prole. Never have I read a book in which there are
so many different romances. I am sure Emy, when
she was alive, found it difficult to keep track of so
many bedfellows.

Biddy didn't mind me reading about historical
bed-hopping, but she did fuss about contemporary
sexy books. Sandra, a girl I knew at dancing
classes, told me that '*Peyton Place* was a shocking
book, her friend had showed it to her at school. I
asked Mum if I could read it but she said wait till
you're 16.'

441

I didn't waste time arguing. I knew Biddy wouldn't let me buy it and I wasn't sure the staid librarians in Kingston library would let me check it out. So I secretly borrowed *Peyton Place* from Sandra.

Wednesday 13 April
This morning I phoned Cherry to arrange about the flicks, and then spent a good half hour reading 'Peyton Place' which is <u>strictly taboo</u>. As I flipped through I found the interesting bits Sandra referred to, but oh, what a storm in a teacup! The parts about Alison's adolescence are a little boring, as in thousands of books it mentions, sometimes being far more frank, these things. I thought Stella conceiving her stepfather's baby a little peculiar, but when it told you about Betty's seduction, and her tight shorts being easy to slip off, well, I thought it sheer trash. In fact I had a good laugh to think that sensible adults are 'shocked' by this 'outspoken book'. I think my dear parents would get a shock if they knew some of the books I read that are far worse.

Thursday 14 April
This morning I finished skimming through 'Peyton Place'. It went on in the same manner as before, ending up when Alison finally launches upon 'The

Fate Worse Than Death', and discovers that she loves Peyton Place and is no longer afraid of it.

The next day was Good Friday – and I wanted something else to keep me going all over the Easter weekend. My longest book was *Gone with the Wind*, over a thousand pages, but for some reason I'd lent it to Uncle Ron – Biddy's friend, not a real uncle.

Friday 15 April
I phoned Ron up to ask him if he was coming over on Saturday. He said he definitely was so I asked if he would return my book 'Gone with the Wind' when he came. He promised he would, then I rang off after chattering a little. I hope he does remember to bring it as I am stuck over the weekend without any books to read, as I have either finished my library books or else they're boring. I cannot bear persevering with a book when I don't like it.

Re-reading *Gone with the Wind* kept me going right through Easter and beyond. I guzzled my chocolate eggs and then tried to suck my tummy in, sighing over Scarlett O'Hara's minuscule waist. I didn't envy her any of her men. I didn't even care for Rhett Butler – but I *did* envy Scarlett her green velvet gown and all her rustling petticoats.

Ga and Biddy and I all unusually agreed that *Gone with the Wind* was a great read. We all also liked Monica Dickens.

Friday 8 April
I finished reading 'Joy and Josephine' by Monica Dickens. It was a <u>very</u> good book, with a really smashing plot.

I spent the day at my grandma's on 20 April, helping her with the spring cleaning at Fassett Road.

Ga armed me with a ladder, a rag, and a bucket of hot water and Flash. I washed down all the upstairs doors and frameworks, then all the banisters, both the landing and the stairs, and the cupboard door, and all that enormous panel, and in all the little crevices where dirt miraculously collects. Ga was very pleased, and paid me 4 bob! Then after a fish and chips lunch (home cooked) Ga and I lay out in the sun in deckchairs. My, it was as warm as the middle of Summer. I stayed out there so long that

I regretfully finished reading a very funny book. 'One Pair of Feet' by Monica Dickens.

I met Monica Dickens many years later, when we were both judging a children's writing competition, and I shyly told her how much I'd enjoyed her books. She was lovely to me, but a terrible stickler for correct grammar and punctuation while judging those children's stories, worse than any teacher!

Ga owned very few books herself, and she didn't belong to the public library. She had a subscription to Boots library and fed her reading habit that way. Sometimes she lent me her library books too.

My father brought me books from Westminster library. He worked at the nearby Treasury. He was such a strange man. He could be so moody and unpredictable, losing his temper violently and then sulking, sometimes for weeks. He rarely chatted with me and never tried to understand me – and yet he had an unerring knack for picking out unusual books for me that I *loved*.

It was through Harry that I discovered Rumer Godden, a favourite author of mine for many years. He brought *The River* home for me first, a beautiful bittersweet story of a family in India, narrated by thirteen-year-old Harriet, who wants to be a writer.

It took me a few pages to get into the story. I was a little dismayed to see the Latin declensions and conjugations for *love* and *war* on the first page. I hated Latin lessons even more than maths – but wonderfully, Harriet seemed equally hopeless at Latin.

I read *The River* over and over, begging Harry to renew it for me. He then found Rumer Godden's *The Greengage Summer* on the library shelves, and I liked this even more. I identified with Cecil this time and suffered painfully with her. I was angry with her elder sister, Joss. I envied Joss her beauty and confidence. I especially envied her because Eliot was attracted to her. I adored Eliot, even when it turned out he was a criminal.

The Greengage Summer was a story about children but it was told in the most adult way. It was wonderful when I bought my own copy with my pocket money. I could read it whenever I wanted. I soon knew the first paragraph off by heart. It starts: 'On and off, all that hot French August, we made ourselves ill from eating the greengages' – and on and off, all that year when I was fourteen in 1960, I read that book until it seeped into my soul.

I don't think I've ever read as widely as I did then. If I particularly liked a library book I'd copy out appealing passages and then stick them into my diary.

Wednesday 30 March
I got a good book from the library called 'Dress Rehearsal' by Monica Sterling. Parts of it are boring, but the rest is very, very good. I like chapter seven best, about Olive, an Irish girl, who first obtained Jocelyn's admiration by shouting at her teacher 'Oh you and your damn Girl Guides.'

There are then two pages of weeny biro writing to remind me why I liked it so much. It looks embarrassingly mawkish now.

However, I did occasionally show good taste in literature. Harry bought a copy of Vladimir Nabokov's *Lolita*, a very controversial literary novel much tutted over in Biddy's *Daily Mail*. It was the story of a middle-aged man who runs away with a twelve-year-old girl, a subject justifiably considered shocking. I was told I was far too young to read it. Harry started it at once but gave up after the first chapter.

'It's not really my sort of thing,' he said, and handed it over to Biddy. I wrote in my diary: 'At the moment Mummy is sitting with her nose buried in the book taking in every word!' There were rather too many obscure baroque words for Biddy's taste. She abandoned *Lolita* just a few pages in too.

'It's stupid, all this fancy stuff. You can't tell

what he's on about,' she said. She skimmed through the book, pausing here and there. 'There doesn't seem anything in it anyway.'

'Then can *I* read it?' I asked.

'No, you can't! And you wouldn't understand a word of it anyway,' said Biddy.

Again I didn't argue. I waited until I was in our flat on my own, and then I flew to the bookcase and started reading – and reading and reading and reading. It was a revelation. I hadn't known language could be used in such a rich and elegant way. I whispered each sentence, tasting the words on my tongue.

I knew I simply *had* to read the whole novel. I was a fast reader but I couldn't possibly whiz through it before Biddy came home from work. The dust jacket was a distinct brown, with the word LOLITA in enormous capitals on the front. The solution was simple. I took the cover off, and swapped it for a Catherine Cookson novel of a similar size.

I took my disguised copy of *Lolita* everywhere, reading it at the tea table, on the bus, in the playground. If any of my friends glanced curiously over my shoulder, they didn't see anything on the page to make them gasp or giggle. It wasn't a so-called 'dirty book', one to pass round with all the rude pages carefully marked with old bus tickets. Humbert and Lolita were alarmingly *real*.

448

Lolita was very like some of the tough, pretty, scary girls at school and I thought I understood why Humbert was so enchanted by her. I wasn't particularly shocked, just enormously interested. It's strange, nowadays I find the whole story so troubling, so distressingly offensive, that I can't bear to read it. I strongly recommend that you don't read it either. It's truly not a book for children.

Very occasionally a child *wrote* a book that got published. When I was nine or ten I'd enjoyed reading Pamela Brown's *The Swish of the Curtain*, written in her early teens. I was very impressed – but there was a good five-year gap between us then. But that June when I was fourteen I borrowed a book called *Strange Evil* from the library.

Monday 13 June
At the moment I'm reading a book by a fourteen-year-old, Jane Gaskell. The girl's a genius. She must be terribly mature for her age: I won't be ready to attempt to write a book for at least another four years.

I don't know why I wrote that. I seemed to be starting to write a book almost every week of 1960 – starting, but never finishing!

8
Writing

I was often inspired to write by the book I was currently reading.

Saturday 16 January
I did a little homework like a good girl and then read some more of 'I Capture the Castle' by Dodie Smith. It is a very good book. I also started writing a story. It has its possibilities.

Sunday 17 January
I continued writing my story. I'm quite pleased with it. The trouble is that I'm neglecting my homework because of it.

I wish I'd said what the story was *about*. I wrote hundreds of thousands of words when I was twelve, thirteen, fourteen, fifteen . . . and they've nearly all vanished now. I threw them out myself, ashamed because they were so childish, so awkward, so derivative. Biddy frequently had a purge of my

451

possessions too in one of her regular spring cleans. Once or twice as I got older she sneakily read something that infuriated or offended her in my diaries and journals and notebooks and she threw them down the rubbish chute.

However, she didn't ever throw any of my writing away if it was in a school notebook, so *The Story of Latina* survived. Maybe Biddy thought it was an English project rather than my own private scribbling. I think I'd probably stolen the big blue notebook from the school stationery cupboard.

At the top of the first page I wrote in capitals 'A BOOK OF TEN STORIES FOR TEENAGERS' which seemed overly ambitious. I only managed thirteen pages and three lines of the first story, and that was mostly preliminary passages before Latina herself came into the story. *Latina!* Why did I make up such a weird name? I didn't like Latin, I hated it. I suppose Latina was one stage better than Mathematica! I just had time for a detailed description of Latina before I lost interest in the story.

Her eyes gazed into his, a soft, intelligent bright blue, which reminded him very much of the sea for although they were now calm and peaceful they had tints of violet, green, grey and black which showed

452

they could change colour in accordance to her mood.
They appeared big in her pointed sensitive face
which was framed with a tumble of dark straight
hair that fell in a cascade past her shoulders. She
was of average height as far as he could judge, and
slim. Her skin was a golden tan and she wore a
faded cotton dress.

I rather think I must have based Latina on a
clay model of a girl's head that I'd had as a holiday
present from St Ives. I called *her* Tasmania
(goodness knows why – I think I just wanted it to
sound exotic) and kept her on my bedside table.
While I did my homework or wrote my stories, my
hand would reach out and I'd stroke Tasmania's
shiny black hair, smooth her arched clay eyebrows,
and finger her pointed chin.

Now here she was, re-christened with an even
odder name and given an indeterminate age. I had
her at fourteen at first, but I clearly intended her
to have a full-blooded romance with my hero so I
added another three years to make it more
respectable.

I called my hero Alan. I was still feeling very
fond of the Alan who had been my boyfriend when
I was in Year Six at Latchmere, my primary school.
My fictional Alan was a grown man, not a young

boy, and, as the opening pages make clear, going through a pretty traumatic time. I'll embarrass myself and give you another quote:

As soon as Alan found out, after thinking for a while and knowing that he could not keep it a secret, he notified the authorities and then returned home. He undressed and had a shower and a shave, and redressed in clean underwear, clean blue open-necked shirt and navy trousers, and an old windcheater. His socks were also clean, and his sandals well polished. A knife in a sheath was fixed to his belt, a comb, handkerchief, map, wallet and some chocolate went into his trouser pockets and his windcheater pockets were filled with a packet of sandwiches, and two bottles, one containing brandy and one of plain water. He then packed a small case with a change of clothes, pyjamas and washing things.

He glanced around at his small flat littered with possessions, and a surge of affection for it rose in his breast. He moved towards the mantelpiece and tenderly picked up a photo of an attractive, smiling girl and kissed it. Then he replaced it gently and moved slowly towards the door. What would Barbara say when she knew, he wondered? What would they all say? He paused with his hand on the door knob. Suddenly he leant on the wall and closed his eyes. Yes, what would his friends say? Would they despise him, use his name as a revolting word? He pressed his knuckles against his eyes so that all he could see was a revolving whirl of darkness. Through this he could clearly see the faces of his friends, Barbara, his boss, his parents. All were pointing at him, accusing him, wrinkling their noses in distaste. Was it so terrible? Did it make all that difference? He savagely gnawed at his knuckle. All right, he would show them. Damn them all, what did they matter? What did anyone matter? Barbara floated into his mind, and a sob rose in his throat and choked him. Never again would he be able to hold her in his arms, or never firmly shake a man's hand. Thinking of hand shakes he tentatively glanced down at his own hand, his right one. A tear glistened for an instant on his tanned cheek, but it was wiped away as quickly as it had come. The clock struck the hour. Alan straightened himself, his ears strained to the door. Sure enough, just as the nine chimes had died away there came a long firm ringing on the doorbell. Although his face was now pale, it was composed. He took a quick last glance around the room, and then flung open the door. There stood two burly men dressed in black suits, shirts, shoes and hats. Alan swallowed,

455

picked up his case, and then stepped on to the landing and closed the front door behind him. 'I am ready,' he said almost inaudibly. The men put on black rubber gloves and then stood either side of Alan holding his arms in their firm cruel grasp. They marched him slowly along the streets to the city's dock. As they went passers by stood and stared and the youths laughed and shouted in derision. Alan clenched his teeth and tried to shut his eyes to the jeers. A few of the onlookers felt sorry for this brave handsome young man who stood so erect, and whose set face did not give way to his grief. Only a few days ago he had been one of those ordinary people, who now stood and stared at him. But he had never been one of the mob of onlookers because he had felt only pity for the miserable wretches taken by the black police. One of the youths threw a stone, and its sharp edge cut Alan's cheek. He flinched, but his face was still set. Whatever happened his pride would not let him relax his face from the composed mask, or to falter his steady step, although his mind was in a terrible ferment. Oh God, he thought, let it be over soon. Let me get on the boat. Oh God, let this Hellish walk be over soon. The black police's hands gripped right into his arms bruising the flesh, and the blood from the cut started to trickle down his cheek.

OK, let's play guessing games. Why has poor Alan in his clean outfit, old windcheater and polished sandals (!) been manhandled onto this boat by the black police? After passing out on the boat all night Alan regains consciousness in the morning.

When Alan awoke the first thing he saw was three eyes staring into his. He started, and realised that his life with The Disease had begun. Just as there had been Bubonic Plague in the Middle Ages, in the twentieth century there was also a disease, but in many ways a more deadly one although it did not cause death, and was not infectious. It was a disease which, if one caught it, would make one grow another part of the body. In Alan's case it was not so bad because he had only grown another finger on his right hand, but others grew another leg, arm, eyes, nose, ear, sometimes even another head. The authorities formed a party of men called the black police named thus because of their black uniform, who were responsible for finding the disformed men and women. The men were sent to a far off island to the west and the women to a far off island in the east. They were not allowed to go to the same island because a man and a woman might fall in love and have children who would naturally be disformed. The authorities naturally had to be very careful about this, because if it was allowed to happen there might become a whole race of badly disformed people.

This seems a startling idea for me to have thought up. I'd be quite proud if it was original – but I'd read John Wyndham's brilliant science fiction book *The Chrysalids*, where the characters also sprout extra digits or endure other deformities and are rounded up and sent to the badlands. John Wyndham manages to make his scenario convincing. A few of his characters discover they can read each other's thoughts. This has always seemed such an appealing idea that from time to time I've tried to do this with people I'm very close to, even though it's probably scientifically impossible.

Perhaps it was just as well I didn't develop the relationship between my six-fingered Alan and sensitive Latina or we'd all get the giggles. I don't think I *ever* finished a story when I was fourteen, but it didn't stop me trying again and again. On 5 February I wrote: 'Cherry sold me a lovely black file for only a bob.' A bob was slang for a shilling – that's 5p in today's money. 'I'm going to get cracking on a new story now.'

I was always happy to do any kind of writing, even English essay homework.

Friday 19 February
Miss Pierce was the only one to give us weekend homework; all the other teachers let us off because next Monday and Tuesday are half-term. Luckily I adore English Essay so I'm not complaining, but it's a damn shame for the others. The subject is 'The Village Street' and Miss P requests some vivid description. I wish we had a really decent subject to write about, most of my essays have to be so childish. Oh, how I long to get a book published, just to show Miss P. I have one in mind at the moment, a rather sordid story about teenagers. I long to shock Miss P and show her that her quiet shy Jacky isn't what she thinks she is.

I used the word 'damn', which sounds quaint now, but when I was fourteen it was the worst four-letter word any of us used out loud (though we might whisper or spell out the really bad ones).

When I was a little girl I took great delight in buying fashion pattern books with my pocket money. I'd cut out all the particularly interesting girls and ladies and invent elaborate games for them. I was still doing this when I was a 'big' girl.

I justified this by insisting it was for legitimate writing inspiration – and sometimes it worked.

On Tuesday 23 February I wrote:

Yesterday at dinnertime I bought a fashion book, and the people I cut out of it today have given me a wonderful idea for a book. It is set in the future and . . . Oh I won't go into details, it is sufficient to say that at the moment I think it is a good idea.

I've no idea whether I wrote it or not – I can't remember it. I'm interested that I don't want to go into details about it in my diary. I feel exactly the same way now. If I get a good idea it's fatal to talk about it, and even writing too many notes can destroy it. Story ideas need to stay in my head, gently glowing in the dark, developing for a long time before they're ready for the light of day. I like the wise note of caution even though I'm obviously bubbling over with enthusiasm: '*at the moment* I think it's a good idea'. So often today's sparkling and original idea seems tarnished and second-rate the next day!

I bought another big fashion book in April – and the *following* April, when I was fifteen and going out with my first steady boyfriend, I wrote: 'I still haven't managed to grow out of buying fashion books, and cutting out the people and making families of them.' My handwriting is more like a five-year-old's than a fifteen-year-old's on this page but I add: 'By the way, excuse the occasional left hand writing, but I am putting nail varnish on and I don't want it smudged.'

I'm impressed that I was reasonably ambidextrous then. I've just had a go at writing left-handed now and find it very difficult. It would be such a *useful* thing to be able to do, especially when I've got a very long queue of girls wanting their books signed. My right hand starts to ache horribly after an hour or so. It would be wonderful to be able to swap my pen to the other hand and give the right one a rest.

Later that April of 1960 I told Chris I still loved playing with my fashion book:

She seemed shocked – and I must admit it does sound a bit queer – a grown girl of fifteen playing with cut-out figures. No-one but me knows the enjoyment I get out of it though, and also playing around is some constructive use. Each model has a special character and personality – I don't have to invent this, it just comes. Then when I'm writing a story I've got a lot of ready made characters

461

complete with names. I especially like the 'Style' fashion books – the drawings are clear and attractive and a lot of the figures have very strong personalities. I'm not talking rubbish; it's true. As I've been playing with fashion books ever since I've been about six I have some very firm favourites that have lasted through the years although most of the old ones aren't included now as they're too old-fashioned.

Judging by the following diary entry my fashion-book games and stories weren't childish at all – quite the opposite: 'Yesterday I had a lovely morning in bed with my fashion book. I discovered a lovely new person, Carola.' I can *remember* Carola – she had long hair, and as the fashion artist wanted to show off the unusual waist on her tight skirt he drew her without a blouse top. So there she was, as bold as brass in her bra and skirt and high heels. I obviously felt she was what Biddy called 'fast'. So I wrote:

I've decided she can have an affair with John, and I've given her Betty and Katy to look after. [They were small girls with very carefully cut-out pigtails. Did I cast Carola as a single mum with two daughters already?] *She goes around with Nicky and Sherry's crowd. I spent three contented hours with my fashion book.*

The next day:

I bought myself a lovely hard 2H pencil, a thing I've been wanting for a long time. I drew a picture of Carola, Nick, Katy and Betty from memory. I know you should use a soft pencil for drawing, but I hate dark smudgy messy lines, and much prefer neat precise lines. Also the children look much more delicate with a hard line. I want to write about Carola etc., etc.

The drawing and the story and the fashion books were all thrown away but they've stayed indelibly clear in my mind to this day.

I used my own life as inspiration as well as all my paper girls. On 1 March Miss Pierce, our English teacher, told us all about people who lived on barges (in preparation for introducing *Maiden's Trip* by Emma Smith as our class reader). I wrote: 'It was interesting and worth keeping in mind for a story, except that I have just started one

463

about a co-ed school based on my many <u>experiances</u> at Latchmere.'

I spelled experiences wrong and underlined it heavily. I'm not sure what extraordinary experiences I was thinking of. I'd obviously got fed up with it five days later, because on Sunday 6 March I wrote: 'I started writing a story, but got a bit fed up with it.' That could be a valid diary entry nowadays, though now I just grit my teeth and carry on writing – on and on and on – until six months later the story is finished, polished, typed out and sent off to my publishers.

At least now I can reassure myself that I've produced a lot of novels that children enjoy reading. When I was fourteen I was plagued with doubts about my writing.

I wrote in March:

Is it just a form of escapism? Am I burying my head in the sand like an ostrich, is my writing just an adolescent craze? No, it <u>can't</u> be just a phase. Well, I've settled it that at least I'm serious about my writing. But is it any good? Is it? Oh, how I wish I knew. I have a reasonable grasp of writing, <u>but</u> am I any good? I mean <u>really</u> good? I just don't know. I want very much to prove to myself that I can write good material. I would like <u>very</u> much to *hold a finished story in my hands. So I am not going to be weak-willed and sit here wishing, I'm going to think of a plot and – START WRITING! Blast homework, blast everything, I must prove it to myself. Oh let me think of a good plot, some realistic characters, and let me produce a really good book.*

I was so frantic, so earnest. It's a relief to flip the page in my diary and read:

We had a really stinking sum to do for Geometry homework. Chris and I just sat back and laughed it got so complicated. I've now cooled off from my writing outburst yesterday, but I am still determined to write a good novel. Imagine the sheer bliss of printing 'THE END' on the umpteenth sheet of manuscript paper.

A week later I wrote:

Remember my writing outburst on Wed 9th? Well, I have thought of a really good idea for a novel, using my own experience – so that I can know what

I'm writing about. Now I must get on and – WRITE.

The next Sunday we went to visit my godparents, Gladys and Sid, who had just adopted three-year-old twins. I wrote that night:

Gladys says their mother is married, but the children are from another man. How can she just abandon them? They are such lovely pretty kids, perfectly healthy, happy and normal [obviously *not* little Tracy Beakers!]. *The mother idea could be a new angle for a book . . .*

I was brimming with new ideas, new angles. On Saturday 2 April 'I bought a red fat shilling exercise book for my new story. It is coming along nicely at the moment.'

I wasn't limiting myself just to novels:

Reading a good book has brought out the writing urge in me again, but this time in a different form. A book of short stories has given me the idea to try writing for this medium. Besides in book form, short stories are always needed for magazines – so now

I must study all my old copies of 'Woman's Own' to see what type of story is most popular.

I usually only read the problem pages, although in March Biddy had recommended that I read an article in *Woman's Own* called 'The Way to Healthy Womanhood'. I don't think it would have been about eating lots of fruit and veg and walking to school instead of getting the bus. In those long ago days 'healthy womanhood' meant sex education. I don't know how helpful this was to me. I say, very limply for a would-be writer, that the article was 'quite good'.

I was more interested in proper teenage magazines. On 11 April I wrote:

I bought the new teenage magazine 'Honey'. Back home I spent one and a half hours reading it solidly. By the way, I disagree entirely with what the writer of the article 'CONFIDENCE' has to say. I don't think trying to be a writer will ruin my self confidence. <u>I am not going to say to myself that it isn't important. IT IS! I'M GOING TO TRY AND TRY AND TRY UNTIL I GET SOMEWHERE</u>.

I knew perfectly well that I wasn't ready to write for publication. I *did* enter the *Daily Mirror* Children's Literary Competition in 1960, sending off my entry with fervent wishes and prayers. Jill at school entered too. I didn't win, I wasn't a runner-up, I didn't come anywhere – though I did receive a note saying, *This is to certify that the attached entry reached the final stages of selection.* I was pleased for Jill, if a little jealous, when she received a *Highly Commended* certificate.

Jill was the only girl I knew who loved writing too. She kept a fictional diary about two sisters called Doffles and Bluebell and let a little group of us read the latest entries. She was happy to share it with us, even letting me contribute an entry or two.

I was still writing just for myself, taking it terribly seriously. I worked pretty hard in English lessons at school, trying to please Miss Pierce. I wrote: 'I love Art, but English is still my first love. Not English Grammar, of course, that's foul, but English Essay is heavenly.'

Miss Pierce was an inspirational teacher with a passion for English that was infectious. She had us ordinary, not especially academic fourteen-year-olds reading *Jane Eyre* and *Pride and Prejudice* with joy and enthusiasm, discussing the merits of Rochester and Darcy as eagerly as if they were Elvis or Adam Faith.

She was very exacting when it came to the art of writing. She said that an English essay should be like a perfect string of pearls, each paragraph leading on to the next and the next and next until it doubled neatly back to the very beginning.

'What's she *on* about?' Chris mouthed.

I raised my eyebrows and shrugged my shoulders, just to be companionable, but *I* knew. I understood Miss Pierce's lesson on metaphors and similes too. She quoted 'a squirrel sat on the lawn like a coffee pot' – and I *saw* that squirrel and the perfect spout of its paws and handle of its tail. It was like discovering a glorious new game.

I wasn't very good at it at first. Miss Pierce told us to form pairs and describe each other, using metaphors and similes. I squinted long and hard at Chris, gazing into her eyes until we both got the giggles. Her eyes are pale blue – and I couldn't find an original simile to save my life. As blue as the early morning sky? Oh please! As blue as sapphires? How many times has that been used? I ended up with some appalling suggestion about paint water! I'd thought about the first time you swizzle a paintbrush thick with cobalt blue into a clean jug of water and make delicate swirls of pale blue. Chris thought I meant that awful grey sludge colour your paint water becomes after a long painting session and wasn't especially thrilled.

Miss Pierce wasn't either. I tried so very hard with my essays, linking each paragraph together and making my ending fit neatly into my beginning like a clasp, but my essays were nearly always returned with clipped annotations in red pen: 'Too colloquial! Slang! I don't like your tone. This isn't suitable!'

I was always so down-hearted then. I didn't understand that my natural writing style simply wasn't appropriate for a school essay. I'm pretty sure if Miss Pierce were still alive and I gave her one of my books, she'd reach for her red pen after the first paragraph (albeit beautifully linked to the next) and repeat her comments. In fact she'd probably underline them.

However, just occasionally she made my heart leap.

Friday 4 March
In English I got 'Very good work indeed. Well done' which raised my writing hopes as Miss P usually gives mouldy remarks.

And on a golden night in June I wrote:

In the evening Mum went to a parents' meeting at

the school to discuss what subjects we are going to take in the G.C.E. Miss Pierce told her that I was very excellent at English and that she personally would think it a crime if I didn't stay on to the 6th form and take A level English Literature!!!! When Mum told me I was so happy I nearly cried. I might be good as a writer after all.

I had the determination. Then on 14 April I became more focused: 'I bought a WONDERFUL little book called 'Teach Yourself to Write' by Kathleen Betterton. It is wonderfully encouraging and has given me absolutely heaps of ideas.'

I still have my copy of that little book now, well thumbed, with the cover in tatters. Kathleen Betterton says:

> No book can teach you how to write, much less how to succeed as a writer. It can teach you only how to teach yourself to write: the rest depends on you. Literary success springs from an unusual combination of originality, luck and industry – especially industry.

I was an odd one out, a strange, shy, weird, imaginative girl who seemed to think differently from everyone else. Did that make me original? I was prepared to be ultra industrious. All right, I

471

could hardly bear to open a school textbook and I was pretty hopeless at helping Biddy with the dusting and vacuuming – but I wrote for hour after hour in my notebooks and diaries.

I wasn't so sure about the luck element though. It's the one thing you can't really control. You can do your best to make your own luck, keeping an eye on literary trends and always being one step ahead. You can force yourself to write an artful letter, make a phone call, approach the right person at a publishing party (though it's agony if you're shy like me). But it's still mostly a matter of luck whether you get your manuscript accepted or not, whether it wins awards and races up the best-seller charts.

My biggest best-seller has been *The Story of Tracy Beaker*. It was a reasonably original idea to choose to write a story about a fierce little girl in a children's home, desperate to be fostered. I certainly worked hard at it. There was no problem with Tracy herself. She sprang to life the moment I made up her name. It was as if she'd seized my pen in her own hot little hand, determined to write her story her way, in her own voice.

I needed to check my facts and find out about fostering. This is where the first piece of luck flashed forth. My friend Bryony works for the

Fostering Network and has very successfully fostered children herself. I asked her if she had any pamphlets about the whole procedure. She gave me a handful, including a yellow booklet specially for children called *My Book About Me*. As soon as I opened it and saw: MY NAME IS . . . I AM . . . YEARS . . . MONTHS OLD. MY BIRTHDAY IS ON . . . my heart started thumping. This was the way to write my book. I imagined my fidgety, stroppy Tracy being sat down by an overly earnest social worker and told to start writing her life story in her special book. She'd start messing about almost at once, telling fibs, going off into little flights of fancy. She'd doodle little drawings all over the page too. I knew I wanted those drawings in the published book.

I nervously asked my then editor, David Fickling, if I could have lots of black and white illustrations throughout the text. This was quite unusual in those days and I worried about it being an extra expense.

David just beamed at me. 'An *excellent* idea, Jacky,' he said. 'I tell you what, I think I know exactly the right person.'

That right person was Nick Sharratt, now my dear friend, who has illustrated every one of my books for nearly twenty years now, and provided each one with an imaginative, distinctive, colourful

473

cover. I am sooooo lucky to have Nick as my artistic partner.

I've written around ninety children's books now and people often ask me if I've ever thought of writing for adults. I *did* actually write five dark and depressing crime novels for adults long ago but I'm not the slightest bit tempted to write for adults now. I only ever want to write for children and teenagers.

However, I didn't *always* feel that way. I read Kathleen Betterton's chapter on 'Writing for Children' and felt disheartened. Kathleen states dogmatically that 'the writer for children must not attempt subtlety of character in which good and evil are blended'. That was precisely what I found disappointing in many children's books. The children just didn't seem *real*. She suggests that children like to read fantasy or adventure or school stories. I hadn't especially enjoyed *any* of these genres. I decided the fault lay with me. I'd simply been a very weird child.

I wrote in my diary:

I have been reading Enid Blyton's autobiography again, but this time far more cynically. She doles out advice again and again to would-be writers – yet surely her books are not all that great. If I ever write I won't write for children. I can't understand how Enid Blyton can write all day, yet leave out everything about real life. Her families don't quarrel, her parents don't nag, her teenagers aren't interested in lipstick and boys, her children never listen to dirty stories or wet themselves, and she ignores babies and pregnancy and sex. Surely all these things must have some part in her life. I just don't see how she can go on about little Noddy and the Famous Five, etc., etc.

Coombe County Secondary School for Girls

9
School

I *hated* school. I didn't mind Latchmere, my primary school, but I couldn't bear my five years at Coombe County Secondary School for Girls. I've been back to Coombe quite a few times to give talks to the girls. I've even presented the prizes at the end of term. I've talked about my school days and I've been polite and tactful, because Coombe now is a very different school. It's warm and relaxed and all the girls (and now there are even *boys* in the sixth form) seem cheerful. They get excellent exam results and they're very sensitive to any girl with special needs. They tick every box and get ten out of ten, full marks for a fine school.

Coombe way back in 1960 was a very different sort of school. *All* schools were different then. There were pointless rules, fierce regulations about uniform, a strict standard of behaviour. You were expected to *conform*. I've never been very good at that.

I loathed most of the lessons too. I disliked PE most of all. Every Friday morning I'd wake up and stick my head out from under my eiderdown,

477

straining my ears. What total joy if I heard rain pattering against the window! Friday was double hockey in our yellow shirts and green shorts – '*G-r-e-e-n and yellow, G-r-e-e-n and yellow, oh Mum be quick, I'm going to be sick, just lay me down to die,*' we sang in the changing rooms.

I had no idea how to play hockey. Miss French, the formidable new PE teacher, had told us the rules, but I'd never listened properly. I simply ran when she blew the whistle – *away* from the ball and the likely whacks from everyone else's hockey sticks. Then she'd blow the whistle again and shout, 'Jacqueline Aitken! What are you *playing* at?'

I didn't want to play at anything. If it poured with rain, making the playing fields too muddy, we couldn't have double hockey. We had country dancing instead, and I adored any kind of dancing.

Hockey was the worst torture, but netball was almost as bad, shivering on the court in the middle of winter, our bare legs beetroot red. I couldn't see the ball until it practically knocked my head off. One day it caught the side of my glasses and sent them skew-whiff, so I went around looking lopsided for weeks.

The scariest ball of all was the hard little rounders ball. Miss French became fed up with me lurking way out on the edge of the pitch as a deep fielder. For one terrible term she insisted I man first post at every game. This was a key position. It was vital that you caught the ball to get the batter out. Miss French was such a sadist. She *knew* I couldn't catch the ball to save my life.

'Come on, Jacqueline Aitken, wake up, watch that ball, catch it, catch it, *catch it*!' she screamed.

I dropped it. I dropped it. I dropped it.

The batting girl hared round second post, third post and was home with a rounder before I'd stopped fumbling. Then Miss French would scream some more, and the other girls on my team would yell at me too. I'd stand there, trying to hold my head high, acting like I couldn't care tuppence whether I caught the stupid ball or not – but I'd be trembling, sometimes dangerously near tears.

Then there was gym. For some inexplicable reason we weren't allowed to wear our green shorts and plimsolls in the gymnasium. We had to run round in our bare feet in just our ugly yellow blouses and our grim grey knickers. We were all shapes and sizes – fat, skinny, wobbly, hairy – so this was bad enough. But in those long-ago days none of us yet used tampons when we had our period. We used sanitary towels hooked onto belts – awful pads like nappies, so of course the shape of them showed right through your knickers.

Sometimes if Miss French was in a very good mood you might whisper to her that you had a very heavy period and then she *might* let you wear your shorts, but not always. You *could* get out of showers if you said you had a period, and that was a relief. Who wants to parade around stark naked so that all your enemies can nudge each other and giggle at your sticky-out tummy or your non-existent chest? We huddled under our towels, and Miss French would shout, 'Get those towels *off*, girls, and get in the showers. Don't be so ridiculous!'

Did Miss French whip her cosy tracksuit off and gambol naked in the showers in front of everyone? No, she did not.

Biddy once suggested that if I was frightened of a teacher I should imagine them naked. I was frightened of our Latin teacher, Miss Cambridge. She looked comical standing pink and plumply bare in my mind's eye, but I was still frightened of her in real life – and oh, how I hated Latin. I never got to grips with it. If we'd been taught about ancient Rome as an introduction I might have become interested. If we'd had a simple conversation book it might even have been fun. (When my daughter learned Latin, the first two words she was taught were 'Hello, sailor!' which made all her class collapse laughing, though they all remembered *Salve nauta* for evermore.)

Miss Cambridge went straight into those bewildering grammatical declensions and conjugations, giving us long lists to learn almost every night. Then we started translating a very long text about Hannibal and his elephants crossing the Alps, and that *should* have been interesting too, but as I understood one word in fifty (probably just Hannibal, elephant and Alp!) I never mentally joined them on their journey. I doodled in the margin, I daydreamed, I made up the next part of my story, I thought about the boy on the bus that morning – and then jumped violently when Miss Cambridge yelled, 'Jacqueline Aitken, are you sure you're paying attention? Translate the last four lines!'

Although I hated Latin I rather liked Miss Cambridge, even though I was scared of her. She used to be funny in a highly sarcastic way, and if she was in a mellow mood she didn't mind if we tried to be funny too.

On Monday 18 January I wrote:

In Latin we had 28 vocabs to learn! Not homework, mind you, but just to be done in our spare time! Honestly, isn't it ridiculous? I'm just dying to leave school. Miss C was complaining that we ought to read more literature, and someone said 'How

can we when you give us all this homework?'
We, including Miss C, roared with laughter.

But you had to judge her mood very carefully. She could squash you flat if she wanted. She had the ability to march into the rowdiest classroom in her sensible polished shoes and get instant respectful silence. She didn't shout or clap her hands, she just *looked* – and every girl shut her mouth and sat up straight.

The only way we could get the better of Miss Cambridge was to sigh and say, 'I wish I knew what the Colosseum really looked like,' and then Miss Cambridge would be *off*, telling us about her many holidays in Rome. Her eyes went dreamy and her cheeks would flush as she talked, sitting on the edge of her teacher's table, her large legs planted on the desk in front, talking away half the lesson while we sat back happily in our seats. Maybe we weren't getting the better of her at all: she was probably as bored with the lesson as we were and was happy to stride back down Memory Lane to all those carefree Italian summers.

I hated maths too, but again I liked Miss Rashbrook. She wasn't fierce like Miss Cambridge, she was sweet and softly spoken with curly red hair. She was very pretty, though she was disfigured with a hunchback. This made her look lopsided and she walked with a little limp. With unusual delicacy we never once referred to this, even amongst ourselves, and anyone imitating her would have been ostracized.

However, we could be hateful to some of the teachers. There was poor Mrs T, who couldn't keep control at all: 'Every time Mrs T turned her back for us to write on the blackboard we slung dishcloths at each other. Soon five or six dishcloths were in orbit!'

We thought we were so funny. I expect she wanted to stuff the dishcloths down our stupid throats.

I did enjoy *some* lessons though. I was always happy in history lessons, especially with a new teacher.

Thursday 7 January
We had Mr Stokes for History for the first time today. He's quite nice but a bit Welsh, look you. He's young, but already he's going a bit bald. I sit next to Jill right in the front. She can be ever so funny. For instance she put on a gruff voice and proceeded to relate to me how she hated Parliament, and was a strong Charles supporter, and how she wanted to throw a brick through the window of 10 Downing

Street at the Mackintosh person. I couldn't help laughing at the 'Mackintosh' and Mr Stokes looked at us two and grinned.

I loved art. I struggled to make my line drawings as delicate and beautiful as Mr Jeziewski's. He had the knack of pressing firmly at the point of a leaf, the turn of an elbow, the corner of a table, that made everything look three-dimensional. I struggled with shading. Sometimes my drawings worked, sometimes they didn't.

We were occasionally taken on sketching parties, which were great fun, but not necessarily productive: 'This afternoon we went sketching to Hampton Court. I drew the ducks most of the time on the pond – I think they're sweet.'

I could have been sketching those fantastic twisty Tudor chimneys, the sculptured yew trees, the gnarled Great Vine, the white classical statues, the fountains, the knot garden . . . and I drew the *ducks*!

I drew a lot at home too, making up my own imaginary people, drawing them in a long line, sometimes muttering to them as I coloured them in. No wonder Biddy sighed over me.

I loved English lessons the most of course, though I could be scathing at times:

Then we had English in which we read a babyish play. I wish we could do a really <u>modern</u> play like 'A Taste of Honey', 'The Grass Is Greener', etc., etc. Even Shakespeare would be better. Last term all our group went to see 'As You Like It'. I enjoyed it very much. I also enjoyed the train ride going home when we poked a comb into the adjoining carriage in which there was a highly amused boy.

Now what would I call *that* behaviour? *Babyish!* And how irritating of me not to write more about the play and who was playing Rosalind. It was heroic of Miss Pierce and her colleagues to shepherd us silly giggly girls up to London to the Old Vic. We sat right up in the gods in four-shilling seats, which were really just like big wooden steps. Your back ached unbearably and your bottom got pins and needles, and if you were short-sighted like me the little figures down on the stage were just a blur. But in spite of all this we found those performances thrilling. I was lucky enough to see the young Judi Dench playing Juliet, and that time going home on the train we didn't play silly games with combs and boys, we discussed her brilliant, passionate performance and tried to talk in the same soft sexy voice.

Miss Pierce didn't just take us to plays – she had us perform them too. She ran a drama club on Monday nights. Anyone could join. She chose plays with very large casts to make sure everyone could have a part. They weren't all speaking parts of course.

I secretly hoped I'd get chosen for a main part. I loved English and I was good at reading aloud, but I don't think Miss Pierce thought I was extrovert enough to rise to the occasion. I was always Village Girl or Courtier or Extra Child. It wasn't too taxing standing about on stage, laughing or gasping as required. We generally had a little dance too, and at least we could wear stage make-up and a proper costume.

Monday 11 January
After school I went to Drama Club. At Easter we are going to do a Chinese play, and I saw my costume material today. It is a nice silky pink, far better than my last costume which I had to make out of old brown curtains. But actually the brown didn't look too bad as I wore a lime-green sash and ribbon so it brightened it up.

We rehearsed every Monday evening, but as Easter drew nearer we needed to make more time.

Wednesday 16 March
After school I had to stay for __45__ minutes for a Drama rehearsal. Honestly, Miss Pierce is the limit, she had told us that we would only need to stay for 10 minutes. The play is coming on slowly but surely. We have a lovely silver cage and a stuffed nightingale as props. For the nightingale's voice Geraldine Taylor blows (behind stage) a sort of whistle filled with water. It sounds beautiful.

The two performances of *The Imperial Nightingale* took place on 5 and 6 April.

Tuesday 5 April
THE PLAY!
All the drama club were let off the last lesson so they could get home, have their tea, and get back to school in time. I got off at Norbiton with Cherry and went home. Mum (she's got a stinking cold) got me some scrambled egg on toast, some tomatoes and some currant slices, and then after a good wash I was ready. I cut through the back of our flats and down Crescent Road and called for Cherry. Her house is very untidy but has a nice lived-in feeling, and I like the way that even if she's in on her own there's always the television blaring, the budgie

487

*cheeping, and the cat providing company as well
as noisy miaows. She got ready quickly although
she was very nervous as she had quite a big part,
and then we set off, two little girls neat and tidy in
grey uniform. On the way we met Mrs Eldridge and
saw Roger Foulds twice. On the bus we met Mary
Todd and Susan Wooldridge. We enabled them to
smuggle Miss Pierce's fifteen-shilling bouquet into
school without her seeing it. Then we went upstairs
and got dressed in our costumes. I wore my pink
oriental dress and my pink Alice band with a pink
flower on each side. (I was told I looked pretty.)
Then we were made up. It was fascinating watching
ordinary schoolgirl faces turn into startling Chinese
courtiers or suspicious old men, etc. Actually the
play didn't go as well as we thought it would, and
quite a few girls forgot their lines. But it didn't
matter so much today, so long as we are okay
tomorrow when the Mayor etc. and the 'Surrey
Comet' come.*

*Wednesday 6 April
It is all over. We have performed our play, and,
thank God, it went <u>beautifully</u>. During the afternoon
Miss P called the Drama Club together and tactfully
told us what went wrong yesterday, and told us how
to put it right. Mrs Eldridge gave us a lift to school
at six o'clock, and Cherry and I dressed and made*

up. I made Cherry say her lines to me, because last night she forgot them and said, 'I'm so sorry, I seem to have lost my memory,' getting, incidentally, the biggest laugh of the evening. Miss P took tons of photos of us, including one when the ladies are kneeling down in the spotlight. Anyway, the play really went down <u>well</u>. The audience was very good and laughed at all the jokes Everyone said it was extremely well done, and that the acting, costumes, scenery and properties were all <u>very</u> good.

The day after we were allowed to take it easy.

Thursday 7 April
It is History. As there is only one more day left of the term we have been left to get on with whatever we like. We are all lying sprawled at our desks as we have just had a very strenuous game of Netball, and I, for one, have my blouse sleeves rolled up. It is peaceful in here, except for our low (well, perhaps not!) chatter. Oh! The class below us have just started their rather loud singing. Mr Stokes (not a music lover in spite of his Welsh blood) gives us a look both cynical and ironical. Jill sitting next to me is writing a melodramatic love story. I have just looked up to find Mr Stokes' eyes peering into mine.

He gets up and starts pacing round. He's coming towards me! Help! I must cover this up! Phew – ! He's gone past. Oh no! He's just chalked the word 'Homework' on the board! We gasp in agony. He gives us another of his smiles. I think he's only joking, cross fingers.

I so *hated* homework. It seemed such a terrible waste of time. I could struggle all evening with my maths – even risking Harry's wrath by asking him to help me – but it didn't help me understand how to do it. I could mutter Latin vocabulary over and over and over again, but I was so bored by grim repetition that I couldn't remember a word the next day. I muddled through biology and science and geography and French, sighing and moaning. I tried hard with my English essay homework, though of course I worked *much* harder on my own private writing. At least we didn't get homework for our form lessons, singing, music and PE. Oh God, imagine PE homework!

We tormented little Miss St John in singing, a minute lady who drove to school in an equally minute bubble car: 'For singing we had Miss St John. Everyone ragged her and sang out of tune. I felt rather sorry for her as it must be awful for her to lose control completely.'

Poor Miss St John had such courage. She played the cello, a very large instrument for such a small woman.

Friday 18 March
Honestly, in assembly this morning Miss St John played her <u>cello</u>. She was so sweet and little behind it, and oh she played so terribly. The notes were all little and queer like she is, and her high notes were about four notes below the right one. I could hardly control my hysterical giggles and at first there reigned a strained silence in the hall except for the fumbly little cello noises. Then one girl gave an awful snort, and that started us off. There was a bellow of six hundred suppressed giggles, all turned into coughs. I had to bite hard on my fingers to stop myself laughing. I couldn't look to my right as Chris was going red in the face suppressing herself, while Sue on my left was openly sniggering. Even Miss Haslett had to laugh, so she bent her head and pretended to be praying!

Miss Kingston took us for our actual music lesson, and she was a very different type of teacher. No wonder she was snappy with us. We were not a musical bunch, many of us barely progressing beyond the first book of recorder music. We all tooted away valiantly until the spit dribbled disgustingly out of the end of our recorders but we rarely made melodic progress. I remember trying to play Handel's 'Water Music' and all of us collectively drowning in a sea of squawks.

Miss Kingston made us listen to crackly old gramophone records of real musicians playing Handel, Bach and Beethoven. I rather liked this part of the lesson, especially when the music seemed to tell a story. I loved Beethoven's Pastoral Symphony, but tried hard to hide my enthusiasm. If you sat with too rapt an expression, everyone would laugh and tease you and label you a swot. It wasn't cool to like classical music, though we all adored dancing to a record called *Asia Minor* which was a jazzed-up version of Grieg's Piano Concerto.

Sometimes the records seemed to go on for ever. It could get very boring just sitting there, so we worked out ways of communicating with each other. We didn't dare whisper in front of Miss Kingston. Passing notes was decidedly risky. Chris and I had learned the rudiments of sign language for the deaf from a schoolgirl diary and this proved useful during protracted school assemblies, but Miss Kingston was on to us the minute we tried it in music.

Wednesday 27 January
Chris, Lyn and I were doing deaf and dumb
alphabet in music, and Miss Kingston saw us. At
the end of the record she asked (or rather shouted!)
what had we been doing. We sat silent. 'Answer me
at once!' We still sat silent. 'The girl on the end'
(me) 'you tell me!' Silence. 'At once!' 'Well, er, you
see,' I said, trying in vain to think of some excuse,
'Christine was, er, playing with her fingers.' The
whole group roared with laughter and we three got
a severe telling off.

I didn't mean to tell tales on poor Chris, I just
blurted out the first thing that came into my head
– but she wasn't best pleased with me. She still
sometimes teases me about it now, hundreds of
years later.

I hated the whole *atmosphere* of school. My heart
would sink as I trudged up the path and went
through the glass doors into the cloakrooms. There
was always a fug of damp grey gabardines and old
shoes as soon as you walked in. As the day
progressed the smells got worse. Our school dinners
were made on the premises and in retrospect were
totally delicious:

Monday 8 February
We had chips, corned beef and American salad and mince and apple tart for dinner today, not bad for school dinners.

Tuesday 9 February
Dinner was steak pie, greens and mashed potato, and semolina and jam for pud. Pretty awful, n'est-ce pas?

Wednesday 10 February
After dinner (porky sort of meat, peas, roast potatoes and caramel pie) Carol, Cherry and I went up to the library to do homework.

Cherry was the dinner monitor on our school dinner table that year. If everyone had finished their platefuls the dinner monitor could put up her hand, and when the supervising teacher had given her permission she could charge up to the kitchen counter and ask for seconds. We might moan about our school dinners but *some* seconds were definitely worth having. Mrs Legge, our school cook, made delicious fish and chips on Fridays, and her pastry was total perfection. She made beautiful steak and kidney pies; her fruit pies – apple, apricot and plum – were glorious; and her occasional-for-a-special-treat lemon meringue pies always made my mouth water. So we obeyed Cherry as she urged us to bolt our food down in five minutes so we would be in with a chance of more. It's a wonder we didn't hiccup our way all through afternoon school.

Mrs Legge worked miracles – imagine baking enough pies for hundreds of girls – but her budget was limited and mince and stewing steak were served up very regularly. I hated both. You started being able to smell them cooking by break time, and by twelve o'clock the whole school reeked of this strong savoury smell, appallingly reminiscent of body odour.

The corridors were frequently filled with a horrible burning smell too. Mrs Legge never burned her dinners. This was all the fault of the incinerator in the girls' toilets. We all used sanitary towels and in those days they weren't properly disposable. If you had your period you were supposed to go in the special end toilet, which had an incinerator – but it was a tricky customer and if you didn't insert your disgusting towel just so, it would spitefully send out smelly smoke. Everyone would look at you and point when you came out of the toilet.

We all smelled too, in various ways. The girls smelled of bubble gum and hairspray and nail varnish and Goya's Entice scent and fresh tangy sweat. The teachers smelled of chalk and talcum powder and Polo mints. The men smelled of tobacco, and the French master reeked of unwashed body. We hated having to go up to his desk – and when you stood there breathing shallowly he'd often slyly pat your breast or bottom.

Some brave girls in another form went to Miss Haslett and complained about this teacher's wandering hands and suggestive remarks. Miss Haslett told the girls they were making disgusting allegations because they had warped minds and sent them away in disgrace.

I was only in really serious trouble once in my five years at Coombe. It was a sporty school and Miss French and her colleague Miss Snelling were proud of the hockey and netball teams. They were particularly keen on athletics and our school was entered for the County Championships at Motspur Park.

Chris and Carol and Cherry and Sue and Jill and all my other friends weren't at all interested. They weren't quite such duffers at games as me but they knew they were nowhere near speedy enough to represent the school at athletics. *I* came last in any race, I couldn't do the high or long jump, I was downright dangerous with a discus or javelin in my hand and I couldn't even *lift* the shot, let alone put it anywhere.

I went off in a daydream whenever Miss French talked excitedly about the wretched Motspur Park athletics. She was outlining the arrangements – it seemed the school was hiring coaches so we could all go and watch – as if it was a serious treat.

Miss French told us we had to tell her at the next PE lesson whether we needed a seat on the coach or not so that she could book it.

'Of course, if you don't wish to go you don't have to. It is entirely voluntary,' she said.

Chris nudged me. 'Did you hear that, Jac? What does that mean, exactly?' she whispered.

'It means we don't have to go!' I said happily.

'But we'll get into trouble,' Cherry said. 'You know she *wants* us to go.'

'Yes, but do *you* want to go?'

'Of course not!'

We conferred with all the other girls in the class. *None* of the non-team girls wanted to go. So we decided to tell Miss French politely that we simply didn't wish to attend. She couldn't really object, could she? She'd *said* the trip was voluntary.

Miss French was in a bad mood the next PE lesson.

'Come along, you lazy girls, you're five minutes late already. Change into your kit in double-quick time and then go and sit in the gym. No talking now!'

497

We got changed quickly without so much as a whisper. We sat cross-legged on the polished wooden floor. Miss French squeaked towards us in her gym shoes. Her whistle bounced on her chest. She clutched a clipboard and pen.

'Right, I need to get this coach business sorted and then we'll get on with our lesson.' She consulted her register. She was going to do us in alphabetical order. Oh God. Guess whose name was right at the top.

'Jacqueline Aitken!' Miss French called. 'Do you want a seat on the coach?'

Her pen was poised, ready to tick me. Everyone was staring at me. I swallowed.

'No, thank you, Miss French,' I said.

Miss French drew in her breath so that the whistle bounced on her bosom. 'Are your parents taking you to Motspur Park in their car?' she asked.

'No, Miss French.'

'So *why* don't you need a seat on the coach?'

'Because I don't want to go, thank you,' I mumbled.

'You don't want to *goooo*?'

Oh God oh God oh God.

'No, Miss French,' I said in a squeak.

'Well, that's just *typical* of you, Jacqueline Aitken! It isn't enough that you're a disgrace in every single PE class. You never even *try* to catch a ball and you won't run to save your life. You're bone idle and lazy. But what about all your friends and colleagues? How can you be so selfish? Don't you *care* about all the girls competing? Don't you *want* Coombe to win?'

I couldn't care less, but I could see a truthful response wouldn't be wise.

'I've got used to you being useless in my classes, never trying hard, never taking PE seriously, but I thought at the very least you cared about all the other girls. I even thought you might have just a little loyalty to *me*.'

I stared back at her, wondering how she could seriously think this.

'Take that expression off your face, you insolent girl. I'm sick of the sight of you. You'll never amount to anything, do you hear me? Do you know why? You've no team spirit. You don't care about anyone else. Well, believe you me, no one will ever care about you. Very well, *don't* come to Motspur Park to support your team. Now, who's next?' she said, consulting the register again.

I went to sit down.

'No, you stay standing, Jacqueline Aitken. You'll stand there till the end of the lesson.' She frowned at the register. 'Jill Anderson. Do *you* need a place on the coach?'

499

Jill said yes. I didn't blame her. I'd have said yes too if I'd been second on the register. Everyone said yes. I was stuck standing there, the girl who'd said no.

I held my head high and clenched my fists, telling myself I didn't care. But my heart was banging *boom-boom-boom* inside my chest and I knew I was trembling. It all seemed a ridiculous fuss about nothing and blatantly unfair as she'd said attendance at Motspur Park was voluntary. As if it made any difference to anyone whether I was there or not. She kept glancing in my direction, acting as if I'd deliberately tried to poison the entire athletics team.

I didn't really believe her remarks about never amounting to anything – and to be fair, I don't think she really meant it. She was just furious, worried that all the other girls would follow my example and she'd be left looking a fool without any girls cheering on her wretched team.

She was right about one thing though. I don't think I *do* have any team spirit. I never identified with school. I never felt proud of my uniform. I never sniffled when we sang the school hymn at the end of term. I never cheered with genuine enthusiasm. I loved my special friends, I liked some of the teachers, but Coombe as an institution meant nothing to me.

Coombe's lovely now. Maybe it was lovely for all the other pupils back in 1960. I was just the odd one out.

A dance class party

10
Dancing

Miss French thought I was the most bone-idle, lazy girl at Coombe. I wasn't at all. I walked to school every day, a good two- or three-mile hike from our flats in Kingston all the way over to New Malden. If I'd spent my week's bus fare on a paperback or Woolworths notebook I'd walk all the way home again too.

Sometimes I walked with Sue next door, sometimes I walked with another Susan, a girl from Kingsnympton, the council estate up the hill. I liked both Sues. I could have a cosy chat with Sue next door about our dancing class and a moan about our mums. I knew the other Sue less well, but she was interesting, telling me all about the feuds and gangs and punch-ups on the Kingsnympton estate. She also passed her *Bunty* comic on to me every week. I considered myself way beyond the *Bunty* stage but it wouldn't have been polite to say so – and I was happy to read anything.

I think I liked the walk to school most, though, when I was on my own. I'd always been a very dreamy girl and yet nowadays there was very little opportunity to dream. I was supposed to stay on red alert, listening and concentrating at school, and then in the evenings I had to struggle through my homework before rushing out to go dancing or to the pictures.

But if I walked to school on my own I could daydream for nearly an hour as I marched along in my Clarks clodhoppers, swinging my satchel. Sometimes I made up stories. Sometimes I pretended I was being interviewed by a journalist: 'I'm simply bowled over by your first novel, Jacqueline. I've never encountered such remarkable talent in one so young,' etc., etc.! Sometimes I peered at the houses all around me and imagined the people inside and the lives they were living. The first half of the journey was much the most interesting because I stepped from one world into quite another.

Cumberland House was a small 1950s council estate, three six-storey blocks of flats. It was quite genteel as council estates go. A window would get broken once in a while or someone used the lift as a toilet, but mostly we were a timid, law-abiding tribe, though still relatively poor. Biddy and Harry had only just got a car and a telephone. We still didn't have a washing machine or a fridge and owned just a very small black and white television. We went for a holiday once a year but we hardly ever went out as a family otherwise.

We had the special treat on Sundays of a shared bottle of Tizer and a Wall's family block of raspberry ripple ice cream after our roast chicken. This was High Living as far as we were concerned. The flat was still furnished with the dark utility table and chairs and sideboard bought just after the war, with a gloomy brown sofa and two chairs filling up the rest of the room. We weren't allowed to sit on the sofa because it would disturb Biddy's complicated arrangement of decorative cushions. She sat in one chair, Harry in the other, while I perched on an unpleasant brown leatherette pouffe.

We didn't have a garden to relax in but we *did* have a balcony. Biddy didn't go in for tubs of flowers or window boxes as she said that plants would shed their leaves and make a mess – but she let me have a hammock slung precariously from one end of the balcony to the other. I'd begged for a hammock for my birthday, thinking it would be romantic to swing idly while reading a book, just like all the girls in Victorian storybooks. I hadn't bargained on the fact that swinging, idly or otherwise, made me feel queasy, and if I wasn't cautious enough the hammock would go *clonk* against the side of the concrete balcony and give my hip a nasty bruise.

But once I'd walked out of the flats, crossed the very noisy main road and passed the pub opposite, I stepped into George Road, which could have been on a different planet. It was a private road, part of the Coombe estate, the very poshest part of Kingston where celebrities lived in enormous houses and played on the exclusive golf course. I wasn't so keen on the modern houses, palatial though they were. I liked the enormous Victorian houses, some now turned into private schools. I'd imagine myself back in time, living there, the bookish daughter of the house, *not* the grubby scullery maid.

Then I'd turn down a smaller road and reach my favourite house. I describe it in a June entry in my diary:

Down the Drive there are some absolutely beautiful houses with enormous gardens – my favourite has a great big pond, almost a lake, with willows all around and a little waterfall leading onto a much smaller pool surrounded by bluebells. There is a fence and hedge all round so you can only see bits at a time. At the moment their rhododendron bushes are all in bloom, a lovely crimson.

I found out that this beautiful house, Kingfishers, had once been part of the John Galsworthy estate. I didn't read his Forsyte Saga books until they were serialized on television in the late sixties. It was enough just knowing that the house had once been owned by a *writer*.

I wrote a lamentably bad poem about the house:

KINGFISHERS

I peer through the bamboo leaves;
No privet hedges here.
The sweet pea on the trellis weaves;
Bees, satisfied, appear.

The gabled house stands proudly
Embraced by tender creeper.
Only a chaffinch, singing loudly,
Ignoring me, the peeper.

Small curious paths brazenly wind
Beneath the silver birches,
Scattered round, to the garden's rind.
Peace here, as in churches.

A feathery aged willow protects
The quiet unruffled lake.
A tiny woodsy island injects

Itself, obstinately opaque.

The water trickles, filters through
To a secret mossy pond,
Springtimely fringed by bells of blue
And the fern's lacy frond.

Oh house, generations-long secure
With your cosy ingle-nooks.
Your magic easily did procure
John Galsworthy and his books.

Would that I might live here too,
Free from cares and danger;
So easy, Jeevesy. Troubles few;
But I am just a stranger.

As I trudged on through the less exciting suburban streets of New Malden I'd daydream about being a famous best-selling author one day – and maybe *I'd* live in a house like Kingfishers.

Dream on, little Jacky Daydream! I live in a beautiful house now and I wouldn't want to swap it with anyone, but my lovely home looks like a little cottage compared to Kingfishers.

I was clearly exercising my imagination as well as my legs as I walked to school. I also went dancing at least twice a week, sometimes more. Not *ballet* dancing, though I'd have loved to learn. When I was little I longed to wear a neat black practice dress, a pink angora bolero and pale pink ballet shoes like some of the girls at my primary school. Biddy thought ballet a waste of time and didn't want to get lumbered with making my costumes.

She sent me to old-time dancing classes instead, mainly because they were held just down the road on a Saturday morning and I could go with Sue. There were fourteen or so other pupils, all girls. We paired up, and because I was a little taller than Sue I had to be the boy. I'm *still* better at being the boy at dancing and have to fight not to take the lead and steer my partner around the floor!

We didn't have to wear special outfits like ballet dancers. We didn't even have to wear special shoes, though lots of the girls wore silver or sparkly strappy dance sandals. I longed to have a pair, but had to make do with boring black patent. Perhaps that's why nowadays I have such a weakness for silver or sparkly shoes!

Sue and I went dancing together for years. I started to feel I was getting too old for it – and we weren't really progressing. We'd got our bronze and silver and gold medals but we were never going to be real competition standard. I skipped dancing class the first two Saturdays in January, but on the sixteenth I wrote:

For once I went Old Time dancing with Sue. I quite enjoyed myself although I prefer Friday night dancing. [Of course I did – it was ballroom, and there were boys]. *I wasn't the oldest for once because Sandra came* [the girl who lent me *Peyton Place*]. *We danced the Quadrilles and it was ever such good fun. Also we did the Maxina which I enjoy doing as it is so unusual.*

I can't for the life of me remember how to do the quadrilles or the maxina now. I can vaguely remember old-time favourites like the valeta and the Boston two-step, and I still get tempted to whirl about the room whenever I hear a Viennese waltz – my feet go forward-side-together-back-behind-front of their own accord.

Mr Crichton, the old-time teacher, threw a party for all his dancing students at the end of January.

It was very good fun and I had a lovely time, but not as good as last Saturday! [I'd been to a party. I'll be writing about it later in a chapter on boys.]

We had some good novelty dances and some ballet shows that Sandra was in. Then all these lifeboat men in raincoats and sou'westers came in through the door pulling a rope and singing 'Yo heave ho'. Then into the hall on the end of the rope was pulled a man on a potty reading a newspaper. Everyone was so amazed they just stood open-mouthed. Guess what! Sue and I won the Maxina competition and got a lovely gold medal each!

I wore this gold medal the next Saturday when I went dancing.

We did a good square dance called the Caledonians. Next week we are all taking sandwiches and staying on in the afternoon to train for the Kingston dancing competition to be held at the Coronation Hall.

The following Saturday

We did the Quadrilles; I love the music to that. We had a picnic lunch there, and then had another hour's dancing, this time competition work. We had some exercises to do, and next week we've got to bring old sheets to put on the ground as we're going to do exercises on the ground. It's going to be jolly indecent raising stockinged legs in front of Mr Crichton!

Saturday 20 February
Went dancing. We learnt some new dances, but not very nice ones. When it was time for the Beginners to go home and for us to have our picnic lunches this gorgeous boy and an enormous Afghan hound came and collected one of the little girls. Naturally, I went up and stroked the hound, then stared up into the boy's face and smiled. Am impatiently waiting for next week to come. We had a good chat eating our lunch in the cloakroom gathered round the oil stove on old benches. Sandra, who is 15 in July so nearest in age to me, told us she had three brothers. 'How old?' came a chorus. 'All younger than me,' Sandra replied. 'Ooh!' came disappointedly from the chorus. Afterwards we had to do some horrible exercises lying on the floor. We all had terrible giggles!

Saturday 27 February
When I woke up I thought it was Friday like I do every Saturday and tried to force myself out of my lovely warm nest. Then the gorgeous realisation swept over me and I was able to go back to sleep.

I went dancing. Sandra, Christine, Wendy, Sue and I had a good chat. The dog turned up again to collect the little girl but with a middle-aged man instead of its <u>other</u> owner. Honestly, the exercises were <u>so</u> funny. Doing bicycles was bad enough, but when we had to lie on our tummies and just balance on our hands and the tips of our toes, and also when we had to raise both our chest and our legs off the floor so that we were curved, and only lying on our waists; <u>well</u>, we were just prostrate with giggles. Sandra told me that her hair was not naturally curly. I was amazed as it looks so pretty. I must try putting mine up in rollers. Also she said she goes to a co-ed school, and learns typing as well as ordinary lessons. Isn't she <u>lucky</u>!

Saturday 5 March
Lay in, and then got dressed in white jumper and pink and mauve mohair skirt and went dancing. We learnt a new square dance called the Tango Quadrilles. Now we know four: the Quadrilles, the Lancers, the Caledonians and now the Tango Quadrilles. The middle-aged man turned up with the dog <u>again</u>. Sue didn't stay the third hour. She might have let me know beforehand. After we'd eaten our picnic lunches we chattered a while, and then really slogged away at the Filed Waltz, Valeta,

513

Latchford and the Military Two Step. The competition is in a month's time! Mr C was giving us all butterflies when he told us about the strict rules. As Sue wasn't there I had to dance with Mr C. Honestly, such a fuss about a little thing like a salute. Mr C had us all in front of him, and finally we could do it as 'snappy' as he wished. My poor arm aches now.

Saturday 12 March
I went dancing with Sue this morning. Sandra has had her hair cut, it looks nice, but I preferred it long and curly, it made her look more pretty. We had our picnics and then slogged for another hour at the Lola Tango, Fyle, and the Premia. Ga and Gongon said they would like to come and watch me at the competition on 2 April. I cannot think of an excuse to prevent them coming without making them feel hurt, but I shall be very embarrassed, especially if I am knocked out the first round. (It sounds like boxing!)

Saturday 26 March
I dressed in my new sprigged violet cotton skirt, and Mum's mauve Spring coat and went to Kingston with Carol and Cherry. Then I went dancing. We _slogged_ and _slogged_ (the competition is next week) and then Mr C played my new record

on his record player for me. At our picnic lunch Sue
and I talked to Sandra a lot. Then another hour of
<u>*slogging*</u> *– and it was time to go home.*

The competition was on 2 April. After all that
build-up I wrote precisely two lines about it: 'In
the afternoon went to the Comp. but Sue and I
didn't get anywhere.'

It had been a total nightmare. There were lots
of girls who danced together, but they all had
specially made matching net costumes in excitingly
violent colours: purple, crimson, shocking pink,
with matching sequinned bodices.

Our mums didn't do dressmaking. My grandma
used to sew beautifully but now her arthritis was
so bad she couldn't tackle elaborate dance
costumes. We wore our mums' party dresses, which
were vaguely similar blue florals. We looked
ridiculous with these big matronly dresses hanging
off our puny shoulders. Our hair wasn't styled in
a chignon, our faces weren't made up, and we didn't
have the right shoes. We did our best, dancing with
fixed smiles and desperate eyes – and we were
eliminated in the first round.

Friday night ballroom dancing was much more
fun. We didn't take the dancing part too seriously
– and there were boys. Not many boys. None of my
crowd went with a boy – but we were in the same

515

room with them, and occasionally changed partners and danced with them, solemnly waltzing or quickstepping up and down the ballroom (a long bleak hall in Surbiton where Sainsbury's now stands).

Friday 8 January
A whole crowd from Coombe went dancing – Carol, Sue, Jill, Cherry, Judith and I. Carl (Mr Bryant) taught us thank goodness. I can't bear that awful Len that sometimes teaches us, when he dances with you he breathes a whole barful of beer over you. Peter and the other reasonable boys weren't there but dear Laura and co. were. She's very common [oh God, I sound like Biddy!], *but I like her hair when she doesn't scrape it into a French roll. It is a sort of long pageboy. I think I'll grow my hair and have it like that; that is if it will go into a pageboy.*

Laura was Peter's girlfriend. He was the only decent boy at dancing. We all raised our eyebrows and shook our heads over her short skirts and high heels – but we secretly envied her like anything.

Friday 15 January
In the evening I went dancing with Carol and Jill. Peter wasn't there again, and neither was dear Laura etc. this time. I've come to my own conclusions about those two. Carl wasn't there so that Len character took us, but it was quite good fun actually. It was great fun walking home through the snow singing at the tops of our voices.

We didn't go dancing the next Friday: this was when we all flocked to the cinema to see *Expresso Bongo*.

Friday 29 January
Sue came dancing with us this evening. Carl took us thank goodness. No Peter again, he hasn't come for ages. Not that I care, now I've got Ken. Laura and Veronica turned up in tight skirts above their knees. Sue's eyebrows went up when she saw them! I might wear my straight skirt to dancing, my blue one.

Ken was a boy I'd just met. There'll be more about him later. Lots more.

Friday 12 February
In the evening I went dancing. Sue didn't come, or Judith, but Carol and Jill did. I wore my new nail varnish and new flatties which were lovely for dancing in. We did a lot of complicated Samba steps and I had Peter for a partner. After Ken I think he's terribly ordinary. He's taking his silver medal next week. Jill asked him if he had enjoyed 'Expresso Bongo' and he said he had. Peter forsook Laura and accompanied Anne home this week. She looks about sixteen, wears sloppy jumpers, very tight skirts and crimson nail varnish.

Friday 19 February
I went dancing with Carol. We made friends with a Tiffins girl and she told us the amazing news that Anne (see last Friday) is only in the first year at Tiffs!!!

Friday 26 February
Jill, Carol and I went dancing. I asked Peter whether he had taken his silver medal yet, but he said he was taking it next week. We did some funny new cha cha steps and some new rhythm dancing.

Friday 4 March
After school Carol, Jill (in a new tartan skirt) and I went dancing. Laura came, but Peter didn't, so

that was one in the eye for her. She is really common, but some of the things she says are very funny. When Len was trying to be funny, she said, bored, 'What a queer old man.' Carl knows my name! He called me Jacqueline!

Friday 11 March
Sue came dancing with Carol and I. None of the girls seem to like Carl, but I think he is sweet. He's certainly 'all there'. Going home Carol said my mother sounded a pushing type. The bitch! I don't care what she says about me, or even my friends (e.g. Chris and Jill) but I will not have her saying things like that about my mother.

I wonder what she *said* exactly. I don't know why I got in such a state. I loved Biddy very much but I couldn't possibly deny that she *was* pushy. She called this having *gump* – short for gumption – and lamented the fact that I possessed no gump whatsoever.

Friday 1 April
As I was standing at the bus stop ready to go dancing I turned towards the flats and waved at Mummy. Guess who was standing at the next door window.

Jeremy! He must have thought I was waving at him! A new boy actually turned up at dancing, but not anything particular. Peter did not come and neither did Laura. We did the quickstep again. I could do it when I danced with Carl and with other girls who could do it, but not when I did it with someone who couldn't do it, as I was a girl and could not take the lead. On the way home I bought a red fat shilling exercise book for my new story. It is coming along nicely at the moment, thank you.

Friday 8 April
Jill, Carol and I went dancing. I wore a summer dress for the first time. We did a new dance that was good fun. Jill, Carol and I had to show the others how to do it.

There was no dancing over Easter, and when we went back it didn't seem so beguiling. I didn't bother to write about it for several weeks, then:

Friday 27 May
After school I didn't go dancing as I'm getting a bit sick of it. So is Carol, so I think we'll start going to the Lagoon on Fridays instead.

We'd been to the lagoon the day before. It was called Surbiton Lagoon but it was actually in Tolworth, a bus ride away. It was a wonderful white art deco lido with a big open-air pool and a proper diving board. I *wish* it was still there now. I'd spent most of the long sunny summer of 1959 going to the lagoon. It was only sixpence (2Hp) to go in, so Biddy would give me a shilling (5p) each day and that covered my bus fares and a packet of crisps as a treat. We'd stay there all day long, chatting, reading, eyeing up the boys and diving in for a swim whenever we got too hot.

Obviously the lagoon was closed during the winter but it opened up in May.

Thursday 26 May
After school Cherry, Carol and I went to the Lagoon. It was SMASHING. We certainly picked the right day for going, as it was lovely and warm. It was cold at first in the water, but after a minute or two it was delicious. We all brought our teas so we could stay in till gone seven, when the session ended. We all wore our glamorous swimming costumes and painted our toenails.

But it didn't stay warm. Carol and I went to the lagoon at half-term.

Tuesday 7 June
In the morning Carol and I optimistically went to
Surbiton Lagoon. It was f-r-e-e-z-i-n-g, and when we
eventually plucked up courage to jump in the water
we were very nearly frozen solid. I was surprised
that there weren't any icebergs floating around.
Anyway, when it began to pour with rain it was just
the limit, and C and I packed up and ran for the
warmth of the changing rooms. After we were warm
and dry and changed we decided to go. As we were
standing at the bus stop guzzling our packed lunches
my front tooth filling came out again, blast it.

Oh, that front tooth! It was the bane of my life,
always falling out at awkward moments. Long ago,
when I'd first learned to swim at the age of six, I'd
bashed my mouth against the stone side of the
swimming pool as I struggled to get out. Both my
front teeth were chipped, and when I reached my
teens my dentist sent me up to the Royal Dental
Hospital in Leicester Square to see if they could
fix me up with a rudimentary crown. If anything
went wrong I had to trail all the way up to London.
So the next day:

In the morning I went up to the Royal Hospital of

Dentists and had my tooth seen to. This time I didn't have Mr Arnold but a fat chubby student who reminded me of a teddy bear. He was very nice though, and I could have hugged him when he asked if I went out to work yet!

I'm rather impressed that at fourteen I was able to make that journey on the train up to Waterloo and then take the tube to Leicester Square. I was always supposed to come straight back after my dental treatment but I didn't always, especially if it was a school day and I could miss maths and PE. I'd sit on a bench in Leicester Square and read my book, hoping that everyone would think me a young secretary on my lunch break. I didn't have enough money on me to buy myself lunch but I'd look longingly at the menu in the window of the Golden Egg restaurant. Then, to distract myself from my hunger pangs, I'd wander along to the Charing Cross Road and peer even more wistfully in the windows of the second-hand bookshops.

11

Boys Boys Boys

Oh dear. This is the hardest chapter to write. I was so *silly*.

Chris asked me if I'd like to start going with her to the Youth Fellowship group at her local Methodist church. I wasn't a Methodist, I wasn't any kind of church-goer , but Chris said there were sometimes interesting discussions – and lots of boys went. So on Sunday 3 January I ate my Sunday roast chicken hurriedly, got myself dressed up (the eau-de-nil outfit) and caught the bus over to New Malden.

The Youth Fellowship discussion group was run by a gentle bald man called Mr Golden, who welcomed me warmly.

Mr Golden based his talk on stars, and told us about horoscopes etc. Afterwards I had to give my name and address to Michael Young to be put on the register. Chris pipes up 'Why not give him your vital statistics as well?' and M.Y. and I promptly blush scarlet. When we got outside the Church we saw

Johnny Wilkins smoking a pipe! I couldn't believe my eyes as he is only about sixteen. He looked so funny, puffing away self consciously. We now call him Sherlock Holmes amongst ourselves.

I settled into going to Youth Fellowship every Sunday. I don't think I ever contributed to any discussion. I was far too shy, though I was Miss Gabby Gossip with Chris.

Sunday 17 January
Before the service everyone natters away to each other, and Chris and I were engrossed in conversation. We suddenly realised that Viv was nudging us and that everyone was staring at us. Poor Mr Golden had been trying to begin the service and had said 'Shall we commence by singing . . .' whereupon Chris had said (in reply to me) 'No!' Everybody burst out laughing and a boy called out 'Big Brother has his eye on you.'

The next day I wrote:

When I got home after Y.F. Mum asked me which

boy I liked best. Little does she know it's John Wilkins! At school Sue told Chris I liked him but Chris has sworn faithfully not to tell him.

I liked John Wilkins the pipe smoker?! But not for long.

Wednesday 20 January
I can't imagine loving a man, not now. Of course I get crushes on boys, but that's not proper love. In Biology Chris told me that she thought J.W. liked Gloria Hastings. That has rather put me off him.

The next Saturday there was a special Youth Fellowship Tramps Party. I've inked red and blue stars at the top of the page. This was clearly a magical occasion for me, though reading my diary entry now, it sounds so touchingly soppy.

Saturday 23 January
Met Chris in New Malden at 10 o'clock. We went round the shops and bought some loaves and marge for the church 'Tramps Party' in the afternoon. We dropped them off in the Church hall and then went

back to Christine's. After lunch Jan, Val, Chris and I sat at the table doing our homework. At 5.30 Chris and I changed into old slacks and sweaters and then went out and met Carol, Lyndsay, Viv and Rosemary. Then we nervously went into the hall and sat on a table together. We were soon jiving with each other. Then Mr G came and the party began. It was lovely! We played some gorgeous games and it was all such fun! We played a sort of Pass the Parcel only there were forfeits like find the boy who is the most ticklish, or find the girl with the smallest waist. This boy measured mine and said I was 21 inches and I couldn't possibly have been as I am 24–25 inches. There was also a husband and wife game in the dark! But one game you had to sit on the boys' laps. Ken said, 'Oh, this is better,' and put his arms round me! I think he's smashing!!!

I went very eagerly to Youth Fellowship the next day.

Sunday 24 January
Went to Y.F. in the afternoon. Carol went too, and seemed to enjoy herself. I sat next to Michael Young. When we stood up to sing Ronnie put a hymn book

on my chair and I sat down straight on it. Isn't he a beast! Ken said, 'Excuse me, Jacqueline.' Oh well, I'm getting on!

Monday 25 January
Today Chris has done nothing but talk and think of Peter Lock, the boy who she danced with on Sat. and I have done nothing but talk and think of Ken. I think he is wonderful, and very good looking in his own way. He is about 16 or 17 and goes to work. He lives in New Malden. He has a little sister Geraldine who goes to Brownies and his father is a Cub master. Ken has a fair sort of long crew cut and lovely eyes. I gleaned this information from Chris about his age and family etc., the rest I observed. I only wish he had been my husband in the game on Sat. because lots of the others were kissing!

Thursday 28 January
We had another Maths theorem test, worst luck. I still think of Ken an awful lot. Chris has told me that Glenda told her in strictest confidence, mind you, that he smoked a lot. I don't care!

Friday 29 January
Saw Glenda at dinner time and casually mentioned Ken. It was obvious she hates him, but she said he

*didn't drink or anything, just smoked. What's
wrong with a boy of seventeen or so that smokes?*

Sunday 31 January
*After roast dinner dashed off to Y.F. It was terribly
hot in that little room, and I almost fell asleep,
except that I was so intent on trying to screw my
head round and look at Ken. We had to discuss
some questions Mr Golden gave us. I had to be in
that horrible S— boy's group. Ugh, I think he's
awful. So overbearing, aggressive, almost fatherly!*

Monday 1 February
*You'll never ever guess who I saw by Norbiton
station. Ken! I almost fell over with surprise! He
was riding a bike and wearing blue jeans. I could
recognise that fair crew cut anywhere. I don't think
he saw me. Next Sunday I'm going to ask him if it
was him. I hope he'll tell me where he works. I only
hope he hasn't got a girlfriend. I know he used to
like Anne Wilkins, Johnny's sister, but I don't think
he does any more.*

Tuesday 2 February
*Saw <u>him</u> again this morning. He looked at me as
if he recognised me this time. Next Sunday looms
ahead! I have a shocking cold, but I don't feel a bit
depressed. I feel very happy, and you can guess why!*

Wednesday 3 February
I went down the hill and saw Ken. Oh, you'll never guess where I saw him go! Kingston Hill Motor Works. Bang next door, almost! I'm ever so excited about that!

Thursday 4 February
Saw my Ken again this morning. Sue can't understand what I see in him as he isn't really handsome. I don't know myself what it is, except that I like him so much.

Friday 5 February
Saw <u>him</u> again. It is wonderful being able to see him every day. It makes the day start off right, and puts me in a good mood straight away.

Sunday 7 February
Woke up early this morning. I put the light on, did my hair, and then settled down to homework. Oh how I HATE it. It rules my life, it does really.

In the afternoon went to Y.F. Us girls were the first there (I got a lift in Carol's car) and Mr Golden asked us to put the chairs out. We only put the girls' out. Mr G asked where the boys would sit and Chris said 'On our laps,' whereupon Mr G replied 'A good idea!' Didn't get a chance to talk to Ken as he came late and went early. We talked about newspapers; it was

*quite interesting. When he stood up to sing Ronnie
and John put a hymn book on Brian Tiplady's chair.
He sat down, and almost fell off again. It was
so funny!*

I was so obsessed with Ken that I thought it
worth writing in my diary on 9 February: 'Saw Ken
but only a glance as I went past him on the bus.'
On 10 February I didn't even see him and thought
this important enough to record: 'Didn't see Ken
today, worst luck. Chris and Sue told me to call out
hello to him next time I see him. I think I will, you
know. I wonder what will happen!'

Nothing much! On 11 February: 'I didn't see
Ken <u>again</u> but Chris told me she saw him on her
way home from school, the lucky thing.'

I didn't mention him for a day or two, and then:

Sunday 14 February
*At Y.F. Mr Golden suggested that we girls should
make a cloth for the table. No fear! I'm hopeless at
needlework. We talked about adverts this week and
it was very interesting. We had to divide up into
two groups and think up as many adverts as
we could in 10 minutes, like 'Cadum for Madam'
and 'Hey diddle diddle there's a hole in the middle'.*

We thought of piles including 'Goodnight, sleep tight, and don't forget to use Harpic every night'. Us girls had hysterics when Mr G started talking about 'home helps'. [Why?] Ken dashed off like last week so didn't get a chance to talk to him. But actually my interest is decidedly waning as he is rather scruffy. I'll just have to find someone else.

It didn't take me long.

Wednesday 17 February
Saw CRAIG going home. Oh, I think he is <u>so</u> nice but I mustn't let on to anyone.

Craig? He was a blond boy who lived in our flats. There'll be more about him later. Much more interestingly to me now, that diary entry continues:

Saw Mr Townsend on the 213 bus. I almost fainted! He looked ever so tanned and handsome and talked to Carol and me. Carol agreed with me that Mr Townsend looked very <u>young</u>. I remarked that perhaps it is only because we are <u>older</u>. He said that we were nearly old enough to go out to the pictures

533

with him. He also asked if Cherry was still as noisy as ever, at which I promptly replied 'YES!!!'

Dear Mr Townsend, my favourite teacher at my primary school. I wrote a whole chapter about him in *Jacky Daydream* – and I was so touched when Mr Townsend wrote to me after it was published. He'd seen me on a television programme going round Latchmere, reminiscing happily about him. I was so pleased to be able to tell him just how much he meant to all of us.

I seemed to have an embarrassingly vast capacity for crushes. I went to the Adam Faith show with Carol on 21 February, the first time I'd ever been to a pop concert. It was a small gig by modern standards, on the stage of the Granada cinema, but I was bowled over:

The John Barry Seven were ever so good. You had to clap, you couldn't help it while the music pounded out, everyone was joining in the beat. I've never experienced anything like it, you don't feel at all self conscious, just madly <u>hep</u>. Of course Adam was wonderful. Honestly, I've never believed girls could scream so loud! Adam looked ever so handsome though!

534

I've stuck a photo of him on another page in my diary, with 'Adam for Always!' and 'Faith Forever' written in lurid green biro.

I still remembered Alan fondly, my first 'boyfriend' back at primary school.

Friday 26 February
Carol told me that she saw ALAN yesterday. Oh, how clear everything is now. Until she mentioned him, I didn't realise how much I still like him. Ken was just a substitute for ALAN because he reminded me a little of him (they both have fair hair, etc.). Likewise my fair Craig. Carol said ALAN had on a seaman's cap and a navy overcoat. He told me when he was ten that he was going in the Merchant Navy, but fancy him sticking to it. I expect he was home on leave.

Alan would only have been fourteen, the same age as me, but I think there was a special boy sailor entry into the Merchant Navy in those days.

Wednesday 2 March
Going home Carol and I reminisced about the old days at Latchmere.

Oh Alan.

Oh Alan, do you remember the dressing room up in the gallery where we used to go? Do you remember the purple velvet crinoline we found there that I dressed up in?

Do you remember our 'sunbathing' with Robert and Eileen, etc.?

Do you remember when I suddenly saw you looking at me, and we looked for a long time and then kissed?

Oh, I wish I was back at Latchmere.

I wasn't really in love with Alan, we'd just been children. I wasn't in love with Craig or Ken or Adam Faith. I was simply in love with the idea of being in love. I was fourteen and it was spring.

Sunday 6 March
I went to Y.F. this afternoon, wearing Mum's cream Spring coat. On the bus I noticed lots of signs that Spring is here. There were many pink apple blossom trees in full bloom. Malden bridge was being mended and the bus couldn't get through, so I had to walk part of the way, but I didn't mind. While we were singing the hymn at Y.F. John Reynolds kept on staring at me. Chris has had her

hair done; it looked very nice. Mr G talked about T.V. It was <u>very</u> interesting, especially when he talked about a programme about teenagers.

John Reynolds now?
I did still have a mind, in spite of all the boy-madness.

Monday 7 March
We had double Art with Mrs Canter. She suggested I take O level Art in my G.C.E. At the same time she pointed out that although my 'Picture of the corner of our living room' was technically good, it was uninteresting. I couldn't agree more about it being dull, but how can one make a window, a radiator, a chair, part of a wall and part of a ceiling look thrilling? Admittedly Van Gogh did a lovely enthralling oil painting of a chair, but I am <u>not</u> Vincent Van Gogh, a genius at Art. For Latin homework we had one sentence 'The Romans seized the Sabine women'. How funny, because last Tuesday I saw the picture in the National Gallery 'The Rape of the Sabines'. Now I know where the word 'rape' is derived from, as the polite word 'seized' in Latin is rapio. In Drama Club I had to be <u>three</u> people all at once!

That shouldn't have been too much of a problem. I was used to playing three versions of myself: I was the dippy boy-mad teenager; the giggly schoolgirl; and the real me, reading and writing in my own secret world.

In Youth Fellowship on Sunday 13 March:

Johnny told us about the hike next Sat. It sounds wonderful fun; Chris says I can have lunch at her house and then – off we go. I hope it will be as fun as the Tramps Party. Ken and Robin were discussing an 'all night' hike. I heard them say 'Two tents?' and give dirty little chuckles.

Saturday 19 March
!!!!! THE HIKE !!!!!
Oh the hike was SMASHING. I went over to Chris in the morning, bought a navy duffel bag and did homework. After dinner Chris and I packed our duffel bags and met Viv. We were a bit nervous, but Viv was as matter of fact as usual. Everyone arrived at Worcester Park Station, and then – we set off! We got out at Box Hill and walked the opposite way towards Ranmore Common. We got lost, and ended up at Abinger in the evening! It was very warm and not muddy, except for one place where it was just a sea of mud. I took a huge step, and all at once my

shoe fell off, and I was standing in the mud in my socks. John Reynolds got it for me, and got his trousers all muddy! I bet his mother cursed me! We went up this hill as steep as a mountain, covered with all brambles like a jungle, and as I scrabbled and grovelled in the earth I felt a hearty push from behind and John's voice, 'Up we go, Jacqueline!' We climbed over barbed wire, ate, and walked and walked until long past dark. Afterwards John Wilkins invited all 23 of us back to his house for coffee and biscuits. When we got there there weren't any empty chairs left, and Ken and Robin invited us to sit on their laps! I don't know which I like best now: Ken, John R or John W.

I think John R sounds a sweetie, wading into the mud to rescue my shoe! We might have stayed out after dark, but we certainly didn't stay out all night. We were all extremely well-behaved. I was rather prim and priggish at fourteen:

Monday 4 April
At dinner Janice B told us that Mr Gander [one of the French teachers] had suddenly said to them, 'Let's have a debate.' The girls in her group were approving as they were naturally willing to have a

break from French. One bright spark suggested they should have a debate on 'Should boys be allowed to do what they like with girls?' Mr Gander was <u>extremely willing</u>. He told them that he thought virginity is an important factor in marriage, and that although he and his wife had intercourse a few times before they were married, he didn't think we ought to. He went on in this way, and then asked if there were any questions. One girl asked 'Why does a woman not have a baby every time she does it?' He told them that if you do it a certain time after a girl's period nothing would probably happen. <u>Honestly, isn't he awful</u>. Janice said that towards the end he got awfully het up and excited. Ugh! I'm glad I don't have him for French. Give me Mrs Coffin every day, you bet. Angela and Irene said that they'd already done it with a boy once or twice, and seemed extremely proud of the fact. They'd have laughed the other sides of their faces if anything had happened.

I saw Craig again on 19 April:

In Kingston I saw Craig who was going into Maxwells. He somehow reminded me very much of a sailor in his blue jeans and shirt, and his fair hair.

Thursday 21 April
I caught the bus home and <u>I saw Craig</u>. Before this
week when I saw him I just thought of him like –
well, an ordinary boy, but today! Wham! Now
PLEASE don't think how awful I am, because I
keep on saying I'm crazy about different boys. I'll
explain. I like Jeremy H and John R and John W
but that is all, I don't <u>particularly</u> like them. At the
time I did like Ken a lot, but now I realise it was
only to keep Chris company. I always knew I could
never like him as much as she likes Peter. Now I
can understand her because I keep on thinking of
Craig and wanting to talk about him every minute
of the day. But don't be mistaken, Alan is still first
with me, and always will be, but it's no use thinking
about him as I'll probably never see him again,
whereas I see Craig every day.

Sue next door used to go to the same school as
Craig: 'She told me he likes Art and History best.
I know he must like swimming for I often see him
go out with a towel tucked under his arm.'

I was like a Mickey Mouse detective, observing,
questioning, following a boy who was serenely
unaware of my existence. I was still interested in
a handful of Youth Fellowship boys. We went for
another hike:

Saturday 30 April

I met Chris at 10 a.m., and we wandered around the shops and went to the park. After dinner we met Carol and went to Worcester Park station. Mr and Mrs Golden and their son and their dog Rory came on the hike. We went to Box Hill station again, and climbed up Box Hill. Then we walked, ditto, ditto, ditto. Luckily it was not muddy this time, in fact it was very dry. This time we had to make our way down a chalk cliff on a neighbouring hill. Rory kept on breaking loose, and J.W. in relation to Rory's lead said 'Grab his whatsit,' and K.W. said 'I beg your pardon!' Everyone swapped jokes, and on the train back there was a paper fight between one compartment and the next. Afterwards we went back to J.W.'s house and watched T.V. and had coffee. Chris and I talked a bit to B.T., J.R. and Pyjamas. J.R. called us both by our names.

Sunday 1 May

I stayed in bed this morning, and after a good read, quickly skimmed through my Latin book. It's amazing the amount I've forgotten. Still, not to worry. In the afternoon I went to Y.F. and Mr Golden talked about 'Tough Guys'. As I sat there while Mr G talked on and on I imagined Mr G in Heaven, with a little golden halo perched on his head. It got very hot in that stuffy little room,

192

and the atmosphere seemed to press down on me. The hard little chairs are very uncomfortable and I couldn't help fidgeting; first with my handbag, crossing my legs, rocking my chair, looking at Chris and J.R., at the ceiling, at the wall. The blue of the cloth on the table, the pink of the wall, the white of the ceiling, and the grey of the boys' clothes all swam together, and I felt dizzy. Then my eyes began to water and I had to rub them. My throat was dry and parched, and I couldn't swallow, my lips felt as if they would never open again and I had to keep wetting them. Oh the blessed relief when we began the hymn!

Sunday 8 May
In the morning Mum and I stayed in bed for a while and Daddy went to tennis. It was very, very hot and in the afternoon I only wore my green shirtwaister. It was the Sunday School's anniversary and instead of the usual Y.F. service we all went down into the church and listened to the children's service in which the Juniors took part. Geraldine Webb, Ken's sister, sang a solo. (She has a nice clear little voice.) I was sitting sandwiched between Carol and John Reynolds. Carol wore her new black and white checked dress again. After the service I said goodbye to Carol and Viv and went to tea at Chris's.

We decided to go for a walk and took little-girl-next-door Margaret's dog Bluey. She is a lovely, very energetic, cocker spaniel. We took her to Beverly Brook which was crowded with New Maldenites. We went past all these boys who made noises after us, and immediately almost bumped into Ken Webb and Robin Marriot! After tea we re-met Carol and Viv and returned to church. Mr Golden is getting quite pally with us and called me 'Jac' and was very concerned about Carol's cold. We all wore lily of the valley posies on our dresses as they are our church's special flower. In the evening service it was the Seniors' turn to perform and they acted the part of nurses, beggars, school children, etc. Dangling from the roof of the church was a painted sun, moon and some clouds and stars to represent the universe, and every time Mr Kelly or anyone got up to preach they got hit on the head by the sun.

I still didn't seem to be making proper friends with any of these boys.

Monday 20 June
I must admit it would be nice to have a boyfriend to boast about, but boys of my own age are so stupid, and boys of about 16 or 17 who are interested in

girls want girls their own age. Oh well, if I'm just
patient I expect one will come along some day.

I had lots of attention from the wrong sort of
boy. Whenever Carol and I went to the pictures,
older boys usually started whistling or messing
around or trying out some corny chat-up line. Carol
looked older than me and had a dark, pouty,
smouldering look they found very attractive. But
we both found these approaches embarrassing and
we were under no illusions – they just wanted girls
to sit in the back row with them. We knew what
was likely to happen.

Tuesday 9 August
In the afternoon Carol and I went to the Granada
to see 'Make Mine Mink'. It was very very funny,
but half the time we weren't watching the screen,
but watching the couple in front of us. A girl was
sitting in the middle of the row and a boy at the
end. The girl got up to go, and as she passed him
the boy looked at her. A few minutes later the girl
returned, only this time she sat next to him. They
started talking, and he gave her a cigarette. Then
he casually put his arm along the back of her seat,
and then onto her shoulder. Then he leant over and
kissed her, then again. She leant back and he leant

over her and they kissed and kissed passionately. Then he slowly slid his hand up her skirt but I don't think she liked that because she tried to push it away. Anyway, when the film ended the boy whispered to the girl, and then went out and didn't come back. The girl sat placidly in front of us and watched the second film. Two perfect strangers!

Boys tried to pick girls up everywhere.

Friday 22 April
I met Carol at half past two and we went to the baths, but they were packed, and there was a very long queue. We resolutely joined the end of it. A Teddy boy ran his hand up my back and I said 'Do you mind?' and dragged Carol away as I <u>hate</u> that sort of boy.

Teddy boys wore their hair in greasy quiffs, they had long fancy jackets down to their knees, bootlace ties, drainpipe trousers and suede shoes with enormous soles. They were nearly all harmless suburban lads, but the very name 'teddy boy' made Biddy think of flick-knives and drinking and sex and doing a ton on motorbikes. She wanted me to find a boyfriend but she'd have fainted if I'd brought home a teddy boy.

Sunday 17 July
Went to Burnham Beeches with Carol. At the swimming pool a boy squirted water from a soda siphon all over us. Then we went round the fair together. I turned round, and noticed that four teds were following. Cas and I walked on to the Rollapenny and the teds followed and stood very close behind us. One of them said, 'I dunno how to play Rollapenny, perhaps one of these young ladies will show us how' so I said, 'Okay, if you provide the pennies.' And believe it or not the ted fished in his pocket and brought out a handful of coppers. I felt awful (I don't know why) so I didn't take any.

This was all pretty tame, but sometimes girls felt very vulnerable back in 1960, when mild sexual harassment was commonplace:

Thursday 4 August
Went to Lagoon with Carol. Four boys kept throwing matches at us and kept on talking for hours. I didn't like them and neither did Carol but we stayed until

one of them mentioned undoing my swimming costume zip, and then we hastily departed.

Monday 8 August
Carol and I went to the Lagoon, but the changing rooms were being sluiced out all day so we had to change in the open. It was horrible. When I had nothing on but a towel on my top some men came along and stared and commented.

I was starting to despair. There were a good handful of boys I liked, but none of them seemed to want to get to know me properly. All the boys who showed an interest in me were too old or too scary or too crude. But at the end of August Biddy and Harry and I went on holiday to Cornwall – and I had my first real romance.

GOOD LUCK

FROM ST IVES

12
Cornwall

We went on a fortnight's holiday, one week in St Ives and one week in Newquay, with Uncle Ron and Aunty Grace. I wonder whose idea it was. Biddy worked with Ron at Prince Machines and they were very close. I'm sure they'd have loved to go off on holiday, just the two of them. It seemed so strange for us all to go in this awkward fivesome. Why didn't Harry or Grace object? I didn't mind for myself. I'd been to Cornwall before on an odd holiday with Harry and had thought it beautiful. (He and Biddy had separate holidays the year I was eleven – I had to accompany both of them in turn.)

Cornwall was considered *exotic* in 1960, before there were cheap package tours abroad. Chris was going on holiday to Eastbourne as usual with Fred, Hetty and Jan. I think Carol and her family were just having day trips here and there.

I met up with Carol the Friday before we went on holiday and we went to the Boys and Girls Exhibition at Olympia. I'd been there before when I was younger, with Biddy. I'd shyly whispered a few words to the children's author Pamela Brown and been traumatized by George Cansdale wrapping a large snake round my neck. I kept well away from any animal stand this time.

I looked hopefully for Pamela Brown, or indeed any other authors. I have a feeling Noel Streatfeild might have been there. I'd loved all Noel Streatfeild's books when I was younger and longed to see her, even if I wasn't sure I'd have enough gump to talk to her – not without Biddy prodding me into action. But we couldn't find Noel Streatfeild. It was hard finding any of the stands it was so jam-packed. We simply shuffled here, stumbled there, eating hot dogs for our lunch, giggling and blushing when any boys spoke to us.

When I got home Biddy had done all my packing for me. She spent hours ironing and folding and arranging every item in perfect patterns until each suitcase looked like a work of art. My white canvas beach shoes and my new pointy black heels touched toes beside my blue and white floral swimming costume and my best baby-doll pyjamas; my underwear was prinked into shape like elaborate table napkins; my two white T-shirts and my startlingly short shorts were carefully folded, still serenely spotless. My pale lilac cardigan was curled round them like a little furry creature, and all my frocks were puffed out and folded over tissue paper: my green shirtwaister and a deep blue floral frock and a new white puff-sleeved dress sprigged with tiny apricot flowers. My favourite lilac skirt floated on top, freshly laundered and immaculately ironed.

'Oh thanks, Mum, but what about my *stuff*? My journal and my notebook and my black folder and—'

'You're not going to be huddled in a corner writing all day long. You're on *holiday*,' said Biddy.

'But what about my books?'

'You can take a paperback for the train,' said Biddy. 'We'll get you some magazines too.'

I didn't argue, knowing it was a waste of breath. I waited until she'd gone to tackle Harry's packing – he wasn't trusted to do it himself either – and then carefully shoved my diary down in the depths of the case, together with *The Greengage Summer*, a Monica Dickens paperback, a little Collins copy of *Jane Eyre* because it was very long. *Gone with the Wind* because it was even longer, and my current favourite book for the train, *Billy Liar* by Keith Waterhouse.

I found *Billy Liar* riveting reading. It's a story about a young Yorkshire lad called Billy Fisher who worked in an undertaker's, had three simultaneous girlfriends and told compulsive lies. I was a suburban schoolgirl who didn't even have one boyfriend and didn't tell *actual* lies, though I was frequently economical with the truth. I identified totally with Billy because he was a helpless daydreamer, forever seeking refuge in his own imaginary world of Ambrosia, he didn't feel he fitted in with his family, and he badly wanted to be a writer. It was a revelation to me that someone else felt exactly the same way I did. I laughed at his jokes, I bit my lip when he got into endless trouble, I learned all his catch phrases, I lived every minute of his life.

Biddy sniffed when she saw me clutching *Billy Liar* the next morning and Harry cursed when he picked up my suitcase (*Gone with the Wind* alone was like a couple of bricks), but I couldn't bear the thought of running out of reading matter. I had two long weeks sitting on a beach with four adults who would be talking amongst themselves. It's a wonder I didn't try to stuff our collected hardback edition of Jane Austen into my suitcase too.

I read my way through *Billy Liar* twice on the train journey down to St Ives. It was always an incredible palaver for the three of us travelling anywhere. Ron and Grace must have travelled separately by car. We certainly had the use of a car on holiday and it wasn't ours. It would probably have been too much of a squash for all of us to travel down to Cornwall in Ron's car, especially as we three Aitkens travelled with four large cumbersome cases and several bags and carriers as well. Biddy had to have *two* large battered Revelation suitcases to spread her frocks out properly, fluttering brightly in between layers of tissue paper like giant butterflies.

We would normally have taken the hourly Green Line bus all the way up to London but we couldn't possibly manhandle so much luggage ourselves so we hired a car up to Paddington. This was such an extraordinary step that Biddy and Harry were extra tense on the journey, and I sat bolt upright, eyes closed, breathing shallowly, praying that I wasn't going to be sick over the hired upholstery.

We felt triumphant when we eventually flopped down on the scratchily upholstered seats in the train. Poor Harry struggled to stow all the cases in the roof racks while Biddy fussed because we weren't facing the engine and pulled hard on the leather strap to make sure the window was tightly closed. It was stifling in the carriage before we'd even started the journey, but she was anxious about smuts flying in and speckling our virgin-white shirts and cardigans with soot. This was the age of steam trains. They let fly a plume of white smoke as they chugged through the countryside, the wheels turning to a comforting tune: *diddle-de-der, diddle-de-der, diddle-de-der*, on and on. And on and on and *on*, all the way to St Ives.

It took all day long then. By the time we eventually arrived and checked into our modest hotel we were exhausted. We met up with Ron and Grace and ate our dinner of brown Windsor soup, boiled beef and carrots, and vanilla ice cream with tinned peaches, and then went straight to our bedroom.

We had to unpack everything there and then and hang it up carefully under Biddy's strict supervision. I quickly hid my extra books in the drawer she'd designated for my T-shirts and underwear. I had my journal and was all set to write up the day while Biddy and Harry were making their treks to the bathroom and back. The hotel was quite posh in our eyes but certainly didn't run to en suite bathrooms. I was so tired I just wrote in pencil: 'Long long long train journey', and then I fell asleep.

We met up with Ron and Grace again at breakfast, Biddy and Ron chatting animatedly, Harry and Grace chewing silently, me spooning up my tinned grapefruit and surreptitiously peering round at all the other guests in the dining room. There didn't seem to be any girls my age. There *were* a few boys, but surprisingly none particularly took my eye.

I was keen to get to the beach. We sunbathed most of Sunday. I wore my minuscule short shorts and white top and later changed into my blue and white swimsuit. Biddy wore her very similar costume on the beach. There are snapshot photos of us looking alarmingly alike, our brown hair blown back by the breeze, showing our high foreheads, our big noses and determined chins. Biddy is small and slim and looks years younger than her age. It must have been galling for Grace, who was older and stockier and much more staid looking. There are no photos of her in her swimming costume.

There are lots of photos of Ron, who is older and overweight and very homely looking, with eyes too close together and flat Brylcreemed hair – and yet he's always got a cheery grin on his face and the only time he's bothered to try to suck in his stomach is when he's standing in the sea with Harry and me.

Harry is the best looking of all of us, his tennis playing keeping him trim and muscular. He tanned easily, going an impressive golden brown within a couple of days. He's smiling in every photo too, which seems astonishing.

On the Monday we had a trip out in Ron's car to Mullion and the Lizard. I was particularly enthusiastic about going to Mullion because I'd once enjoyed reading a book by Mabel Esther Allan about a bunch of children with bizarre names: there was one girl with green eyes called Pussy, and the narrator was called Mullion after the Cornish cove. The Lizard sounded interesting too. I was mad enough to hope for real large lizards lurking on the rocks like a fantasy Jurassic age. Both Mullion and the Lizard were doubtless beautiful but a little disappointing in reality. I'm not sure which is which in the little black and white snapshots. There's one of a vast cliff with Ron straddling a large rock, flabby chest and big belly making him look like a Buddha.

We made another trip out to Land's End. In those days it was attractively bare and deserted so it gave you a feeling of being at the very end of England. The only nod to tourism was a signpost where you could insert the letters of your own home town. So there we are, smiling under a sign that said CHEAM 291 MILES (where Ron and Grace lived) and KINGSTON 283 MILES.

We all look relaxed and are smiling obediently, even Harry and Grace. Harry is wearing a too-tight sweater, baggy tennis shorts and open-toed sandals, *not* a good look. Grace is sitting down, wearing a large frock, skirts blowing in the breeze, a bead necklace round her throat. Biddy is next to her, her grinning mouth dark with lipstick. She's wearing a snug sweater and surprising trousers – she called them trews – in a jazzy zigzag pattern. Ron is standing above her, one arm leaning on the signpost, the other arm round me. My shorts look indecent, I'm showing way too much plump leg. I was always such an anxious, self-conscious girl, fussing desperately over my hair, obsessing about a tiny spot on my nose – how could I have gone out practically showing my knickers?

Our hotel held a dance on Monday evening. I wasn't sure I wanted to go, feeling foolish trailing behind these four ill-assorted adults.

'Can't I just stay in my room and read?' I begged Biddy.

'No, of course you can't! You can't just lurk in the bedroom and read. You're here to enjoy yourself on holiday,' said Biddy.

I *wasn't* enjoying myself. I felt bored and restless and embarrassed trailing round with four adults all the time, and I was terribly aware of Grace's little huffs and Harry's sulks. We were playing this game that we were all great friends having a fantastic holiday, but we all knew that wasn't true.

'I don't want to go to this damn daft dance either,' said Harry. 'I'm going to push off for a walk.'

'You can't! You've *got* to come,' Biddy said, craning to zip herself into her best low-necked frock.

'I haven't *got* to do anything. I don't want to dance with you – and I certainly don't want to dance with Grace,' said Harry.

'You've got to, to be polite. Look, don't just stand there, help me with my zip!'

Harry sorted her out so smartly that the skin of her back got pinched in the zip. Biddy screamed and accused him of doing it on purpose. There was a row, conducted in whispers, because all the bedrooms were in close proximity. Harry stormed off on his walk. Biddy collapsed in tears. I tried inadequately to comfort her, longing to escape back into my book.

But disaster was averted. Harry came back twenty minutes later. He wasn't talking, but he put on a clean white shirt and changed into his best grey suit. Biddy held a damp flannel over her eyes and then patted her powder in place, painting a big lipstick smile on her face. I stopped lolling on my bed with my book and shook out my creased skirts. My white dress set off my tan and I had a new gilt and mother-of-pearl locket as a holiday present.

We lined up to peer in the big mirror inside the wardrobe, Biddy and Harry and me, and we all passed muster. Then we went down the stairs, along the passageway and into the ballroom to join up with Ron and Grace, who were already halfway through their lemonade shandies.

Oh, those long-ago dances! You had a waltz, a quickstep, a slow foxtrot, and if you were really dashing, a cha-cha-cha. There were the novelty dances, the spot waltz where the music stopped every few minutes and the compère asked a silly question and the first couple to answer it got a prize: a bar of chocolate or a tin of talcum powder or a propelling pencil, nothing exciting at all, but the couples whooped as if they'd won the football pools. Then there was the Paul Jones, where all the ladies joined hands in a circle facing outwards and all the gentlemen formed an outer circle facing inwards, holding hands far more awkwardly. When the music started the ladies danced clockwise, the men anti-clockwise, until the music stopped and you had to dance with the man facing you. Sometimes there were more ladies than men and you got a gap, so you had to slink back to your seat until the circles started up again.

But I was lucky that evening. I wrote: 'I had a partner for nearly all the dances, but I'm not particularly keen on any of the boys here although they are really very nice.'

'Very nice' sounds a little limp. I was obviously still feeling depressed. Harry was very quiet too, though he did dance with Biddy several times, and even steered Grace around the room in a jerky quickstep. Biddy and Ron danced too. I wonder if those snatched five-minute sessions on the dance floor made the whole holiday worthwhile.

But the next evening:

We went for a walk around Zennor head. First we climbed up a very high stony hill which was covered with very soft earthy grass that looked rather like lava from a volcano. When you reached the top a tremendously powerful wind almost lifted you off the peak, so that I experienced a sensation almost equal to flying. The wind seemed to cleanse and lift my spirits until I was almost bubbling over.

I can still vividly remember staring up at the stars and wanting to spread my arms and leap upwards.

'*Then we went for a walk along the cliff in the dark and poor Uncle Ron tripped over and sprained his ankle.*'

Did he trip – or was he pushed? Did Harry bump into him accidentally on purpose? Did Grace shove him with a sharp elbow? What were we *doing*, walking along a clifftop in the dark?

But we all got back to St Ives safe and sound, though Ron limped for a few days and wasn't able to trip the light fantastic at the farewell dance on Friday night.

We moved on to Newquay on the Saturday, all booked up for one more week. I'd much sooner have gone straight home to Cumberland House, where I could have a bit of privacy in my own bedroom, read and write whenever I felt like it, and go to the pictures or the shops or the lagoon with Chris or Carol. I even fantasized about seizing my train ticket from Biddy's purse and travelling home on the train by myself.

I tried suggesting this in a very roundabout way – 'It's been a lovely holiday but I'm a bit worried, I didn't take any of my school set work. Tell you what, I could always go home a bit early and get on with it. You don't have to worry about me, you know I *like* being by myself, and I could have my dinners at Ga's, she wouldn't mind a bit.'

'Don't be so *silly*!' said Biddy. 'Come on, start getting your things laid out nicely on your bed for me to pack. You're coming with us.'

'But I don't want to,' I mumbled childishly.

'Well, that's just too bad,' said Biddy. 'Now get cracking with those clothes, pronto, and stop being so ruddy ungrateful. *I* never went away on holiday for a whole two weeks when I was your age. Stop pulling that sulky face. You'll love it when you get there.'

She was right, oh so right!

On Newquay beach

Harry, Jacqueline and Ron

Cookie, his sister and Colin

13
Cookie

Saturday 27 August
Our new landlady, Mrs Philpotts, is an absolute
scream of a character, although she means very well.
She is a very hearty type with an enormous bust
and a horsy face. I think I'm going to like Newquay
and this hotel better than St Ives. The young people
are – two teenage blondes that are nicknamed 'The
Beverley Sisters', a big hefty boy called Jeff, and a
nice-looking boy about 13–14 called Colin, with his
sister and his sister's friend, both called Gillian
and both 16.

I never got to know the Beverley Sisters or big
hefty Jeff – but I *did* get to know Colin.

I got up early on Sunday morning and wandered
downstairs a good half-hour before the breakfast
gong. Mrs Philpotts had said there was a recreation
room with a small library. I still had *Gone with the*
Wind as a standby but I wanted to see what other
books were on offer. I peeped in several doors and
found the dining room all set up for breakfast and

565

a sitting room with big sofas and a small television set – and then I stumbled upon the recreation room. It was just a small room with a shelf of Agatha Christie and Alistair Maclean paperbacks and a lot of board games, Monopoly and Ludo and Snakes and Ladders. There was a table-tennis table crammed into the room – and Colin was standing at the net, madly trying to play his left hand against his right hand.

He grinned when he saw me and clapped his tennis bats together. 'Hurray! Come and play with me!' he said, as if we'd known each other for ever.

'I can't play. I don't know how,' I said.

'I'll teach you,' said Colin, thrusting the bat in my hand.

'I'm not any good at games,' I said. 'I'm sure I'll be hopeless.'

I *was* hopeless, but Colin didn't seem to mind. He was happy to chase after the ball and win spectacularly.

'*Champion, the wonder horse!*' he sang. (It was the theme tune from a children's television show.) He threw back his head and neighed while I giggled uncertainly.

'You are daft,' I said.

'Course I am. Totally nuts,' said Colin happily. 'I'm Colin. What's your name?'

'Jacky.'

'Have you got any brothers or sisters here?'

I shook my head.

'I've got my big sister Gillian. She's with *her* friend Gillian. She's OK but she's sixteen, too old for me. How old are you, Jacky?'

'Fourteen.'

'Well, I'm *nearly* fourteen. Do you want to be my girlfriend?'

I stared at him. I liked him but I didn't want a boyfriend who was younger than me – and totally nuts.

'Let's just be friends,' I said cautiously.

'OK,' said Colin, not seeming to mind. 'I've got this friend Cookie. He's a great laugh. He's got this beach hut. We muck around together. Maybe you could be *his* girlfriend?'

'I don't think so!'

Cookie! He sounded as odd as Colin. I didn't think it at all likely I'd want to be his girlfriend.

'Well, you could still come and hang out with us by the beach hut,' Colin suggested.

'It's very kind of you, but I'm here with my parents and their friends,' I mumbled. 'Shall we have another game of table tennis?'

'Yeah, yeah, great,' said Colin, immediately serving and not even giving me a chance to return the ball. 'One to me. Are you going to the beach today then?'

567

'Yes, I expect so.'

'Are you going to do any surfriding?'

'You bet,' I said.

He looked surprised and wiggled his eyebrows. 'You can really surf?'

'Of course I can,' I said proudly.

I'd been to Newquay two years before and surfed every day. *Not* the surfriding guys in wetsuits do today, standing up and zigzagging over huge breakers. I wish! No, in 1960 in England, surfriding meant basic wooden boards. As long as you were a strong swimmer anyone could wade out, wait for a big wave, lie on the board and be whisked along into the shallows. I might be a total duffer at table tennis but I loved swimming and I'd taken to surfriding in a big way.

'Two to me. My pal Cookie's super at surfing. I'm just sort of so-so,' said Colin. 'I don't like getting my head under the water.' He shook his thick brown hair, pulling a silly face. Then his eyes brightened.

'So what kind of swimming costume have you got, Jacky?' he said, serving again. The ball whizzed straight past me. 'Come on, you can't be *that* bad . . . Is it a bikini?' he added hopefully.

'No, it's *not* a bikini,' I said.

'Oh, spoilsport,' said Colin. As he served he

started singing the 'Itsy Bitsy Teenie Weenie Yellow Polka Dot Bikini' song.

'Mine's a swimsuit. It's not itsy-bitsy or teeny-weeny, and it's not even yellow, it's blue and white,' I said. I actually managed to connect bat with ball and smash it past him.

The breakfast gong sounded and Colin grinned.

'Just as you were coming into your own. Oh well, maybe see you on the beach? Or if not, come and find us along the beach-hut terrace. Cookie's hut is number sixty-eight.' He put his head on one side, squinting at me earnestly. 'You're absolutely *sure* you don't want to be my girlfriend?'

I was still absolutely sure, but I did like Colin a lot. He waved to me enthusiastically when I entered the breakfast room with Biddy and Harry, calling, 'Hello Jacky!' nearly knocking his orange juice over.

'I see you've made a friend here already, Jac!' said Biddy.

'We just played table tennis together,' I said casually.

'You played table tennis?' said Harry, raising his eyebrows. He'd tried very hard one summer to teach me the rudiments of tennis, with spectacular lack of success.

'I'm not very good at it,' I said humbly.

'Never mind, as if it matters,' said Biddy. 'It's

lovely that you're chumming up with someone. You never know, you *might* meet up with him on the beach.' She sounded a little patronizing.

'Well, his friend's got a beach hut. He wanted me to go there, practically begged me,' I said. 'But I'm not sure I want to. In fact I definitely don't.'

'Oh, *Jac*,' said Biddy, exasperated. 'I don't understand you at all.'

I didn't really understand myself. I'd been so fed up traipsing around with Biddy and Harry and Ron and Grace. Now I had a chance of younger, livelier, albeit crazier company and I was wilfully turning it down. I suppose I was just a bit shy, a bit scared. You couldn't be shy or scared of Colin but this unknown Cookie might be a different matter.

So I ignored Colin's gesturing queries and went off to get ready for a day on the beach with Biddy and Harry and Ron and Grace. This involved a lot of packing. Biddy had her favourite Evan Hunter book and her spare white cardigan and her camera and her swimming costume, just in case. Harry had his racing papers and his windcheater and his woolly swimming trunks and a spare towel snaffled from the hotel bedroom. Ron and Grace took beach time even more seriously. Ron had his trunks and his own big stripy towel and his hairbrush and Brylcreem and a beach ball and a big bag of toffees.

Grace had her knitting and a map of Cornwall and a thermos and plastic cups and a damp cloth in a plastic bag and a *Woman's Own*. I had my swimming costume and *Jane Eyre* and my journal.

We wandered down to the beach, lugging our burdens. I saw the rows of beach huts and hesitated for a moment, but I scurried off after the others. I hoped they might settle on the smooth golden sand near the beach huts but they seemed intent on doing a Lawrence of Arabia trek across the sands, seeking an ideal spot.

We eventually set up camp way down the beach, out of sight of the beach huts. I pretended I didn't care. I struggled into my swimming costume under cover of my towel and then lay on my tummy, reading and eating Ron's toffees. Ron tried to tempt us with a game of ball, and for a little while he and Harry tossed it about while I was piggy in the middle. Biddy and Grace made strained conversation while peering at the map, plotting little outings to Polperro and Mousehole and Jamaica Inn.

There were families all around us, some of the boys rushing in surfing.

'Shall we give this surfing lark a go?' Ron asked eagerly. 'Come on, Biddy, I bet you're a dab hand at it. Get your costume on!'

'No, no, I'm much too comfortable,' said Biddy.

'Jac, you'll have a go, won't you? I'll show you what to do,' said Ron.

'Jac's a good surfer already,' Harry said coldly. 'I showed her how on our last holiday to Newquay.'

This was a downright lie. Harry was a weak swimmer and didn't have much clue how to surf, but I smiled at him loyally. The three of us trailed all the way to the surf shack to hire boards. No one bothered to ask poor Grace if she'd like a go.

I clutched my board and waded gingerly into the water, lifting my feet high and jumping every time a wave swelled past me, a total wimp about getting wet. But though it took me ages to get in properly up to my neck, with Harry and Ron shouting and splashing me, I came into my own once I was in. I paddled around on my surfboard, eyeing up each likely wave, and then, just before it crested, I leaped forward and hurtled full tilt all the way into the shallows. I waded out again and again, while Harry and Ron wobbled and wavered and fell off their boards.

Biddy came picking her way to the water's edge, her Brownie camera in her hand. She lined us up and commanded us to smile, bossily intent – so much so that she shrieked when a wave suddenly swirled round her ankles, wetting the hem of her frock. We all smiled easily enough then.

I hated the getting-out-the-water stage, blue and shivering, with the towel wrapped around me, struggling out of my wet costume and into my knickers, trying not to get everything all sandy. But the sun was out and I gratefully drank a cup of tea from Grace's thermos. I combed my straggly hair and fished my coral lipstick out of the pocket of my skirt.

'Haven't we got any sandwiches?' said Ron, rubbing his big tummy. 'I'm starving after all that surfing. Let's have a picnic.'

'Oh, Ron, how can I make up a picnic when we're staying in a hotel?' said Grace.

'*I'll* magic up a picnic,' said Ron, reaching for his wallet. 'I'll nip along the beach to the shops. Who's coming with me to help carry the goodies?'

He looked hopefully at Biddy, but she was stretched out, eyes closed, seemingly asleep. Ron looked at me instead. 'Come on, Jacky.'

So I sauntered along beside him, carrying my sandals, while he laughed and joked and clowned around. He attempted daft conjuring tricks, plucking pennies from my ears, hankies from my hair. People on the beach smiled at us, obviously thinking he was my dad. In lots of ways I wished he *was* my dad. You could laugh and joke and tease him back, you never had to be wary, you could say the first thing that came into your head.

I wrote later, cruelly:

How happy we'd all be if Uncle Ron and Mum married. Dad would have Aunty Grace! (Two awkward ones together.) I am writing a lot of nasty things about him, we haven't had a quarrel or anything but I'm just fed up and truthfully admitting things I've loyally tried to ignore. Later I'll probably want to tear out this page. But if Daddy wasn't my father I wouldn't be the same, as I am very like him in some ways.

I know Biddy tried to read my diary, which was why I kept trying to find new hiding places for it. I do so hope Harry didn't ever find it and read that last passage. Today I went through many files of my old manuscripts, looking for the story I wrote about that Cornish holiday. I came across two letters that Harry wrote to me when I was living in Scotland several years later – lovely, funny, stylish letters that made me want to cry. I couldn't find the story anywhere, though I did find a letter telling me that it had won a competition, the first time I'd ever won anything with my writing. But I don't really need to find that story. I can still remember the holiday as if it was only last summer.

Ron and I went to the general shop and bought five big Cornish pasties, five Scotch eggs, five packets of Bovril-flavoured crisps, two pounds of tomatoes, a bunch of bananas and a bag of apples. He dawdled at the sweet counter and then chose five Fry's Five Boys chocolate bars. There were faces of the five boys on the wrapper, labelled DESPERATION, PACIFICATION, EXPECTATION, ACCLAMATION, REALIZATION. Uncle Ron imitated each one with his big red rubbery features, making everyone in the shop chuckle.

There was a particularly loud hoot of a laugh behind me, curiously familiar. I turned round. There was Colin, choking on his choc ice, standing beside a boy with intense brown eyes, fair curly hair and a smooth golden tan. He was wearing a casual white shirt and blue shorts and his sandy feet were bare. I stared at him and he stared at me.

'This is *Jacky* – you know, the girl I told you about. We played ping-pong this morning,' said Colin. 'I won, both games. Jacky, this is my friend Cookie.'

I swallowed. I smiled. Cookie put his hand out in a charmingly old-fashioned way, shaking mine.

'Hello. Colin's told me all about you. I'm Peter Cookson, but all my friends call me Cookie.'

Did that mean I could call him Cookie too? What exactly had Colin told him? Had he told him I didn't want to be his girlfriend?

Uncle Ron was wiggling his eyebrows and beaming at us, clutching our two big brown carrier bags.

'Are you Jacky's dad?' asked Colin.

'No, he's my . . . Uncle Ron,' I said.

'OK, Uncle Ron, can Jacky come and hang out with us over at the beach huts?' said Colin.

'Well, that's fine with me, but I expect she should ask her mum first. And she's got to come back up the beach with me for her picnic lunch.'

'She could have a picnic at our hut. My mum always has heaps,' said Cookie.

'Or we could come with you and wait till she's had her picnic and then walk back with her,' said Colin, licking the last of his choc ice from the wrapper.

So they ambled along beside us. My heart was beating fast underneath my white T-shirt. It was wonderful having not one but two boys begging for my company – and Cookie seemed so *special*.

Biddy sat up and blinked when we got back to our little camp. There I was, a boy on either side of me. Harry looked startled, Grace mildly surprised. Uncle Ron did the introductions and Colin sat down cross-legged at once and started chatting nineteen to the dozen. Cookie was much quieter, though he politely answered all Biddy's questions. He lived in Sale, he was fifteen years old, he went to a grammar school.

'Mum!' I mumbled. She'd be asking him what his father did for a living next.

Grace took over the picnic, arranging pasties and Scotch eggs on the paper bags and circling them with tomatoes. I was so excited I just nibbled at a Scotch egg and then an apple.

'Don't you like pasties, Jacky? I *love* them,' said Colin blatantly.

Grace offered him one and he wolfed it down.

'I don't suppose there are any crisps going spare?' he said.

Cookie had a few crisps too, and then stood up. 'So it's OK if Jacky comes with us this afternoon?' he asked Biddy. 'We're number sixty-eight if you need to come and find her. Otherwise I'll walk her back to your hotel by six – is that all right?'

'*I'll* walk her, seeing as it's my hotel too,' said Colin.

'Well, just so long as *one* of you gets her back safely. She's such a daydreamer, she'd never find her way back on her own,' said Biddy, but she was smiling. 'Off you go then.'

I ran off with Cookie and Colin. We walked along the water's edge, suddenly all of us at a loss for words, even Colin. He started messing around, barging into Cookie, splashing him, trying to wrestle with him. I edged away, not wanting to get my lilac skirt splashed. Maybe I should have changed back into my swimming costume? No, maybe not. They both stared at me a bit too much as it was.

'What's up, Jacky? Come in paddling,' said Colin, kicking his way through the waves.

'I don't want to get all wet again,' I said.

'Have you been swimming this morning then?' Cookie asked.

'Yep. Well, surfriding,' I said.

'She's really good at it,' said Colin, though he'd never seen me.

'So are you a really sporty girl then?'

'No fear! I *hate* most sports. It's my worst thing at school,' I said. 'I can't catch a ball and I can't run for toffee.'

'But you like swimming?'

'Yes, I love it.'

'Maybe you're a mermaid,' said Cookie. 'Perhaps you've got green scales under your pretty skirt.'

We both blushed. Colin sighed and went tearing along, kicking hard, lost in a plume of spray.

The sun came out from behind a cloud and shone on the blue water. I looked at the sea, the sky, the sands.

'It's so lovely here,' I said.

'I know. We come every year.' Cookie looked up

the beach to the rocks. 'There are caves in there. We could go exploring.'

'I don't think I've ever been in a proper cave before. Do they go back a long way?'

'Some of them do. When I was little I used to like setting up camp in them. I'd take a rug and my spade and some chocolate and stuff and crouch there in the dark, kidding on I was in some Enid Blyton book.'

'*The Cave of Adventure*! I read heaps of those. I love reading. Not Enid Blyton now, of course.'

'What do you like reading now then?' asked Cookie.

I had enough sense not to try and answer him properly as it would have taken all afternoon.

'I've just read a book called *Billy Liar*,' I said.

'Oh, I've read that,' said Cookie. 'It's good, isn't it. Funny. Those calendars!'

He really *had* read it.

'I wish he'd gone to London in the end,' I said.

'I'm going to go to London one day,' said Cookie. 'And I'll come and visit you and we'll go to . . . ?' He looked at me for suggestions.

'We'll go to all the coffee bars and jazz cellars in Soho,' I said, as if I frequented them every day. I thought hard, remembering my trips to the Royal Dental Hospital. 'And we'll have a meal at the

Golden Egg in Leicester Square and then go dancing at the Empire Ballroom.'

'Jiving,' said Cookie, suddenly taking hold of my hand and whirling me round.

'Come *on*, you two,' Colin yelled. 'What are you *doing*?'

'We're dancing,' said Cookie.

'Oh, right. OK, so am I,' said Colin, and he started capering around too, splashing more than ever.

It took us ages to get to the beach hut, but Cookie's parents seemed entirely unfazed. His dad just smiled and waved at Colin and me and then went back to his paper. His mum went into the beach hut and brought back four cans of Tizer and a mound of egg sandwiches in a big Oxo tin. The fourth can was for Cookie's sister, a shy, sweet girl several years younger than me. She looked admiringly at my flowery skirt and coral lipstick. My heart was beating fast again. I wasn't the shy young girl this time. I was the older girl with the cool clothes and make-up, the one the boys liked.

We ate and drank and then played a silly game of deck quoits, where luckily you didn't need much skill at all. Then Cookie and Colin and I went down the beach near the sea where the sand was firm and started making a giant boat with some old spades that had been propped up inside the beach hut. Colin dug wildly of course, flinging sand over his shoulder, but he had bags of energy and got a lot done. Cookie was good at organizing the shape of the boat, smoothing and sculpting carefully. I wandered around collecting shells to stud the sides of the boat and carved stylized waves all around it.

It took us *hours* but it was a truly magnificent boat by the time we'd finished it. We clambered gingerly inside on the sand seat, begging Colin to be extra careful. Then the three of us sat there, feeling proud and yet a little foolish too, because we weren't children any more.

'What are we supposed to do now?' said Cookie.

'We row the boat to China,' said Colin, using his spade like an oar.

We all three rowed wildly, singing the Row-row-row-your-boat song, waiting for the sea to come splashing up around us.

'I wish we could keep it. It's a magnificent boat,' I said wistfully.

'We can build another boat tomorrow,' said Cookie.

'Yeah, we'll build an even bigger boat tomorrow,' said Colin. 'A houseboat, with a proper room inside, with beds and benches and all sorts.'

'No, no, a cruiser the length of the beach,' said Cookie.

'Like the *Queen Elizabeth*. Only we'll call it the *Queen Jacky*!' said Colin, cackling with laughter.

Cookie came with us back to the hotel. 'I wish I was staying here too,' he said.

'Yeah, I shall have Jacky all to myself every evening *and* every morning before breakfast.' Colin thumped his chest Tarzan-style and gave a loud jungle yodel.

I shook my head at him. 'Idiot!' Then I looked at Cookie. 'See you tomorrow then?'

I saw him every single day. I wanted to stay with them all the time but I was forced to go on all the outings Biddy and Grace had planned, though I always had several hours on the beach with Cookie and Colin. I plucked up the courage to go swimming with them – at least I could retire into the beach hut to change into my costume, rather than struggling inelegantly under a towel.

I blushed as I stepped outside in my blue and white swimming costume. It suddenly seemed much too skimpy and revealing. Colin wolf-whistled, inevitably, but Cookie smiled at me and held out his hand to take me down to the sea. We ran right into the water and started jumping each wave and then diving like otters until our eyes were stinging with the salt.

We queued at the surf shack another day and I showed off my surfboard skills to both boys, and then we went back to the beach hut and wrapped ourselves in big towels and ate sandwiches from the Oxo tin.

Biddy was worried that the Cooksons might think I was sponging off them, so she gave me money to treat everyone to ice creams. Mrs Cookson invited Biddy and Harry and Ron and Grace to the beach hut and the adults all had a cup of tea together while we fidgeted and fussed, and then declared we were going off for a walk.

We splashed along at the sea's edge, Colin and Cookie often wrestling and fooling around or telling idiotic jokes or making stupid noises. I'd get impatient and think, *What am I doing here with these two loonies*? and I'd wish myself back with my books and my journal. Then Cookie would suddenly take my hand or Colin would say something so utterly silly I'd burst out laughing, and I'd realize I wanted to be with them more than anyone else in the world.

Well ... I liked Colin very much, fool that he was, but I liked Cookie much more. Whenever Colin whooped off by himself for a minute or two we talked hurriedly, suddenly serious. Once or twice Cookie said, 'Let's push off, just you and me, just for a little while, please.'

'But what about Colin? Wouldn't it hurt his

feelings if we push off by ourselves?' I asked anxiously.

'Oh, never mind Colin,' said Cookie – but he was just as concerned about upsetting him as I was. We stayed a threesome all week.

We went exploring in the caves one afternoon. I was initially disappointed. They were damp and chilly and rather smelly. Every now and then you slipped on empty crisp packets or tripped over beer bottles. Still, it was fun feeling our way through all the winding passages. There was always a thrilling clutch of fear that we would get totally lost and end up going further and further into the dark interior. The constant drip of water from the roof made me wonder if the sea could possibly suddenly come surging in . . .

Colin was very taken up by the echo possibilities in the caves and went running ahead, yodelling enthusiastically. I sighed and went to follow him, but Cookie held onto me, steering me round a rocky boulder. He didn't say anything. He just put his arms round me and bent his head and kissed me. I kissed him back, clinging to him, and for a few moments we were lost in our world – but then a manic cry circled round our heads: *'Jackyyyyyyyy – Cookieeeeeeee!'* We laughed and went to find Colin.

I spent far more time with Colin than with

Cookie, because we had our evening meal back at the hotel. I got changed quickly and went down to the recreation room, where Colin and I played endless games of ping-pong, plus a silly version of Snakes and Ladders, going up every snake and down every ladder.

There was a special dance at our hotel on Friday evening.

'So *I'll* be dancing with Jacky all evening,' Colin crowed triumphantly.

'No, *I* will,' said Cookie. 'I'll come to the dance.'

'It's meant to be for residents only,' said Colin.

'And their guests,' said Cookie firmly. He looked me in the eye. 'I'm definitely coming.'

I didn't fool around playing games with Colin on Friday before dinner. I locked myself in the communal bathroom, ignoring the rattles on the door from the other guests. I washed all the salt out of my hair and had a quick bath. Then, back in my room, I changed into my white dress with the apricot sash. I was really brown now so it looked good on me. I didn't bother with much make-up, just mascara and lipstick. I stared at myself in the mirror. It was as if I was looking at a girl in a picture, not *me*. I seemed to have stepped out of myself into a strange new girl who totally startled me. I clutched the edge of the mirror, wanting to hang onto myself in this moment.

I could barely eat my dinner I felt so excited. We all went into the ballroom and sat at little gilt tables around the edges of the room. I sat with Biddy and Harry and Ron and Grace. Ron bought us all a round of drinks and started clowning about. Biddy laughed at his antics, but Harry and Grace stayed po-faced. I think they were both glad we were going home tomorrow. Biddy and Ron were probably sad. And I was desperate. I wanted to stay here in Newquay with Cookie for ever.

I kept peering all round the room for him but he wasn't there. People started plucking up the courage to dance. I did a waltz with Harry, a quickstep with silly twiddly bits with Ron. Colin clearly wasn't up to any kind of ballroom dancing, but he came charging across the room when they announced a jiving session. He couldn't actually jive either, but he jerked around and clicked his fingers and kicked his legs while I circled him, spinning round until I was dizzy.

I leaned against the wall, the room still spinning even though I was still, and saw Cookie walking calmly through the French windows at the end of the room, in a white shirt and black trousers, his hair gleaming gold.

I rubbed my eyes, wondering if I was just imagining him, but he came right up to me, smiling.

'Hello, Jacky. Do you want to dance?' he said.

I danced with him for the rest of the evening. Whenever there was a jiving session Colin joined in too, the three of us gyrating on the spot in our odd trio.

Then I danced a slow foxtrot with Cookie, the two of us shuffling gently about the room. His arms were round my waist, my cheek was touching his, but we couldn't get really close in front of everyone, especially not Biddy and Harry.

'Shall we go outside for a bit?' Cookie whispered into my ear.

I nodded. We simply held hands and walked through the French windows into the hotel garden. It was so cool and quiet there after the noise and clamour of the dance floor. We stood still, breathing in the sweet smells of stocks and roses. But then we heard giggling behind us, and another couple stumbled out into the garden too.

'Let's go for a little walk,' said Cookie. 'Shall we go to the beach?'

'Yes, let's,' I said.

I didn't go back to tell Biddy where I was going. We simply linked fingers and walked out of the garden, down the road, towards the sea. We looked up at the moon and tried counting the stars.

'Do you know what they're all called?' Cookie asked.

'Well, that's the Pole Star,' I said, peering up at the brightest and biggest star. 'And could that be the Great Bear, that cluster there? And I think that's the Pleiades, seven stars together, the smallest in the sky. One of them's called Maia.'

'You've been reading an astronomy book.'

'No, it's *Mary Poppins*. Maia was my favourite character,' I said. 'Did you read it, Cookie?'

'I think my sister did. I read the Jennings books. And William. They didn't tell you about stars. I know all about space though, from Dan Dare in the *Eagle* comic.'

'Well, we're both well-informed then,' I said as we got to the beach.

The sea sucked at the sands, the shushing sound seeming louder at night. I slipped off my heels and stepped onto the beach.

'The sand feels so much colder now,' I said.

'We won't go for a paddle then, we don't want to freeze,' said Cookie. 'You're not too cold now, are you, Jacky?' He put his arm round me. 'Here, I'll warm you up a bit.'

'I'm fine,' I said, snuggling into him. 'This is lovely. I've never been for a moonlit walk before.'

'I like walking in the dark. There's this graveyard near where I live. When I was a little kid it spooked me out and I thought there were all these ghosts hanging round the gravestones. I felt embarrassed I was so scared. I even had nightmares about it, so one day I forced myself to go there by myself. I was actually shaking like a leaf, but when I got in the graveyard it was fine. It was so peaceful, and I just walked around touching all the gravestones, and ever since then I like to cut through the graveyard and have a little quiet time there. Do you think I'm a bit crazy?'

'No, I think you're the most interesting boy I've ever met,' I said truthfully.

'No, I'm not, I can't be – but you're *definitely* the most interesting girl I've ever met,' said Cookie, and he stopped and kissed me.

We didn't quite have the beach to ourselves. There was a dim glow from a barbecue party down at one end, and several mad surfers were yelling in the water.

'Come with me,' said Cookie, and we went into the caves.

It was so dark I couldn't see anything at all. I had to cling to Cookie and he clung to me, and then we were kissing and whispering and wishing we could stay there for ever.

Neither of us had watches. It was very very late when we eventually walked back up the beach towards the hotel.

'So I suppose this is goodbye,' Cookie said.

'Oh, I wish it wasn't,' I said, putting my arms round his neck.

'I've scribbled my address – here,' said Cookie, tucking a piece of paper into my pocket. 'Will you write to me?'

'Of course I will!'

'And we'll maybe meet up again next summer?'

'Yes!'

'And you won't ever forget me?'

'I'll never ever forget you,' I said, and then we kissed goodbye for the last time.

I did write to him, of course, a long long letter, page after page of my innermost thoughts. He wrote back to me, just two sides of paper, but he addressed me as 'Darling Jacky' and signed it 'Love from Cookie'.

I wrote again. I had to wait a week or more before I got an answer, just a postcard this time, with a lot of boring stuff about his school. I wrote a proper letter – and then another – and another. Eventually I got a letter back – *from his mother*! She was very sweet, and said how the whole family had enjoyed meeting me and that Cookie was very fond of me – 'but I'm afraid he's not very good at writing letters'.

I wrote back to thank her. And that was it. I never heard from Cookie again, and we didn't go back to Cornwall the following summer. I was heartbroken. So what did I do? I wrote about it.

The next year I started a new, more elaborate journal. I wrote in it in February 1961:

Ever since last Summer I've been trying to write a novel. This was vaguely based on last summer holiday, and dealt with Cookie in detail. I was convinced that I was writing what was to become a great classic, and dabbled around with it at the weekends and in the evenings. I now know that it was only very adolescent escapism. I had no boyfriend or anything, and in the Summer I had spent a nice week with Cookie, so I unconsciously comforted myself by my very infantile book about my 'adult' experience.

I was pretty hard on myself! I wish I still had that story now. Later, in April, writing in my diary I said:

Hello. I've nothing much to write about as today was so quiet and ordinary, so I'll write down anything that comes into my head. The nice thing about keeping this diary is that I write about everything without being laughed at; I can write down secrets with no fear of them being told; I can just scribble away to my heart's content. I don't even have to worry about writing or spelling because I don't mind a bit if I'm untidy. You get a lovely sense of freedom this way. It's funny, I'm getting very enthusiastic about diary writing, and yet when I was on holiday I decided to give it up. I'm still terribly conceited – I thought I would write a full length novel based on my Bruges holiday [a school trip that Easter, my first time abroad]. All this time and I'm still not cured. After several attempts to begin I wisely admitted defeat and returned to you. But I'm still not crushed – <u>I'm going to write a book</u>, but not yet, because 15 is too young, too immature. After all, I wanted to write a book at 14, about last summer. I thought I knew it all; now my attitude has changed completely and I feel much more grown up, and yet not so superior. I know I'm just a silly little fool, probably with absolutely no gift for writing at all, yet that doesn't prevent me from trying. I've got to be a writer and nothing else.

seven stories
National Centre for Children's Books

Many of the pictures in this book were featured in a blockbuster exhibition, *Daydreams and Diaries – The Story of Jacqueline Wilson*. The exhibition celebrated Jacqueline's remarkable contribution to children's literature, exploring her childhood influences, her talent for story telling, and how her stories have befriended millions of young people all over the world. The exhibition was designed and curated by Seven Stories. After being on show at the Seven Stories museum in Newcastle upon Tyne, it went on to tour the UK, delighting many thousands of fans.

Seven Stories is the National Centre for Children's Books in Britain. It is the only place in the UK dedicated to saving, celebrating and sharing the art of children's books, the creative talents of the authors and illustrators who make them and the importance of book and story in childhood. Seven Stories saves our literary heritage for children by caring for an internationally important collection of artwork, manuscripts and archives of Britain's most acclaimed writers and illustrators for children, from the 1930s to the present day.

It celebrates this treasure trove by creating playful exhibitions that encourage visitors to explore how books are made – from first scribbles to the finished book. It shares and encourages the enjoyment of books as part of our lives at its lively museum, in schools and communities and by touring its exhibitions across the UK.

Seven Stories is a charity.
Find out more at
www.sevenstories.org.uk

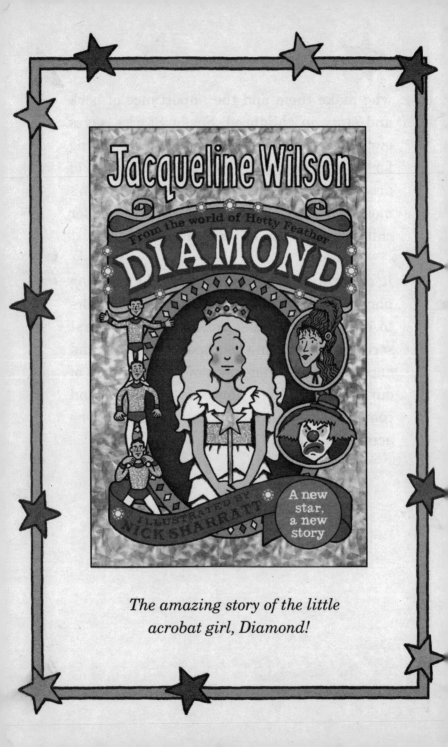

Jacqueline Wilson

From the world of Hetty Feather

DIAMOND

ILLUSTRATED BY
NICK SHARRATT

A new
star,
a new
story

*The amazing story of the little
acrobat girl, Diamond!*

Jacqueline Wilson

QUEENIE

Illustrated by
Nick Sharratt

Who'll look after Elsie when she's left all alone?

*Who will look after Elsie when
she's left all alone?*

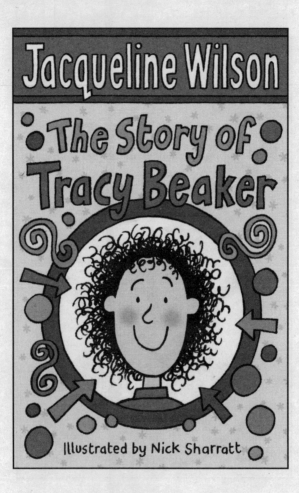

Jacqueline Wilson

The Story of Tracy Beaker

Illustrated by Nick Sharratt

*I'm Tracy Beaker. This is a book all about me.
I'd read it if I were you. It's the most incredible,
dynamic, heart-rending story. Honest!*